CINEMA, PI

The increasingly popular idea that cinematic fictions can 'do' philosophy raises some difficult questions. Who is actually doing the philosophizing? Is it the philosophical commentator who reads general arguments or theories into the stories conveyed by a film? Could it be the film-maker, or a group of collaborating film-makers, who raise and try to answer philosophical questions with a film? Is there something about the experience of films that is especially suited to the stimulation of worthwhile philosophical reflections? In the first part of this book, Paisley Livingston surveys positions and arguments surrounding the cinema's philosophical value. He raises criticisms of bold theses in this area and defends a moderate view of film's possible contributions to philosophy. In the second part of the book he defends an intentionalist approach that focuses on the film-makers' philosophical background, assumptions, sources, and aims. Livingston outlines intentionalist interpretative principles as well as an account of authorship in cinema. The third part of the book exemplifies this intentionalist approach with reference to the work of Ingmar Bergman. Livingston explores the connection between Bergman's work and the Swedish director's primary philosophical source—a treatise in philosophical psychology authored by the Finnish philosopher, Eino Kaila. Bergman proclaimed that reading this book was a tremendous philosophical experience for him and that he 'built on this ground'. With reference to materials in the newly created Ingmar Bergman archive, Livingston shows how Bergman took up Kaila's topics in his cinematic explorations of motivated irrationality, inauthenticity, and the problem of self-knowledge.

Paisley Livingston is Chair Professor and Head of the Department of Philosophy at Lingnan University, Hong Kong.

Cinema, Philosophy, Bergman

On Film as Philosophy

PAISLEY LIVINGSTON

OXFORD

UNIVERSITY PRESS

OXFORD

UNIVERSITY PRESS

Great Clarendon Street, Oxford OX2 6DP
United Kingdom

Oxford University Press is a department of the University of Oxford.
It furthers the University's objective of excellence in research, scholarship,
and education by publishing worldwide. Oxford is a registered trade mark of
Oxford University Press in the UK and in certain other countries

First published 2009
First published in paperback 2012

British Library Cataloguing in Publication Data

Data available

Library of Congress Cataloging in Publication Data

Livingston, Paisley, 1951–
Cinema, philosophy, Bergman : on film as philosophy / Paisley Livingston.
p. cm.
Includes bibliographical references and index.
ISBN 978-0-19-957017-1
1. Motion pictures—Philosophy. 2. Philosophy in motion
pictures. 3. Bergman, Ingmar, 1918–2007—Criticism and
interpretation. 4. Bergman, Ingmar, 1918–2007—Philosophy. I. Title.
PN1995.L5428 2009
791.4301—dc22
2009006280

ISBN 978-0-19-957017-1 (Hbk)
ISBN 978-0-19-965514-4 (Pbk)

Printed in Great Britain
on acid-free paper by
MPG Books Group, Bodmin and King's Lynn

1 3 5 7 9 10 8 6 4 2

Contents

Acknowledgements

My research on the various issues discussed in this book has profited immensely from exchanges with a number of film scholars, philosophers, and students, including Giorgio Biancorosso, David Bordwell, Staffan Carlshamre, Greg Currie, David Davies, Berys Gaut, Mette Hjort, Gary Iseminger, Andrew Kania, Peter Lamarque, Aaron Meskin, Peter Ohlin, Stein Haugom Olsen, Torsten Pettersson, Bo Pettersson, Carl Plantinga, Trevor Ponech, Neven Sesardic, Robert Stecker, Stéphane Symons, Folke Tersman, Tom Wartenberg, and George Wilson. Drafts and earlier versions of some of the material in this book were commented upon helpfully by Maaret Koskinen, Anna Christina Ribeiro, Neven Sesardic, Murray Smith, Robert Stecker, and Tom Wartenberg. Carl Plantinga read the entire manuscript and offered helpful comments. Reports by two anonymous readers helped me to improve the typescript. I would also like to thank Hilary Walford for her excellent copy-editing, as well as Catherine Berry and Peter Momtchiloff for their support of this project.

My work on Ingmar Bergman was enormously facilitated by Margareta Nordström and her colleagues at the Ingmar Bergman Foundation archive housed in the Swedish Film Institute. Many thanks to Fredrik Gustafsson, Håkon Lörgren, and Erik Normann. I am also grateful to Maaret Koskinen and Birgitta Steene for teaching me a lot about Bergman. I have also benefited from commentaries and objections presented by participants in two 'author meets critics' panels, the first at the ASA Annual Meeting in Milwaukee, October 2006 (with Sondra Bacharach, David Davies, Deborah Knight, Hans Maes, and Anna Christina Ribeiro), the second at the Eastern Division Meeting of the APA, December 2006 (with Noël Carroll, William Irwin, Jerrold Levinson, and Daniel Nathan).

Chapter 1 and parts of Chapter 2 are based on my essay 'Theses on Cinema as Philosophy', *Journal of Aesthetics and Art Criticism*, 64 (2006), 1–8; part of Chapter 4 is based on 'Conversational Implicature', 'Discourse Coherence', 'Communicative Intention', and 'Cooperative Principle', in Patrick Colm Hogan, ed., *The Cambridge Encyclopedia of Language Science* (Cambridge: Cambridge University Press, 2011); parts of Chapters 5 and 6 were based on 'On Bergman and Philosophy:

The Kaila Connection', in Maaret Koskinen, ed., *Ingmar Bergman Revisited* (London: Wallflower Press, 2008), 120–39. I have also drawn on parts of my 'Recent Work on Cinema as Philosophy' in *Philosopher's Compass*, 3 (2008), 1–14. I am grateful to Blackwell-Wiley, Cambridge University Press, and Wallflower Press for permission to reproduce these materials.

The work described in this book was partially supported by a grant from the Research Grants Council of the Hong Kong Special Administrative Region, China (Project No. LU3401/06H). I am very grateful for this generous support, which made possible my archival research in Stockholm as well as a much-needed time release.

I am grateful to Lisa Milroy for permission to use her picture *Remembering* on the cover of this book, and for her helpful advice with the cover design; thanks as well in this connection for the courtesy of the Alan Cristea Gallery.

List of Illustrations

Image Permissions
(by image number)

Introduction

The idea that films can be philosophical or even 'do' philosophy has recently found a number of advocates. Somewhat surprisingly, the films described as making contributions to philosophy have not, on the whole, been the more obvious and uncontroversial cases, such as informative documentaries about philosophers or probing non-fictional films dealing with issues more or less directly related to philosophical topics. Instead, the works under discussion have most often been cinematic fictions, including a number of movies, such as *The Matrix*, that clearly belong to the category of commercial, popular cinema.[1] An early and highly influential example of writing in this vein was Harvard philosopher Stanley Cavell's 1981 discussion of Frank Capra's *It Happened One Night*.[2] More recently, Cavell's writings on the philosophical significance of romantic comedies have been identified as a source of inspiration by Stephen Mulhall in his *On Film*, a book in which the Oxford philosopher unfolds an elaborate interpretation of the four films in the thrilling and gory *Alien* series. Many other examples of philosophically oriented interpretations of popular fictional films can be mentioned.[3]

[1] Christopher Grau, ed., *Philosophers Explore* The Matrix (Oxford: Oxford University Press, 2004); William Irwin, ed., The Matrix *and Philosophy: Welcome to the Desert of the Real* (Chicago: Open Court, 2002); William Irwin, ed., *More Matrix and Philosophy: Revolutions and Reloaded Decoded* (Chicago: Open Court, 2005); Matt Lawrence, *Like a Splinter in your Mind: The Philosophy behind the Matrix Trilogy* (Oxford: Blackwell, 2004).

[2] Stanley Cavell, *Pursuits of Happiness: The Hollywood Comedy of Remarriage* (Cambridge, MA: Harvard University Press, 1981); *Contesting Tears: The Hollywood Melodrama of the Unknown Woman* (Chicago: University of Chicago Press, 1996); and *Cities of Words: Pedagogical Letters on a Register of the Moral Life* (Cambridge, MA: Harvard University Press, 2004). For an overview, see William Rothman, 'Stanley Cavell', in Paisley Livingston and Carl Plantinga, eds., *The Routledge Companion to Philosophy and Film* (London: Routledge, 2009), 344–55.

[3] For a start, see Kimberly Ann Blessing and Paul J. Tudico, eds., *Movies and the Meaning of Life: Philosophers Take on Hollywood* (Chicago: Open Court, 2005),

The idea that films, including cinematic fictions, can be philosophical is in one sense wholly unproblematic. It is no surprise that some film viewers find some movies thought-provoking, and, since it is hardly controversial to suppose that some of these thoughts are genuinely philosophical, it is safe to conclude that the films have some kind of philosophical significance, at least for those viewers. It is also wholly unproblematic to observe that philosophers can use aspects of the story conveyed by a work of fiction to illustrate a philosophical problem or theory. For example, the traditional sceptical worry that all of one's perceptions could be systematically misleading finds a vivid evocation in *The Matrix, Total Recall,* and other films and stories.[4] Watching such films and reading such literary works can help some students of philosophy take certain arguments in the theory of knowledge more seriously.[5]

Yet such mild claims are not what some of the advocates of cinema as philosophy have in mind. An oft-cited statement made by Mulhall at the outset of his book is quite noteworthy for its unflinching emphasis on the idea that it is *the films themselves,* as opposed to the philosophical commentator, that should be credited with having done some significant philosophizing:

I do not look to these films as handy or popular illustrations of views and arguments properly developed by philosophers; I see them rather as themselves reflecting on and evaluating such views and arguments, as thinking seriously

Richard A. Gilmore, *Doing Philosophy at the Movies* (Albany, NY: State University of New York Press, 2005), Joseph Kupfer, *Visions of Virtue in Popular Film* (Boulder, CO: Westview Press, 1999), Andrew Light, *Reel Arguments: Film, Philosophy, and Social Criticism* (Boulder, CO: Westview Press, 2003), Mary Litch, *Philosophy through Film* (New York: Routledge, 2002), James Phillips, ed., *Cinematic Thinking: Philosophical Approaches to the New Cinema* (Stanford, CA: Stanford University Press, 2008), Aeon J. Skoble and Mark T. Conard, eds., *Woody Allen and Philosophy: You Mean my Whole Fallacy is Wrong?* (Chicago: Open Court, 2004); Kevin L. Stoehr, ed., *Film and Knowledge: Essays on the Integration of Images and Ideas* (Jefferson, NC: McFarland, 2002), Robert J. Yanal, *Hitchcock as Philosophy* (Jefferson, NC: McFarland, 2005), and Thomas E. Wartenberg, *Unlikely Couples: Movie Romance as Social Criticism* (Boulder, CO: Westview, 1999) and *Thinking on Screen: Film as Philosophy* (London: Routledge, 2008).

[4] For example, literary fictions by Stanislaw Lem vividly evoke sceptical scenarios; for background, see my 'Skepticism, Realism, Fallibilism: On Lem's Epistemological Themes', in Peter Swirski, ed., *The Art and Science of Stanislaw Lem* (Montreal: McGill-Queen's Press, 2006), 117–29.

[5] For an overview of this topic, see Richard Fumerton, 'Skepticism', in Livingston and Plantinga, eds., *The Routledge Companion to Philosophy and Film*, 601–10. Thomas E. Wartenberg describes *The Matrix* as a 'skeptical thought experiment' in *Thinking on Screen*, ch. 4.

and systematically about them in just the ways that philosophers do. Such films are not philosophy's raw material, nor a source for its ornamentation; they are philosophical exercises, philosophy in action—film as philosophizing.[6]

Mulhall also writes that 'the films themselves' do such things as 'addressing questions', reflecting upon conditions, and conducting investigations. In one of Mulhall's formulations, films are even said to have 'metaphysical ambitions'. Contentions along these lines are quite common in the literature on cinema as philosophy. Cinema's contribution to philosophy, it has been claimed, is at once highly innovative and intimately linked to the nature of the cinematic medium and art form. Films, we are told, engage in creative philosophical thinking and in the formation of new philosophical concepts.[7] In one variation on this theme, we read that 'Film possibly contains a whole new system of thought, a new episteme—perhaps the new concepts of philosophy might even find their paradigms in cinema'.[8]

The idea that film has an extremely important or even ground-breaking philosophical role to play raises a number of questions. Who (or what) is to be taken as doing the real philosophical work? Is it literally 'the film itself', and if so, in what sense is this possible? Is a film—in the sense of an audio-visual display—literally the sort of thing that can raise questions, conduct investigations, and make claims about very general topics such as the nature of reality, the good life, and our knowledge of it? If, on the other hand, a film is not literally the sort of thing that argues and theorizes, why do philosophers read their general arguments and theories into imaginative stories that can be associated with the experience of an audio-visual display? When someone writes a lengthy

---

[6] Stephen Mulhall, *On Film* (London: Routledge, 2002), p. 2. This statement is quoted and insightfully commented upon by Murray Smith in his 'Film Art, Argument, and Ambiguity', in Murray Smith and Thomas E. Wartenberg, eds., *Thinking through Cinema: Film as Philosophy* (Malden, MA: Blackwell, 2006), pp. 33–42.

[7] I shall not attempt a survey of this literature here. For a start, see Gilles Deleuze, *L'Image-mouvement* (Paris: Minuit, 1983), and *L'Image-temps* (Paris: Minuit, 1985), and Gregory Flaxman, ed., *The Brain is the Screen: Deleuze and the Philosophy of Cinema* (Minneapolis: University of Minnesota Press, 2000). For a few remarks on Deleuze's enormously influential books on film, see my 'Film and the New Psychology', *Poetics*, 20 (1991), 1–24.

[8] Daniel Frampton, *Filmosophy* (London: Wallflower, 2006), 11. For readers unfamiliar with the term, the Greek word 'episteme' was recruited by Michel Foucault to refer to a vast framework or system of beliefs and discourses that is dominant in a given socio-historical context, or roughly what Foucault himself would later call 'une formation discursive'. For Foucault on *le discours*, see *L'Archéologie du savoir* (Paris: Gallimard, 1969).

essay about a philosophical theme in a movie, is this to be understood and evaluated as film appreciation, or in terms of other, more distinctly philosophical ambitions? If it is the latter, why take the detour through a creative reading of the imaginary goings-on evoked by a fiction film? Is there something about the experience of a film that is especially suited to the stimulation of worthwhile philosophical reflections? Could it be the film-maker, or a group of collaborating film-makers, who raise or try to answer philosophical questions with a film?

My primary aim in this book is to take up these basic issues surrounding film's contributions to philosophy. I try to identify what I take to be characteristic strengths and weaknesses of some of the central claims and approaches in this area. I raise criticisms of some of the bold theses in the literature and survey alternative approaches to the topic. I then go on to advocate and exemplify a type of intentionalist approach, without, however, contending that this is the only viable way to explore the cinema's various possible contributions to philosophy.

The book has three main parts. In the first part I assess positions and arguments on the cinema's contributions to philosophy in general. I make reference to particular examples along the way, but my aim in this first part of the book remains the illustration and clarification of some more general issues raised by the basic idea of cinema as philosophy. In the second part of the book I clarify and defend partial intentionalism, first by elucidating and defending a conception of cinematic authorship, and secondly by describing and defending intentionalist principles of interpretation. The third part of the book instantiates this approach by focusing single-mindedly on the case of Ingmar Bergman. I examine some of his particular films and statements in some detail, drawing on my study of materials in the Bergman archive in Stockholm. The link between the third and first two parts of the book is straightforward: although the chapters on Bergman are of independent interest given the value and significance of Bergman's cinematic *œuvre*, their purpose here is to illustrate and exemplify one of the main approaches to film as philosophy argued for in the first two parts of the book.

A brief outline of the chapters to follow should give the reader a better sense of which questions I shall be taking up in what follows. In Chapter 1 I identify and assess some of the more ambitious claims that have been made about the nature of film's contribution to philosophy. I isolate and criticize what I call the 'bold thesis', which is the conjunction of the idea that films can make an original contribution to philosophy, and the idea that this contribution can be achieved primarily if not entirely through means exclusive to the cinematic medium. I develop a dilemma argument against this thesis: either support for the bold thesis depends on a claim about a cinematic contribution that cannot be paraphrased and so can be reasonably doubted, or it rests on a contribution that can be paraphrased, in which case the clause about medium specificity is betrayed. As an alternative to the disputed, bold thesis, I advocate a weakening of both the originality and exclusivity conditions. The more moderate thesis that emerges holds that films can be used to express and illustrate philosophical ideas, be they significantly innovative or not. Film-makers can do so at least in part by drawing upon devices shared with other media and art forms. In other words, proponents of the moderate thesis hold that a film-related contribution to philosophy can be of value even when the philosophical content is neither original nor conveyed primarily by means exclusive to the cinematic medium.

In Chapter 2 I further develop my argument about film's contribution to philosophy through a discussion of some objections that may be raised against even the more moderate thesis just evoked. The question of art's cognitive merits and demerits has a long and complex history, and it should not come as a surprise that some of the arguments belonging to that history have direct relevance for current debates over the cinema's philosophical value. As a case in point, I have found some inspiration in G. W. F. Hegel's objections to attempts to make works of art serve external ends. In his brief discussion of the topic, Hegel evokes two different kinds of objections that prove to be applicable to the case of cinema and philosophy. One is a *propriety* objection to the effect that it is inappropriate to use art to advance ends other than those that are properly artistic, which, for Hegel, were intrinsic ends. I respond to this objection by stressing the plurality of artistic values. I then turn to a *rationality* objection inspired by Hegel's worry that it is an error to try to use a work of art to achieve an instrumental pay-off whenever some more complete or effective means is available. For the sake of the argument, I reconstruct this objection in a strengthened form by showing how doubts can be raised about the completeness of the philosophical content of audio-visual displays. I then respond to the rationality objection by challenging the assumption that the correct way to assess the rationality of the use of film in philosophy is by means of an isolated, decontextualized scrutiny of the audio-visual display. The way beyond the Hegel-inspired objections is to consider the conditions under which a sufficiently complex and determinate philosophical interpretation of an audio-visual display can be articulated. I identify two such conditions and two corresponding approaches to film's philosophical contributions. In one, non-intentionalist line of enquiry, it is the interpreter who shoulders the burden of *creating or selecting* a sufficiently informative and well-developed philosophical *problématique* (or set of assumptions and questions) in relation to which claims about an audio-visual display's philosophical significance can be articulated. Clearly this is a matter of the use to which an audio-visual display can be put, and not a claim about the film-makers' philosophical achievements. In the second type of approach, the guiding assumption is that it is the film-maker, or a group of collaborating film-makers, who have been guided by philosophical background ideas and questions in the making of the film. The interpreter's goal is to discover, not to create or freely select, these ideas, and when the interpreter is successful, the interpretative *problématique* and the philosophical achievement elucidated are those of the film-maker or of a group of collaborating film-makers.

This second, intentionalist approach is the topic of the second and third parts of the book, where I explore the idea that some film-makers indeed use the cinematic medium to express philosophical ideas of sufficient complexity to be of interest in the context of philosophical teaching and research. Two objections are often levelled against this approach, and these objections are taken up and responded to in Part Two. The first objection challenges the 'application' of what is characterized as a 'traditional' or 'literary' conception of authorship to cinema, either because that conception is deemed faulty in general, or because it is held to be inapplicable to films where many different people contribute to the making of the work. In Chapter 3 I defend a conception of cinematic authorship that embraces a broad range of cases, including joint authorship as well as individual authorship in a context of collaborative work. I do not argue that all films have an individual author, or even a coordinated team of people functioning as a joint author. Yet I do argue that these conditions are sometimes met.

The second kind of objection to the investigation of a cinematic author's philosophical contribution targets intentionalism as such, and, with this in mind, in Chapter 4 I identify and defend a partial intentionalist approach, which is distinct from the strongest forms of actualist intentionalism as well as the kind of conditionalist intentionalism advocated by some of the advocates of philosophically motivated interpretations of art. I argue that partial intentionalism is not vulnerable to the objections levelled against other versions of intentionalism. One of those objections targets the fallibility of intentions and of the art-making actions related to them. Either the artist successfully realizes his or her intentions in the work, in which case talking about the intentions is redundant, or the artist does not successfully realize the intentions, in which case talking about the intentions, as opposed to what the work actually means, is irrelevant. To be viable, intentionalism must have a response to this argument, and such a response requires a claim about the conditions under which intentions are successfully realized in the work. I discuss some different ways of trying to answer this question and develop a proposal involving a 'meshing' or congruence relation between intentions and features of the audio-visual display. The application of this type of success condition is illustrated in a discussion of the determination of the fictional content of Carl Theodor Dreyer's (1943) *Vredens dag* (*Day of Wrath*).

Chapters 5 and 6 constitute the third part of the book, which is designed to exemplify the kind of intentionalist approach discussed in the first two parts. I explore the little-known connection between Ingmar Bergman's films and what he has identified as his major philosophical source—a treatise in philosophical psychology authored by the Finnish positivist, Eino Kaila, in 1934. Bergman proclaimed that reading this book was a tremendous philosophical experience for him and that he found some of Kaila's central claims shattering but true. Bergman added that he 'built on this ground'. Unfortunately, Kaila's book has been translated only into Swedish and Danish, and many Bergman commentators remain oblivious to its contents. I provide a survey of Kaila's positions in Chapter 5 and identify some of the many ways in which Bergman's work was informed by the questions and claims in Kaila's book. More specifically, I focus on Kaila's interest in various types of inauthenticity and motivated irrationality. Scenes from various Bergman films are discussed, but special attention is paid to his (1980) *Aus dem Leben der Marionetten* (*From the Life of the Marionettes*). The discussion of Kaila sheds new light on Bergman's often-misunderstood relation to psychoanalysis.

Chapter 6 returns to the Bergman–Kaila connection and examines in some detail a scene in which Bergman has one of his characters make an allusion to Kaila's views about the status of moral judgements. The apparent thrust of this appeal to Kaila's authority is that there is no right or wrong, only motives and preferences. Yet this allusion is complicated by the fact that the character who makes a decidedly Kaila-esque pronouncement is clearly unreliable. With the goal of achieving a better understanding of Bergman's relation to Kaila's philosophical positions on value and rationality, I discuss Bergman's and Kaila's views on inauthenticity and self-understanding, particularly in relation to *Persona* (1966), a film that plots both the emergence of an episode of inauthenticity as well as an 'awakening' in which genuine insight is gained. Bergman's positions on moral knowledge are explored, especially in terms of characterizations in *Det sjunde inseglet* (*The Seventh Seal*) and an unpublished treatment for a film on the Crucifixion. Bergman's implicit and explicit critiques of certain forms of irrationality are linked to his modernist understanding of the motivation of his own artistic activities. I explore Bergman's reasons for his rejection of cinematic fantasy and his preference for a philosophically oriented and exploratory cinematic art.

In my conclusion I survey the ground covered and consider some of the implications that my discussion of Bergman has for the more general issues canvassed in the first part of the book. More specifically, I explore some of the trade-offs involved in different approaches to cinema as philosophy. Although my discussion of the work of Bergman is meant to exemplify one way in which cinema can contribute to philosophy, it should be obvious that many fascinating questions about the philosophical dimensions of Bergman's films, and of the cinema more generally, remain open.

PART ONE

SURVEYING CINEMA AS PHILOSOPHY

1

Theses on Cinema as Philosophy

Can films make creative contributions to philosophy, and this by means exclusive to the cinematic medium or art form? Although it may be tempting to offer a positive response to this question, a bold thesis of 'cinema as philosophy' is difficult to defend. A better option, I shall contend in what follows, is to accept a more modest conception of the cinema's role in the development of philosophical insight or knowledge. Films can be used to provide vivid and emotionally engaging illustrations of philosophical issues and ideas, and, when sufficient background assumptions are in place, reflections about films can contribute to the exploration of specific theses and arguments, sometimes yielding enhanced philosophical understanding.

THE BOLD THESIS: INNOVATIVE, CINEMATIC PHILOSOPHY

Before I attempt to assess the bold thesis, its components need to be identified. Key conceptual constituents of a type of bold thesis about cinema as philosophy include: (1) a conception of which sorts of *exclusive* capacities of the cinematic medium (or, alternatively, the cinematic art form) are said to make a special contribution to philosophy, and (2) claims about the nature of the latter contribution (such as a strong contention about its originality, significance, or independence). As (1) pertains to means and (2) pertains to the end product, we can call these the *means* and *results* conditions, respectively.

With regard to the results condition, it should be clear that how the multifarious term 'philosophy' is to be understood is a crucial issue. As Murray Smith usefully points out in this regard, some authors who write about cinema as philosophy employ an 'expansive strategy' in which a very loose and all-inclusive conception of philosophy supports the claim that films have great philosophical significance.[1] As Smith indicates, there is nothing to be gained along these lines. Yet I also agree with Thomas E. Wartenberg's contention that it would be pointlessly restrictive to use the term 'philosophy' to refer only to scholarly lectures and publications in academic journals, which would in advance exclude motion pictures from the philosophical picture.[2] So what is wanted is a less narrow, but not hopelessly broad, conception of philosophy that leaves the question about cinema's possible philosophical contributions open. With this in mind, it may be good enough to say that 'philosophy' refers to more or less systematic investigative, expressive, and communicative activities, at a high level of generality and abstraction, pertaining to the world and our knowledge of it; philosophers investigate, discuss, and pronounce upon a range of significant, general topics concerning the nature of reality, and, in particular, human action and value. The privileged, though not exclusive, methods that philosophers use in such investigations and communications include reasoning and argumentation as well as attention to examples, whether actual or imagined, that may be indicative of more general patterns and possibilities.

Such a definition of philosophy is admittedly vague (if only because of the 'more or less general' clause), but it has at least two significant virtues in the present context. First of all, it easily covers many items that are readily identified as philosophy; and, secondly, it is neutral with regard to the relationship between philosophy and the cinema, unless it is the case that the very idea of an investigation into very general questions is somehow inimical to the cinema. I shall discuss this question at greater length below, but, for now, it should be sufficient to observe that it is far from obvious that there is any obstacle to using films effectively in a general investigation. Just think of the 'crash-dummy' films that are used to study the consequences of automotive collisions. Clearly it is not the fate of the particular crash dummy that is of interest to the persons conducting such experiments. This kind of example may seem trivial, but there are arguably some interesting moral and psychological analogues in the art of cinema: perhaps some authors and/or commentators use fiction films to reason imaginatively about the consequences of 'collisions' between types of persons in certain kinds of

---

[1] Murray Smith, 'Film Art, Argument, and Ambiguity', in Murray Smith and Thomas E. Wartenberg, eds., *Thinking through Cinema: Film as Philosophy* (Malden, MA: Blackwell, 2006), 33–42.

[2] Thomas E. Wartenberg, *Thinking on Screen: Film as Philosophy* (London: Routledge, 2007), 28–30.

situations. In Part Three of this study I provide reasons why we should think of aspects of Ingmar Bergman's cinematic works as engaging in imaginative explorations of some general issues in philosophical psychology.

Two kinds of claims can be singled out in relation to the results condition included in a thesis about film as philosophy. The first is a strong condition: the film does not merely illustrate previously published philosophical ideas—in the sense, not of visualizing, but of *recapitulating or recalling* them—but instead realizes historically innovative philosophical contributions. (Moving quickly, we can say that an achievement is historically innovative only if it is new relative to the history of the relevant tradition.[3]) The second kind of claim is more modest: the film brings to mind some well-known philosophical questions and ideas. Clearly, this much is achieved by the scene in Eric Rohmer's *Conte de printemps* (*A Tale of Springtime*) (1990), where it is true in the fiction that a philosophy teacher, Jeanne (portrayed by Anne Teyssèdre), briefly explains some of Kant's basic ideas to a friend.

I turn now to the means condition, or the constraints a bold epistemic thesis places on the specifically cinematic devices by which a suitably innovative and important philosophical achievement is to be realized. Although in a broad sense any feature of a motion picture is cinematic by virtue of being a feature of a film, this is not what philosophers and film theorists have had in mind in using the expression 'the specificity of the cinematic medium', nor is such a broad and all-inclusive notion a component of the bold thesis about cinema's exclusive epistemic value.[4]

---

[3] Margaret A. Boden distinguishes between historical and psychological creativity as follows: an idea is P-creative if it is valuable and 'the person in whose mind it arises could not have had it before'; to be historically creative, the idea must be not only P-creative, but must never have been thought of before. I have weakened this latter condition, and doubt that P-creativity is necessary to historical creativity. See Boden, 'What is Creativity?' in Margaret A. Boden, ed., *Dimensions of Creativity* (Cambridge, MA: MIT Press, 1994), 76. For discussion of this and other accounts of creativity, see Berys Gaut and Paisley Livingston, 'Introduction', in Berys Gaut and Paisley Livingston, eds., *The Creation of Art: New Essays in Philosophical Aesthetics* (New York and Cambridge: Cambridge University Press, 2003), 1–32.

[4] For background on this issue, see Noël Carroll, 'The Specificity of Media in the Arts', *Journal of Aesthetic Education*, 14/15 (1984–5), 127–53; repr. in *Theorizing the Moving Image* (New York and Cambridge: Cambridge University Press, 1996), 25–36; and 'The Essence of Cinema?', *Philosophical Studies*, 89 (1998), 323–30; Paisley Livingston, 'Disciplining Film: Code and Specificity', *Cinema Canada*, 97 (1983), 47–57; Trevor Ponech, 'The Definition of "Cinema"', in Paisley Livingston and Carl Plantinga, eds.,

What, then, does the latter rule out with its conception of the *exclusive* capacities of the medium? Consider an entire film comprised of a single medium-long shot of a philosopher giving a genial talk on synthetic *a priori* knowledge or some other philosophical subject. Some people are tempted to say that this film would not enhance philosophical knowledge by virtue of devices exclusive to cinema.[5] Such a film does not provide any information that a direct or unmediated experience of the philosopher's lecture would not have provided. The cinematic medium makes possible a vivid and informative representation of the lecture, but somehow the philosophical pay-off does not seem to be specifically cinematic in the right sense. And what sense might that be? One thought in this vein is that the cinematic medium's exclusive capacities involve the possibility of providing an internally articulated, non-linguistic, visual expression of content, as when some idea is indicated by means of the sequential juxtaposition of two or more visual displays or shots. So-called Kuleshov effects are an oft-mentioned example. (The Soviet film-makers and theorists, Lev Kuleshov and V. I. Pudovkin, are sometimes reputed to have shown experimentally in the 1920s how an individual cinematic image of an actor with a 'neutral' expression could acquire specific meanings when juxtaposed with another image. Actually, the story is rather complicated and includes the failure of more recent attempts to replicate the experiment.[6]) The category of specifically cinematic stylistic devices or modes of expression is often taken to include montage or editing, then, but also camera movements and selective focus within a shot, and correlations between the soundtrack and moving image (for example, effects involving 'off-screen sound').

It may be important to note that the relevant contrast, as it is often drawn, is not simply between the means available to audio-visual media as opposed to verbal media. The cinema's 'specific' or 'exclusive' devices

---

The Routledge Companion to Philosophy and Film (London: Routledge, 2009), 52–63, and Ponech, 'The Substance of Cinema', *Journal of Aesthetics and Art Criticism*, 64 (2006), 187–98.

[5] A case of this sort was independently conjured up to make a related point by Wartenberg in his *Thinking on Screen*, 77–8. His ruling on such cases is that the film 'merely reproduces in a non-standard medium' the argument the philosopher presents to the original audience of the lecture. An audiotape would have served just as well to record the lecture.

[6] For a concise discussion with references, see Daniel T. Levin and Daniel J. Simons, 'Perceiving Stability in a Changing World: Combining Shots and Integrating Views in Motion Pictures and the Real World', *Media Psychology*, 2 (2000), 357–80.

may be taken to include a juxtaposition of verbalizations (say, in the form of a voice-off narration) and images and/or other sounds. For example, in a sequence in Ingmar Bergman's 1966 *Persona*, a nurse (portrayed by Bibi Andersson) reads phrases from a philosophical essay aloud to her patient (played by Liv Ullmann) (Figures 1.1–1.9). The first shot in the sequence shows the patient's reaction when the nurse asks her to listen; when the nurse begins reading, the spectator hears her voice but is shown a series of five static images of a desolate, stony beach. These images can seem to function rhetorically to corroborate the reflections that are read out, and later contested, by the nurse, who is shown reading only at the end of the sequence. (I shall have a bit more to say about this sequence in Chapter 2.) The overall philosophical import of the sequence is not a function of the verbal discourse alone, but arises at least in part through the combination of different sorts of expressive elements.

Similar assumptions find additional justification if one's focus is not on the specificity of the cinematic *medium*, but on the characteristic and exclusive features of the cinematic *art form*. (Roughly, I take it that a medium is a mode of conveying content; whereas an art form is a category of art works constituted in part by media, in part by artistic conventions and goals.[7]) For example, static cinematic recordings of theatrical, operatic, and other performances may contribute greatly to the performing arts by providing valuable documentation of bygone performances, but they are not generally acclaimed as contributions to the art *of cinema*, for the latter must manifest a skilful use of the medium's expressive and other artistic capacities in addition to exploiting its recording capacity. Thus, filmed operas are contributions to the art of cinema only if they solve specifically cinematic artistic problems, such as that of providing a visual complement to the operatic overture (a shot of the curtain constituting the 'degree zero' stylistic option).

To sum up these considerations regarding the 'means' condition, the proponent of some version of the bold thesis needs to identify and successfully defend some notion of the cinematic medium or art

---

[7] See David Davies, 'Medium in Art', in Jerrold Levinson, ed., *The Oxford Handbook of Aesthetics* (Oxford: Oxford University Press, 2003), 181–91, and Kevin Sweeney, 'Medium', in Livingston and Plantinga, eds., *The Routledge Companion to Philosophy and Film*, 173–83. For an informative survey of discussions of film as an art form and issues of film aesthetics, see Katherine Thomson-Jones, *Aesthetics and Film* (London: Continuum, 2008).

Figure 1.1. In Ingmar Bergman's *Persona*, Elisabet Volger (Liv Ullmann) listens to nurse Alma (Bibi Andersson) reading philosophy.

Figure 1.2.

Figure 1.3.

Figure 1.4.

Figure 1.5.

Figure 1.6.

Figure 1.7.

Figure 1.8.

Figure 1.9.

form's specific or exclusive devices. As there is perpetual dispute on this topic, this turns out to be a heavy burden to shoulder. Someone who is sceptical about the bold thesis can stay neutral regarding the difficult and controversial question of the real 'essence' of the cinematic medium or art form, and ask instead whether, given some specific proposal or assumption about the latter, the bold thesis should be accepted. Such is my approach in what follows.

ASSESSING THE BOLD THESIS

What I am calling the bold thesis is a conjunction of strong claims with regard to the means and results conditions—namely, the idea that some films can make historically innovative and independent contributions to philosophy by means exclusive to the cinematic medium or art form.[8]

---

[8] With regard to this point, Murray Smith and Thomas E. Wartenberg usefully asked me whether the bold thesis is a straw man. My first response to that question is that, even if no actual film theorist fully espouses a version of the bold thesis, the

Different versions of this schematic thesis, as well as various weaker options, will be considered in what follows. I shall argue that this kind of thesis faces a crippling dilemma that takes the following form.

First Horn of the Dilemma. To accept one prevalent conception of the cinema's specific representational devices, while arguing for an innovative and independent philosophical contribution, leads to an insoluble problem of paraphrase.[9] If it is contended that the exclusively cinematic, innovative insight cannot be paraphrased, reasonable doubt arises with regard to its very existence. If it is granted, on the other hand, that the cinematic contribution can and must be paraphrased, this contention is incompatible with arguments for a significantly independent, innovative, and purely 'filmic' philosophical achievement, as linguistic mediation turns out to be constitutive of (our knowledge of) the epistemic contribution a film can make.

Second Horn of the Dilemma. To accept, on the other hand, a broader conception of the cinema's exclusive capacities leads to a trivialization of the thesis that cinema can contribute to philosophy. Suppose, for

bold thesis is still conceptually salient and worthy of consideration. I believe, however, that many actual theorists come pretty close to promoting the bold thesis, though they do not explicitly state or defend it with any great precision. Consider, for example, Jean Epstein's views in *L'Intelligence d'une machine* (Paris: Jacques Melot, 1946); more recently, there is Daniel Frampton's *Filmosophy* (London: Wallflower, 2006). As Trond Lundemo notes, Epstein's speculations about cinema's philosophical import anticipated many of the concepts of later writers such as Gilles Deleuze. See Trond Lundemo, *Jean Epstein—intelligensen hos en maskin—The Intelligence of a Machine* (Stockholm: Svenska Filminstitutet, 2001), 11. For an illuminating discussion of Deleuze's books on film that emphasizes his interpretation of Henri Bergson's metaphysics, see Ronald Bogue, 'Gilles Deleuze', in Livingston and Plantinga, eds., *The Routledge Companion to Philosophy and Film*, 368–77.

   9 Such a problem surfaces repeatedly in discussions of art and knowledge, though not in the precise form it is given here. For surveys, see my 'Literature and Knowledge', in Jonathan Dancy and Ernest Sosa, eds., *A Companion to Epistemology* (Oxford: Blackwell, 1992), 255–8, and Berys Gaut, 'Art and Knowledge', in Jerrold Levinson, ed., *The Oxford Handbook of Aesthetics*, (Oxford University Press, 2003), 436–50. For a more recent emphasis on the problem of paraphrase in relation to film and philosophy, see Murray Smith, 'Film Art, Argument, and Ambiguity'. I agree with Smith's worries about paraphrase as well as the objections he raises to the 'thought-experiment' analogy. As David Davies usefully points out, various contrasting views have emerged in philosophy of science debates over the pay-offs of thought experiments, and, according to deflationist opinion, thought experiments do not really teach us anything, and so can hardly be called upon to elevate the cognitive status of fictional narratives; see his 'Can Film Be a Philosophical Medium?', *Postgraduate Journal of Aesthetics*, 5/2 (2008), 1–20.

example, that we allow that an exclusive and valuable feature of the cinematic medium is its 'recording and representational' capacity, the idea being simply that the cinematic apparatus can be used to make shots of items in front of a camera (and microphone), which representations can then be used to provide an artificially generated 'detached display' that visually (and sometimes aurally) depicts those items.[10] Only the cinema can provide moving images of past events, and such images can be informative in ways other representations cannot.

This contention need not rest on an extreme realist or transparency thesis about the cinematic medium. Rather, we need only recognize that an accurate verbal transcription of what a philosopher said in a lecture does not give us the same type of experience as that provided by a motion picture recording of that lecture, as the latter can convey visual and aural evidence pertaining to the speaker's delivery, which could in turn have implications for one's understanding of the philosophical content of the lecture. Such a conception of the cinema's representational capacities will be compatible, then, with the observation that audio-visual recordings of a philosopher's lectures are an exclusively cinematic resource. It follows that the cinema can make an exclusive contribution to philosophy by providing vivid audio-visual representations of genial philosophical conversations and lectures. Yet this tepid result trivializes the idea of yoking this very broad conception of film's capacities to the bold thesis about the medium's (or art form's) contributions to philosophy.

To expound on this dilemma argument a bit more, we may return to the first horn and ask how linguistically mediated arguments can describe or otherwise demonstrate the existence of an innovative philosophical contribution that *in principle* transcends the expressive capacities of linguistic media. If the 'properly cinematic' contribution to philosophy can be referred to but not stated with words, proponents of a bold epistemic thesis have to fall back on appeals to an indescribable cinematic *je ne sais quoi* that they believe they have experienced, in the hope that others may have a similar experience and come to agree that philosophical insight or understanding has been manifested in a film.

---

10 Noël Carroll, 'Towards an Ontology of the Moving Image', in Cynthia A. Freeland and Thomas E. Wartenberg, eds., *Philosophy and Film* (New York: Routledge, 1995), 68–85; cf. David Davies, 'Ontology', in Livingston and Plantinga, eds., *The Routledge Companion to Philosophy and Film*, 217–26.

Yet here is where reasonable doubts arise. Although it may be plausible to report that an experience of a work's montage or motion picture style has given rise to a vivid, visually mediated recollection of some previously known philosophical thought, it is fair to ask whether such appeals to experience can offer good grounds for believing that a significantly new idea, general thesis, or argument has emerged. If such a claim is made, it is only reasonable to ask for an articulation of these important 'clear yet indistinct' ideas. If such a request is thought unfair or question-begging, it should be noted that the situation is not simply a confrontation between advocates of two contrasting claims, that is, between those who believe in ineffable cinematic insights and those who happen to have some unfortunate doubts about their existence. The problem here is not essentially a social one, but that of providing reasons or evidence for belief in a new and valuable philosophical insight, be it for oneself or for others. The burden of proof rests on the shoulders of anyone who comes to suspect that there exists a new and controversial source of philosophical knowledge. He or she should be able to give reasons in support of the belief that appeals to verbally indescribable experiences or entities should exert a significant influence on philosophical opinion on such subjects as personal identity, freedom, meta-ethics, moral dilemmas, or epistemology (all of which are topics that have been central to the cinema and philosophy literature). Here we chart the gap between the cinema's various pedagogically useful illustrations or evocations of previously published philosophical reasonings, and the bold claim that, in its ineffable, exclusively cinematic form of expression, some work of cinema has significantly advanced philosophical knowledge in a way supporting some suitably strong version of the cinema as philosophy thesis.

It should be noted here that I am not trying to rule out the *logical* possibility that someone's experience in either making or watching a film could involve the acquisition of a kind of ineffable wisdom. In other words, there is nothing contradictory or incoherent about that idea. Also, it is not simply false or incoherent to write, as Daniel Frampton writes, that 'film possibly contains a whole new system of thought, a new episteme'.[11] It is also coherent to say that *possibly* film does not contain any such new system or episteme. As such a new, ineffable system of thought cannot, in principle, be articulated verbally; what is ruled out is the possibility of having or providing any linguistically mediated grounds

---

[11] Frampton, *Filmosophy*, 11.

for believing in the existence of a particular case in which wisdom of this sort has been acquired. It is also logically possible that the experience of acquiring such wisdom could take place while standing outside the process of formulating, asking for, and giving discursive reasons. Yet a private, 'self-evident' event in which wisdom is acquired should not be recognized as an *independent and innovative* philosophical result because the question whether a philosophical thought is new hinges on a large body of prior philosophical contributions. Sufficient information about this rather difficult contextual question can hardly be provided by an ineffable experience occasioned by a film, since it is at bottom a matter of recalling knowledge acquired, for example, through conversations and extensive readings of philosophical publications.

If it is allowed, on the other hand, that cinematic insights can be paraphrased, other problems for the bold thesis become salient. I take it that a paraphrase of something is the result of an attempt to provide an interpretative statement or thinking-through of that item's meanings. To convey an interpretation of some item's philosophically relevant meanings, one must employ linguistically mediated philosophical background assumptions and arguments.[12] Thus, if our aim is to provide an interpretation of René Descartes's *Meditationes de prima philosophia*, we must relate what we take to be the text's linguistic meanings to assumptions about the philosopher's intentions and philosophical background, or to other relevant philosophical works and arguments (such as St Augustine's arguments against scepticism). It seems plausible to assume that similar considerations hold for philosophically oriented interpretations of the meanings of a picture or a film. So, even if specifically cinematic devices, such as montage, were essential to a film's philosophical content in the sense that this content could not have been fully articulated in another medium, the successful *philosophical* function of that device remains importantly dependent on linguistically articulated background thoughts mobilized in both the creation and the interpretation of the film's philosophical significance. In the absence of such background ideas, questions about personal identity, free will, the

---

[12] This basic assumption about interpretation finds a clear statement and justification in Jerry R. Hobbs, *Literature and Cognition* (Stanford, CA: Center for the Study of Language and Information, 1990). There is, of course, a looser sense of 'interpretation' that also covers musical and other performances. My remark focuses on critical interpretations, not performances. See Jerrold Levinson, 'Performative vs. Critical Interpretation in Music', in Michael Krausz, ed., *The Interpretation of Music* (Oxford: Clarendon Press, 1993), 33–60.

possibility of knowledge, and so on could not be cogently pondered by either the film-makers or the spectators. The same point holds, *a fortiori*, for more sophisticated and systematic argumentations about a film's implications for such topics.

As I shall argue at greater length in the next chapter, a philosophically oriented interpreter of a film must take up the task of importing a well-defined *problématique* (a set of assumptions and questions) if aspects of the film's thematic and narrative design are to resonate with sufficiently sophisticated and well-articulated theses or arguments. There are, of course, films where some of this work has already been done by the film-maker, at least in part by means of the audio-visual display itself. The one film I know of that explicitly indicates some of the relevant bibliography in the audio-visual display is Pier Paolo Pasolini's (1975) *Salò o il centroventi giornate di Sodoma* (*Salo or the 120 Days of Sodom*), where a reading list appears in the title sequence. Some of these readings are cited by the characters along the way, but that is, of course, quite different from a thorough presentation of the theories in question. Another interesting case is Alain Resnais's *Mon oncle d'Amérique* (*My Uncle from America*) (1979), which cuts back and forth between shots from an interview with Henri Laborit and scenes from a series of interlaced fictional stories that may be taken as both exemplifying and challenging Laborit's freewheeling socio-biological propositions.[13] Sometimes it is the director whose writings or interview pronouncements provide the crucial background that creates a philosophical context for understanding the film's points, such as references to specific philosophical writings and positions. I explore this option in my discussion of Ingmar Bergman in the third part of this book.

A crucial question for the bold thesis, then, is whether the film's treatment of philosophically relevant topics manifests any *historically innovative* insights. It is impossible to address ourselves reasonably to such a question in the absence of a specific interpretative proposal along those lines, and this fact indicates that a linguistic interpretation is a necessary constituent of a philosophical acknowledgement of any such contribution. Yet this is fatal to the bold thesis, which requires that a film's epistemic contribution to philosophy be

---

[13] For discussion of this example, see Seymour Chatman, *Coming to Terms: The Rhetoric of Narrative in Fiction and Film* (Ithaca, NY: Cornell University Press, 1990).

paraphrase-independent and historically innovative, and not parasitic on either the film-maker's or the spectator's linguistically articulated determination or interpretation of the film's content.

To sum up, if the bold thesis rests on a narrow conception of cinema's specificity, the upshot is an insoluble dilemma of paraphrase. Either the properly cinematic insight, narrowly construed, cannot be paraphrased, in which case its existence is doubtful and/or cannot be argued for sufficiently; or it can and must be paraphrased, in which case it is on its own insufficient to the philosophical task assigned to it by the bold thesis. If, on the other hand, a much broader conception of cinema's exclusive capacities is opted for (namely, one that acknowledges cinema's representational and recording capacities), the epistemic thesis is trivialized, as films that include audio-visual recordings of philosophical lectures or conversations are included.

In a probing essay on film as philosophy, Aaron Smuts has contended that my arguments against the bold thesis succumb to a counter-example. The counter-example on which Smuts bases this claim is not an actual cinematic work but a possible counterpart to Sergei Eisenstein's *October* (1928)—one produced in a world where the intellectual history prior to 1928 is significantly different. Smuts focuses his remarks in particular on the 'For God and Country' sequence in that film. This is a notorious sequence in which shots of buildings and objects associated with Christianity are followed by shots of various religious artefacts (for a sample of shots from this lengthy montage sequence, see Figures 1.10–1.17).[14] According to Smuts, in this sequence the Soviet director used the specifically cinematic means of 'intellectual montage' in order to express general philosophical ideas and to give an audience reasons to accept them—precisely the sort of thing that one would be warranted to classify as the doing of philosophy. Smuts contends that what Eisenstein effectively presented with this sequence is an analogical argument similar in thrust to one set forth by Friedrich Nietzsche in the *Genealogy of Morals*: 'Eisenstein is offering a genealogy of sorts, comparing Christianity to its supposed precursors. The viewer understands that the two classes of artifacts are being compared, and that the overall suggestion is that the Christian artifacts are no better than pagan statuary.' Smuts further comments that this message corresponds quite closely to the

---

[14] Aaron Smuts, 'Film as Philosophy: In Defense of a Bold Thesis', *Journal of Aesthetics and Art Criticism*, 67 (2009), 409–420. I thank him for kindly sending his thoughtful paper to me.

director's intention, at least as it was put by Eisenstein in the following passage:

Maintaining the denotation of 'God', the images increasingly disagree with our concept of God, inevitably leading to individual conclusions about the true nature of all deities. In this case, too, a chain of images attempted to achieve a purely intellectual resolution, resulting from a conflict between a preconception and a *gradual discrediting of it in purposeful steps*.[15]

Smuts adds that this atheistic argument presented in *October* was comprehensible to the audience independently of their knowledge of any prior theoretical publications, and *could have been* innovative, even though it was in fact anticipated by other thinkers. Smuts invites us, then, to imagine a counterpart to *October*—namely, one produced in a context with a strikingly different intellectual history. It is Smuts's contention that the possibility of such a case supports the bold thesis.

In response, I hasten to agree with Smuts that the *actual* Eisenstein intended to use visual parallelism to liken Christian and other religious artefacts, and thereby to make some kind of criticism of religion; he also wanted to make a point about the link between religious belief and counter-revolutionary nationalistic ideas: at the end of the sequence some of the same religious images are intercut with images of a 'magic' reassembling of the statue of Alexander III that was shown being dismantled by the revolutionaries earlier in the film (Figures 1.18–1.19). I have doubts, however, about the claim that the actual Eisenstein film satisfies the independence condition involving the use of means unique to the cinematic medium. Moreover, the conditions that made it possible for Eisenstein to express a philosophical message in *October* would be lacking in the case of the imagined, radically innovative counterpart, which is why the claim about the possibility of such a case does not genuinely support the bold thesis.

In the context of the actual Eisenstein's *October* (setting the issue of censorship aside), the 'For God and Country' sequence indeed helps convey a specific claim about religion, but it does so only in relation to the director's assumptions and intentions. The fact that Christian imagery is followed by shots of a Buddha and then what look like various African sculptural figures does not on its own specify what the intended relation between these images is meant to be; in another context, the

[15] Sergei Eisenstein, 'Methods of Montage', in Jay Leyda, ed. and trans., *Film Form: Essays in Film Theory* (New York: Harcourt, Brace & World, 1949), 72–83, at 62. For background, see David Bordwell, *The Cinema of Eisenstein* (London: Routledge, 1993).

Figure 1.10. Intellectual montage in Sergei Eisenstein's *October*.

Figure 1.11.

Figure 1.12.

Figure 1.13.

Figure 1.14.

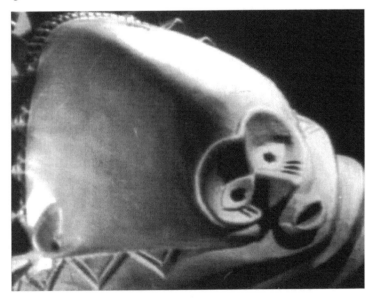

Figure 1.15.

Figure 1.16.

Figure 1.17.

Figure 1.18. Counter-revolutionary magic in *October*.

Figure 1.19.

point of such intercutting could be to *contrast* Christian and other types of statuary as they are obviously dissimilar in many ways. If the montage sequence on its own gives the audience good reason to believe anything, it is that *the director* had made some kind of fairly vague comparison between Russian orthodox Christianity and other religions, as well as the blunt idea that religion is counter-revolutionary. Consider, for example, the following statement of intention that appears a few pages later in the essay by Eisenstein that Smuts cites:

An example of this [intellectual overtone] can be found in the sequence of the 'gods' in *October*, where all the conditions for their comparison are made dependent on an exclusively class-intellectual sound of each piece in its relation to God. I say class, for though the emotional principle is universally human, the intellectual principle is profoundly tinged by class. These pieces were assembled in accordance with a descending intellectual scale—pulling back the concept of God to its origins, forcing the spectator to perceive this 'progress' intellectually.[16]

What, in the context of the film of which it is a part, does the montage sequence indicate about the origin of the concept of God? And, more pointedly, what does it 'force' the spectator to think? Very little. It is worth pointing out that many of my Hong Kong students report on the basis of a first viewing of the film that they find the montage sequence highly puzzling. They wonder, for example, why the image of a statue of Buddha figures where it does in the montage. Are the images that are associated with a counter-revolutionary Christianity contrasted negatively to images associated with more peaceful and enlightened religions? Spectators who, unlike these students, have the requisite background knowledge pertaining to Eisenstein's intellectual background and stated intentions may understand the sequence as a more specific attack on Christianity as a form of repressive ideology 'just like other religions', including those that are 'lower' on some tendentious 'intellectual scale'. They might also then understand the visual rhetoric as expressing Hegel-inspired prejudices about sculpture and the lowly place of African and Asian art within world-historical development. Something like this seems to inform Eisenstein's above-quoted remark about how the later images in the sequence disagree with 'our concept of God' and its relation to deities on a 'lower intellectual scale', where the first-person-plural pronoun presumably was meant to refer to Russians or non-Asians.

---

16 Eisenstein, 'Methods of Montage', 82.

While the example of Eisenstein's 'intellectual montage' reinforces the thought that a film-maker can use the cinematic medium along with other means to urge some familiar Marxist point (all religion is the 'opiate of the masses'), it hardly supports the bold claim that film has a unique ability independently to express significant and innovative philosophical reasoning, such as a new thesis about the origin of the concept of God. Smuts reasons that if no one had ever set forth a critique of Christianity as one religion amongst others, a counterpart to Eisenstein's film would have been philosophically original, and that the possibility of such an imagined case is good enough to support the bold thesis. Yet reasonable doubts can be raised about this claim. The possible case imagined by Smuts is crucially different from the actual case of Eisenstein's film, because the relevant philosophical background and independently articulated authorial thoughts and intentions must be absent. Otherwise, the counterpart film could not provide an independent and philosophically innovative critique of religion. We can only speculate about such a counterfactual scenario, but it is far from obvious what determinate message about the origin or status of specific religious doctrines could have been expressed by the audio-visual display of *October* in a context where the relevant argument about religion had not yet been formulated non-cinematically (either by the non-Marxist counterpart Eisenstein himself or by anyone else). It is highly dubious that in such a context the montage sequence could have been used to articulate an innovative and independent philosophical critique of Christianity or of religion in general.[17]

If the bold thesis is to be given some genuine support, what must be found is a case where a film-maker uses cinematic devices alone successfully to formulate and express an innovative and sophisticated philosophical line of thought or argument. And that is the requirement that leads to the problem of paraphrase and the dilemma argument outlined above.

[17] Noël Carroll discusses the philosophical content of this film in his 'For God and Country', *Artforum*, 11/5 (1973), 56–60; repr. in *Interpreting the Moving Image* (Cambridge: Cambridge University Press, 1998), 80–91. He writes that 'It is within the context of Marxist theory that we can appraise the importance for Eisenstein of the sequence of shots entitled "For God and Country" in his film *October*' (p. 81). As is obvious above, I am in agreement with this point, but, for the reasons sketched above, I am sceptical about the attempt to extract a specific *reductio ad absurdum* argument from the montage sequence; Carroll denies, in any case, that Eisenstein 'invented a new and interesting atheological argument' (p. 88).

If the bold thesis is dubious, what other options are there? As the bold epistemic thesis is a conjunction of exclusivity and epistemic requirements with regard to means and results, respectively, three main alternatives can be considered: (1) giving up on exclusivity while maintaining strong epistemic requirements; (2) maintaining exclusivity while giving up on strong epistemic requirements; and (3) giving up on both the exclusivity and strong epistemic constraints. I shall advocate the third option.

I turn first to reasons that motivate a weakening of the epistemic component of the bold thesis—namely, its expectations with regard to the philosophical significance of cinema's contributions. My recommendation here is that the bar should not be set too high. There is no good reason to spurn or belittle the pedagogical functions to which films can be put in the philosophical curriculum. The appeal of the medium and art form, as well as the affective and persuasive force films can have, help make films an effective *complement* to a philosophical *pensum* or required reading list comprised of difficult writings by philosophers. The stimulation of students' imaginative engagement with philosophical issues, which engagement in turn heightens motivation for renewed encounters with the items on the reading list, is probably the single most valuable contribution the cinema can make to philosophy.[18]

An alternative to the bold thesis need not contend that cinema's contributions are *exclusively* pedagogical, or a matter of redundant restatements of familiar ideas. It is possible that some film-makers have used film as part of a creative exploration of philosophical problems. Arthur Danto argued that Andy Warhol's 1964 film *Empire* makes a philosophical contribution by helping the spectator reflect on the concept of cinema, and, in a similar vein, both Noël Carroll and Jinhee Choi have convincingly argued that some avant-garde film-makers have used their films to make implicit and insightful interventions in ongoing debates about the very nature of the cinematic medium.[19]

---

[18] This is hardly a new point, but it bears restating. For an earlier pronouncement in this vein, see Kevin L. Stoehr's fine introduction to the collection of papers he edited, *Film and Knowledge: Essays on the Integration of Images and Ideas* (Jefferson, NC: McFarland, 2002), 5–6.

[19] Arthur Danto, 'The Philosopher as Andy Warhol', in *Philosophizing Art: Selected Essays* (Berkeley and Los Angeles: University of California Press, 1999), 61–83; Jinhee Choi, 'Apperception on Display: Structural Films and Philosophy', in Noël Carroll and Jinhee Choi, eds., *Philosophy of Film and Motion Pictures* (Malden, MA: Blackwell, 2006), 165–72; Noël Carroll, 'Philosophizing through the Moving Image: The Case of Serene Velocity', in Smith and Wartenberg, eds., *Thinking through Cinema*, 173–85.

While such cases are interesting, I do not think they support a robust and sweeping version of the bold thesis. That a few non-fiction and avant-garde films have been used to make points in debates over the nature of cinema hardly instils confidence about the cinema's capacity to make exclusively cinematic and innovative epistemic contributions on philosophical topics more generally.

As I shall argue at greater length below, films may have a *heuristic* role in the context of ongoing investigations within a number of avenues of philosophical enquiry. Thinking about the issues raised by a cinematic (or other) work of fiction could help a philosopher come up with some new hypothesis or argumentative strategy, perhaps by giving rise to creative imaginings about patterns of behaviour or interaction. I take it that this is core insight behind discussions of fictional works as 'thought experiments', a topic that has a complex tradition that includes Émile Zola's hyperbolic and imprecise use of the notion to promote his novels, which he labelled *des romans expérimentaux*. Questions can be raised, of course, about the soundness of an analogy between controlled scientific experimentation (such as the inordinately costly experiments designed to detect the Higgs boson), on the one hand, and imaginative conjectures based on possible cases, on the other. While the identification of possible cases can be taken as a direct exploration of *conceptual* possibility, that procedure should not be conflated with the discovery of imagination-independent empirical regularities. Yet, as David K. Lewis points out, sometimes we already have the evidence we need, but do not appreciate its significance, and a fiction can play a crucial role in helping us to think about this evidence correctly.[20] Note, however, that, if we are to reason soundly about the actual world on the basis of the content of a fiction, we must work with sound assumptions about the resemblance between the fictional cases and known features of actuality. For example, particular behaviour in the fiction is recognized as belonging to a category of actual behaviour, and it may turn out to be sound to assume that the

For a commentary on Danto's discussion of Warhol and for a related claim about philosophical argumentation in Tony Conrad's *The Flicker*, see Wartenberg, *Thinking on Screen*, ch. 7.

20 David K. Lewis, 'Postscripts to "Truth in Fiction"', in *Philosophical Papers*, vol. i (New York: Oxford University Press, 1983), 276–80. In the context of discussions of film's epistemic value, Bruce Russell has usefully stressed the fact that a fiction film cannot provide empirical confirmation of general philosophical claims. He allows, however, that imaginary cases can evoke possible counter-examples to a general thesis. See his 'On the Philosophical Limits of Film', in Carroll and Choi, eds., *Philosophy of Film and Motion Pictures*, 387–90.

conclusions of reasoning about the former can be carried over to the latter.

Clearly, however, there are abstract problems in philosophy of logic and metaphysics that are not likely to be illumined with reference to cinematic storytelling; on the other hand, as the stories that films convey generally deal with people's unusual problems and efforts to solve them, it may be expected that pondering such matters can contribute to conjectures and observations related to a range of topics pertaining to agency and value. I discuss this topic at greater length in what follows, especially in the third part of this book, in which I explore Bergman's interest in issues in philosophical psychology and ethics.

Turning now to the exclusivity requirement, what good grounds can be given for limiting the philosopher's interest in cinema to any of the notions associated with the expression 'the specificity of the cinematic medium or art form'? One argument in this vein is based on assumptions about the nature of art appreciation. The key idea here is that, to appreciate a film as a work of art adequately, one must ask (amongst other questions) how successfully its themes have been expressed or embodied by its style and by devices specific to the medium.[21] Given such assumptions, some philosophical raids on movies' philosophical contents have the otherwise undesirable characteristic of being very poor instances of critical appreciation. In an effort to bring explorations of 'cinema as philosophy' back in line with what is generally perceived as sensitive or even moderately competent film appreciation, attention is focused on medium and art-form specific devices, on the stylistic 'how' as a necessary means to the thematic 'what'. A problem with this line of thought, however, is that it underestimates the practical difficulty of simultaneously pursuing what are two rather distinct ends. One goal is that of providing a critical discussion of a film that best elucidates and assesses its artistic value and use of the cinematic medium. A distinct goal is that of asking whether and how the film expresses or gives rise to thoughts contributing genuinely to some philosophical debate on a specialized topic. Attentive critical appreciation of a particular work of art rarely requires the importation of the requisite philosophical

---

[21] For background, see Gary Iseminger, 'Aesthetic Appreciation', *Journal of Aesthetics and Art Criticism*, 39 (1981), 389–99; and his 'Experiential Theories of Aesthetic Value', in Richard Shusterman and Adele Tomlin, eds., *Aesthetic Experience* (London: Routledge, 2008), 45–58; and Stein Haugom Olsen, 'Criticism and Appreciation', in Peter Lamarque, ed., *Philosophy and Fiction* (Aberdeen: Aberdeen University Press, 1983), 38–51.

background with its complex array of terms, positions, arguments (and, at times, formal notations). To do so is to employ the work, and, most commonly, aspects of the story the work can be taken as conveying, as an illustration of some part of a theory or argument; whereas to engage in careful appreciation of the individual work is distinct from the properly philosophical goal of exploring and constructing more general arguments. The two goals are not logically incompatible, but it is at least rhetorically very difficult to pursue them simultaneously. To couch this more general point in terms of an example, do we really learn anything about complex arguments and counter-arguments surrounding specific versions of scepticism by paying close attention to the cinematography, acting, montage, lighting, special effects, and production design in *The Matrix*?

In conclusion, a defensible alternative to the bold thesis is the moderate contention that results from a significant weakening of both constituents of the bold thesis. A film can usefully express or illustrate philosophical ideas and arguments, be they significantly innovative or not. It can do so by means of verbal or other devices that the cinema shares with other media and art forms. A film can be philosophically valuable even when its philosophical content is neither original nor conveyed by means exclusive to the cinematic medium. Interpretations that refer to aspects of a film in order to illustrate philosophical ideas can, but need not, focus on the film's specifically cinematic devices.

In this chapter I have presented only the beginnings of a schematic framework for thinking about cinema as philosophy. Although I have presented objections to a prevalent, bold thesis about film's contribution to philosophy and have provided a moderate alternative to that thesis, I have not provided a detailed description and justification of that alternative. In the next chapter I turn to some objections that can be raised even to this moderate thesis.

2

Arguing over Cinema as Philosophy

In his 1835 lectures on aesthetics, G. W. F. Hegel warned that it is a mistake to make an art form serve external ends, such as 'instruction, moral improvement, or political agitation'.[1] As his remarks pertain to any attempt to interpret or evaluate a work of art along instrumental lines, they can be understood as challenging not only the extreme idea that all good art must serve the 'correct' political cause, but also, by extension, the relatively moderate thesis, which was broached in the previous chapter, that films can be appropriately used to illustrate philosophical topics and positions.

Even if one believes—as I do—that this Hegel-inspired challenge can be met, his remarks provide a useful (albeit seemingly anachronistic) point of departure for framing and taking up some important questions about the philosophical significance of film. When considered carefully, Hegel's brief criticism of instrumental uses of art can be understood as raising two separate objections. The first is a contention about art's *proper* value, which, according to this passage in Hegel's voluminous writings, is intrinsic and not a matter of art's advancement of non-artistic goals. For the sake of convenience, we can call this the 'propriety objection'. A second, logically separate contention—which in my view is the more interesting and challenging of the two objections—has to do with the wisdom of employing art to serve non-artistic means. Hegel's point in this regard is that it is a mistake to use art to try to serve

[1] G. W. F. Hegel, *Vorlesungen über die Ästhetik III*, in *Werke in zwanzig Bänden*, ed. Eva Moldenhauer and Karl Markus Michel (Frankfurt am Main: Suhrkamp, 1986), xv. 268–9; *Aesthetics: Lectures on Fine Art*, trans. T. M. Knox (Oxford: Clarendon Press, 1975), ii. 995. As I am not attempting Hegel scholarship here, I set aside questions about the relations between these remarks and the German philosopher's other writings. There is an obvious tension between Hegel's emphasis on art's final value in the cited passage and his more general discussions of art as an expression of truths that can be expressed by religion and philosophy. For some background on this point, see Stephen Houlgate, *An Introduction to Hegel: Freedom, Truth and History* (Malden, MA: Blackwell, 2005), ch. 9, and esp. p. 220.

non-artistic ends because they are better served by other means. This can be labelled 'the rationality objection'.

I shall pursue the following agenda in this chapter. First I set forth and respond to the propriety objection. The discussion hinges on assumptions about the nature of artistic value and relations between instrumental and intrinsic value. I then discuss two ways to understand the rationality objection, which leads to a discussion of the conditions under which a cinematic work can be appropriately said to have a determinate, philosophical content. Taken in its strongest form, the rationality objection usefully underscores the need to understand how a work's content is determined. Although we may be tempted to reject the assumptions about rationality that subtend the Hegel-inspired objection(s), I contend that there is another and better way to respond to his challenge.

MEETING THE PROPRIETY OBJECTION

In the context of a general discussion of film's philosophical value, one response to the propriety objection is to grant the point about art's proper value while observing that not all films are works of art. In the case of non-artistic films, there can be no conflict between a work's properly artistic goals and whatever epistemic or cognitive ends it might serve. For example, it would be ludicrous to oppose the making of a crash-dummy film for the sole reason that such footage is not very likely to have any great artistic value, and an analogous argument may be applied to many highly useful and effective documentaries or non-fiction films. It follows that, with regard to at least some films, there is no successful propriety objection to exploring their cognitive merits, and that includes whatever philosophical value these films might have.

This first response to the propriety objection, though accurate, does not apply to the many films, including some non-fictional ones, that fall within the category of 'art' (broadly construed). The thrust of the challenge is that such art films should be evaluated and understood primarily, or even exclusively, in terms of criteria pertinent to their artistic goals and merits. Hegel's thinking, at least as it finds expression in the passage referred to above, seems to be that art has its own *intrinsic* or *final* value. Thus Hegel writes that the very concept of art stands in conflict with art's reduction to instrumental servitude or

Zweckdienlichkeit. Hegel also evokes the 'free heights where poetry lives for its own sake alone', or, somewhat more literally translated, 'sets its own course'.[2] Hegel is relying here on a well-known and influential philosophical contrast between instrumental and final values. Roughly, something has instrumental value just in case it serves as a means to some other end; something has final value when it has non-instrumental value, or, as the expression goes, when it is valuable 'for its own sake'. Hegel's key thought here would, at least on this reading, be that to assess art *qua* art (or, in other words, in its capacity as art) cannot in any case be a matter of appraising its instrumental rewards.

The Hegel-inspired propriety objection rests on the assumption that artistic value is a proper subset of intrinsic or final value, and that there are therefore no (legitimate) instrumental, *artistic* values. One way to respond to that thesis would be to contend that in fact *all* artistic value is instrumental: a work of art has no artistic value other than the use people make of it. Yet such a strong counter-thesis is hard to establish, and the debate over it has led to inconclusive discussions of contrasting intuitions about arcane examples. A better response to the Hegelian assumption is to make the more modest contention that, while it may very well be the case that some artistic value is intrinsic in some sense, it is also sensible to recognize that at least some artistic value is instrumental, and not a matter uniquely of the kind of 'end in itself' that Hegel seems to have had in mind when he rhapsodized about art's 'free heights'.

It may be worth noting that at least some of the things artists tell us about their artistic aims square with that modest philosophical thesis. For example, in a 1970 CBC interview, Ingmar Bergman contended that his films should be useful to the spectators, and he proposed that they should in this sense be thought of like ordinary artefacts, such as chairs and cups. (Elsewhere he quipped that what he was making might be just like a pot, but at least it was *his* pot and not quite like anyone else's.[3])

---

[2] 'Denn kommt es ihr wesentlich auf dergleichen Absichten an, welche in diesem Falle aus der ganzen Fassung und Darstellungsart herausscheinen, so ist sogleich das poetische Werk aus der freien Höhe, in deren Region es nur seiner selbst wegen dazusein [sich] zeigt, in das Gebiet des Relativen heruntergezogen, und es entsteht entweder ein Bruch zwischen dem, was die Kunst verlangt, und demjenigen, was die anderweitigen Intentionen fordern, oder die Kunst wird, ihrem Begriffe zuwider, nur als ein Mittel verbraucht und damit zur Zweckdienlichkeit herabgesetzt' (Hegel, *Vorlesungen*, xv. 268).

[3] This remark is found in an unpublished typescript in the Ingmar Bergman archive, 'Blad ur en obefintlig dagbok'.

The kind of 'use' that Bergman stressed in such remarks is emotional, for he insisted that one of the great things films can be used for is to stir up valuable emotional responses. And indeed people commonly say that they found a work moving or stirring, and such remarks are usually taken as counting as a reason why the work should be thought as having some artistic merit, just as saying 'it left me cold' would normally be understood as a mark against a film. It strikes me that we ought to agree with Bergman and many other artists in saying that at least some of the emotional (and other) experiences works of art give people under certain circumstances constitute a central type of artistic value.[4]

A good response to the propriety objection may, then, be based on the claim that some, if not all, of art's properly artistic value is instrumental, since it is a matter of serving as a means to a valued end, such as the occasioning of valuable emotional experiences, or, again, of influencing other artists to make valuable works. Given that at least some 'properly artistic' value is instrumental, why not further allow that one of art's legitimate artistic pay-offs is the advancement of cognitive or epistemic goals? And, if that is legitimate, why not include whatever philosophical insight or knowledge we might stand to gain from our experience of a work of art?

To sum up, the propriety objection fails because it has not been shown that someone who makes use of art films in an attempt to advance philosophical (or other) knowledge must make the mistake of turning his or her back on the films' artistic value. In happy cases, discovering philosophical insight in a work could contribute to the project of appreciating aspects of its artistic value. Recognition of the themes or content of a work puts us in a position to gauge whether the specific artistic devices employed in the work are effective or not. There may, however, be other cases where a philosophically oriented interpretative raid on a cinematic or other work amounts to a colossal failure to appreciate the work's artistic merits or demerits. It remains to be shown, however, why someone who develops such an interpretation *necessarily* makes a mistake. There could, of course, be cases where an overemphasis on some philosophical theme leads the interpreter to fail to realize his or

---

[4] On emotion, and art and emotion in general, see Jenefer Robinson, *Deeper than Reason* (Oxford: Oxford University Press, 2005); on emotion, affect, and the cinema, see Carl Plantinga, *Moving Viewers: American Film and the Spectator's Experience* (Berkeley and Los Angeles: University of California Press, 2009).

her goal of articulating a comprehensive appreciation of the film's artistic values—if only because the approach to the work is so highly selective. Assume, however, that some philosophically minded interpreter of a film does not pursue any such goal. He or she just wants to refer to aspects of the story in order to make some philosophical points. On what basis could that person's interpretation be evaluated or criticized? It would be unfair and inappropriate to complain that the person has failed to write good film criticism, as no such aim was envisioned. It is here that the second Hegel-inspired objection becomes pertinent.

THE RATIONALITY OBJECTION

At bottom, the rationality objection is a matter of doubting the practical wisdom of choosing to use a work of art as a means to some non-artistic end. Hegel's suggestion is that it is somehow a mistake to try to make art serve 'external' or non-artistic ends because those very ends can be pursued *more effectively or more completely* (Hegel writes 'vollständiger') by other means.

Two key questions are raised here: is this Hegel-inspired point about the relative effectiveness or completeness of artistic and non-artistic means correct? And, if it is correct, does it genuinely follow that it is always a mistake to try to use an art form to advance such non-artistic goals as the acquisition of knowledge?

With regard to the first question, it is hard to believe that no work of art could ever serve *any* important non-artistic end at least as well as some non-artistic means could serve that end. Although the wording of Hegel's text seems to advance such a bold, but empirically dubious, contention, it is more interesting to explore the merits of a related, yet more cautious, claim. In the current context, a more relevant question would be whether films ever serve as a rational means to the acquisition or transmission of philosophical insight or knowledge. One way to defeat the rationality objection, then, would be to argue convincingly for the existence of such cases. And one way to clarify and strengthen the rationality objection is to give reasons why we should not expect to see any such cases. In the next section, I shall try to do just that in order to bring forth what I take to be a key point about the idea of cinema as philosophy.

As I indicated above, Hegel's text is ambiguous between two ways of reading the rationality objection. On one reading, a film would be a *less effective* means of doing philosophy than engaging in discussion or writing a philosophical essay, and so having recourse to cinema would be an irrational choice. On the other reading, use of the cinematic medium would be the wrong choice because its realization of the philosophical end is less 'complete'. Although the German word *vollständig* covers both readings equally well, there is a sense in which it is the 'completeness' reading of Hegel's challenge that best suits the topic at hand. The basic thought runs like this: if it can be established that a film does not allow us to realize a non-artistic goal as completely as some other, non-artistic means, it could be argued that, in at least a range of cases, the degree of realization made possible by film is not 'complete enough' to be sufficient; on this assumption, it would be irrational to choose a means that does not make possible a sufficiently complete realization of the goal.

How might this completeness objection be applied to the case of cinema as philosophy? The first step is to identify the relevant goal. I take it that, even on a highly liberal and vague understanding of what kind of philosophical contribution is necessary to a film's doing philosophy, a basic requirement is that the film has—or, better, expresses—a significant, determinate philosophical content. In other words, it is not good enough to say that a film has 'done philosophy' because watching the film prompted a baffled and unsuccessful search for the philosophical ideas in the film. Such a search could even benefit the spectator, but that would not mean that the film should be credited with having made a significant contribution to philosophical understanding or insight. Nor would it be good enough to say that a movie was vaguely thought-provoking, or that it motivated the spectator to go out and read some philosophy. It would not be satisfactory to be told that a film was philosophical because the director, scriptwriter, or other persons who were instrumental in its design were in a philosophical mood. Instead, specific philosophical ideas must have been expressed by the film, and, under the right circumstances, they would effectively be communicated to some of the viewers. So a first requirement motivating the completeness objection is one that could be called the 'content-completeness' requirement.

Under what conditions, then, does a film express a determinate philosophical (or other) content? And under what conditions can it do so in a manner that is sufficiently complete to defeat the rationality objection? If we ask about the locus of the philosophical (or other) content of a film, the quick answer is that the content is, as the very word suggests, 'in' the film and is part of it. Yet this is not good enough, since the idea that an audio-visual display has a determinate meaning or content by virtue of its intrinsic properties *alone* is open to a number of devastating objections. First of all, some of a work's meanings are conventional in the sense that they depend on the relation between features of the display and the relevant linguistic and other conventions. This is perfectly obvious when comprehension of a film requires knowledge of one or more natural languages heard spoken in the film. The meaning is only *in* the film in the sense that the dialogues have determinate meanings for people who can apply the appropriate linguistic conventions—namely, those that were effectively acted upon in the making of the film.

The relation between the display's content and external, linguistic conventions is but the tip of the iceberg. Consider a more unusual, and purely visual example. Someone who has the ability to recognize a flag seen on the horizon could normally rely on this same ability to tell whether a shot in a motion picture depicts a flag or not. In the context of a black and white film meant to convey a story set in Sweden, an image of a rectangular piece of cloth with a lighter, contrasting cross on it could be aptly recognized as a representation of a Swedish flag (Figure 2.1). Yet that same black-and-white image is visually indistinguishable from an image of a Danish flag (which has a red field and white cross, as opposed to the Swedish blue and yellow colours). Change the context (that is, shift to a film about Danes in Denmark) and the very same black-and-white footage could function equally well as an image of a Danish flag. It follows that the cinematic content is not uniquely determined by the visual properties of the image. Nor is the content determined simply by the actual context in which the film was made. In a black-and-white film made in Sweden about Denmark, the image could serve perfectly well as an image of a Danish flag, even if a Swedish flag had, for the sake of convenience, been used by the film-makers.

My flag example is obviously unusual if only because it involves black-and-white pictures. Yet many other examples support the more general point, which is that the content of an audio-visual display is determined by a relation between features of that display and various other factors that it is convenient to call 'contextual'. To grasp that content it is necessary to recognize such factors and relations. It is important to observe that this same general point about the determination of content obtains with reference not only to the content of audio-visual displays,

Figure 2.1. Visual ambiguity: a Danish or Swedish flag.

but also, and with even greater reason, to that of a cinematic work, where the difference between the display and the work is again determined by historical and contextual factors, such as the purposeful activities of the relevant film-makers.

To begin to grasp the need for this distinction between works and displays, consider an example that was inspired by a question put to me once by Noël Carroll. An avant-garde video artist presents a film comprised entirely of one thirty-minute-long shot borrowed from a tape made by a security camera in a parking garage. Presenting this audio-visual display in the context of an art gallery, the artist endows it with artistic status and invites spectators to appreciate it as a work of art. The work has certain artistic properties and meanings, such as being minimalist, deliberately provocative, and non-narrative. The film's images of concrete walls and automobiles could have allegorical or symbolic meanings. Now, we do not have to acclaim this work as having high artistic value, but, even if we want to criticize it, we have to recognize that it has certain artistic properties. We can say this while allowing that the footage in question is visually and aurally indistinguishable from an ordinary thirty-minute sequence filmed by a parking garage security camera. An indistinguishable copy of the security footage has no artistic properties or symbolic meanings in the context of its mundane production and use for security purposes. The same sequence could, moreover, take on additional meanings should it be employed by another film-maker who puts it to a different artistic use in another context. It could, for example, be recruited as illustrating what happens in part of a fictional story, where one of the cars is to be imagined as belonging to a particular character. In short, Carroll's example joins many similar thought experiments that underscore the importance of distinguishing between the artistic object or structure (in this case the video footage) and the work of art.[5]

The importance of distinguishing between works and displays is particularly apparent when we reflect over the content of a *fiction* film. What is visually presented to the spectator by the audio-visual display does not map in any simple way onto the contents of the fiction. Consider the following types of exceptions to any simple one-to-one correspondence between the perceptible contents of the display and the contents of the fiction:

1. Intrusive microphones are often depicted inadvertently in films, but these are not part of the content of the fiction. For example, in Louis Malle's 1963 film *Le Feu follet*, two characters are shown having a conversation on a sidewalk in Paris, but it is not true in the story that someone is lurking in the corner holding a boom mike in their direction, even though such a microphone is visibly reflected in the shop window behind the actors.

2. Some of the depictive content of an audio-visual display is meant to give rise to a meta-fictional response. For example, in Sofia Coppola's 2006 film *Marie Antoinette*, a pair of Converse All-Star basketball shoes is clearly visible in a shot of the young queen's closet. This anachronistic detail is not meant to prompt the spectator to imagine that it is true in the story that such shoes existed in eighteenth-century France; instead, it is to be taken as expressing a joke about the very business of making a historically accurate costume drama.

---

[5] For an early articulation of contextualism in aesthetics, see C. I. Lewis, *An Analysis of Knowledge and Valuation* (La Salle, IL: Open Court, 1946), 475–7. For background on the motivation behind such a distinction, see David Davies, 'Works, Texts, and Contexts: Goodman on the Literary Artwork', *Canadian Journal of Philosophy*, 21 (1991), 331–46, Gregory Currie, 'Work and Text', *Mind*, 100 (1991), 325–40, and my *Art and Intention: A Philosophical Study* (Oxford: Clarendon Press, 2005), ch. 4.

3. While it may be true in the story that the characters kill each other, unless something very unusual and horrible has happened, the actors we see performing in the film are not actually killing anyone during the filming. It would be a mistake, however, to reason that, since the audio-visual display is not a representation of any actual killings, it is not 'true in the fiction' that characters get killed.

4. The film actor (for example, Jackie Chan) was badly injured during the shooting of some footage, but this very footage represents a fictional series of dangerous events in which the character portrayed by the injured performer comes out unscathed.

5. Sometimes it is definitely true in the story conveyed by a cinematic fiction that a given character has been murdered, even though the event is not visually represented in the audio-visual display: the spectator has to draw an inference to the effect that a murder has been committed in the story conveyed by the work.

The conclusion to be drawn, then, is that, while there is an intersection between the set of events depicted in the display and the set of events belonging to the content of the fiction, these two sets are conceptually distinct: some events depicted in the display are not part of the content of the fiction, and some events that are part of the content of the fiction are not depicted in the display.

Admittedly, the idea that we have to distinguish between the audio-visual display and the cinematic work is to some degree counter-intuitive, or at least not in immediate harmony with some ordinary ways of talking about film. The work, we tend to say, is just what can be seen on the screen and heard from the loudspeakers. And there is also a tendency to assume that this display 'has' its content as a kind of intrinsic feature. To get the meaning, all the viewer has to do is look and listen. The history of the work—how it was made, by whom, and in what context—is not generally recognized as literally being part of, or included in, the work. Yet there are very good reasons to conclude that ordinary talk about simply 'seeing' or 'hearing' *the work of art* (and by extension, its meaning) does not really stand up to our best theoretical understanding of the status of a work's artistic features and meanings. To appreciate a work adequately, the spectator has to relate what is literally presented—the audio-visual display or 'input', which can be heard and seen—to something that is not directly presented to our senses in the display.

Drawing the foregoing considerations together, we can restate the completeness objection as follows: taken on its own, an audio-visual display does not have a sufficiently determinate content to warrant any claims about the film's contribution to philosophy. One way to put this point is to say that it is *people* who do philosophy, not symbolic artefacts, such as words or sounds or pictures. As Thomas E. Wartenberg puts it, saying that a film philosophizes 'is really a shorthand expression for stating that the film's makers are actually the ones doing philosophy in/on/through the film'.[6] To grasp the reasoning behind such a clarification, it may be helpful to recall that an audio-visual display or film is a sequence of two-dimensional moving images. Someone can use such a sequence of images in order to make a philosophical claim or in order to get someone to entertain some ideas, but it is a mistake to think that it is the audio-visual display *on its own* that carries the relevant thoughts. Someone has to bring the images in relation to a 'cognitive stock' (to use Richard Wollheim's term) if any philosophy is to be done, assuming, as before, that the doing of philosophy requires the expression or even the communication of some determinate thinking.

Before I go on to provide my response to the completeness objection, I want to illustrate and expand upon the argument by referring to examples, which may help to attenuate the abstract character of the discussion. Both examples are, I believe, of independent interest in any case.

I have in mind, first of all, a striking scene in Ingmar Bergman's *Persona*. On one of those rare and most welcomed, bright summer days on the Swedish coast, nurse Alma (Bibi Andersson) and her patient, the actress Elisabet Vogler (portrayed by Liv Ullmann), are sunning together on the beach. (For readers who have never seen the film, it may be necessary to add that the depressed actress has been sent to spend some time at a beach house with Alma as part of her recovery from what might be labelled a 'nervous breakdown', her most obvious symptoms being a refusal to talk and a generalized condition of despondency and sorrow. The specific nature of this crisis in the life of this successful actress is one of the film's central issues.)

Alma is reading a book, the title of which is never made known to the spectator. As far as I have been able to surmise, the text in question

---

6 Thomas E. Wartenburg, *Thinking on Screen: Film as Philosophy* (London: Routledge, 2007), 12.

is the product of Bergman's imagination.[7] Finding a passage of special interest, nurse Alma asks Elisabet whether she would mind if she read something aloud to her. The passage she goes on to read loses something in translation, but runs roughly as follows:

All of the anxiety we bear within us, our thwarted dreams, the incomprehensible cruelty, our angst about extinction, the painful insight into our earthly condition, have slowly eroded our hope in an otherworldly salvation. The howl of our faith and doubt against the darkness and silence is one of the most awful proofs of our abandonment, of our terrified, unuttered knowledge.

Having read these lines, Alma asks Elisabet whether she agrees with these thoughts, and when Elisabet nods affirmatively, the nurse protests that she cannot accept such a conclusion (see Figures 1.7–1.9).

Like the nurse who quotes these lines without endorsing them, this sequence from *Persona* conveys these thoughts to the sufficiently well-informed viewer without making any assertion about them, unless, that is, we have in mind such propositions as: 'It is true in the fiction of *Persona* that nurse Alma contests these thoughts, and that the actress Elisabet nods in agreement with them.' Reference to the cinematic style or rhetoric of the sequence is important. As Alma begins to read, Bergman cuts to five successive, static shots of the harshly lit rocky beach (see Figures 1.2–1.6). As these images correspond to the kind of desolation and indifference of nature to which the passage refers, the visual rhetoric suggests a kind of confirmation or corroboration of the utterance: the rocks are indeed silent in response to human doubt and suffering. When nurse Alma stops reading, we hear the sound of the waves and cries of gulls, again indifferent to the human search for meaning. Yet these observations, while relevant, need not be taken as decisive: the rhetorical devices just mentioned could simply be a matter of dramatic emphasis, and need not be interpreted as some kind of implicit endorsement of the phrases by the director.

On its own, then, the audio-visual display's evocation of thoughts or propositions falls rather short of anything like the film 'doing philosophy'. What would it take to bridge the gap? Actually, there are at least two gaps to be considered: one involving the fictional status of the work, and a second having to do with the difference between

---

[7] This surmise has been seconded by Birgitta Steene (personal communication). Viewers familiar with Bergman's films and writings may recognize that the style resembles that of some of the speeches in his scripts, such as a speech included in an early draft of the script of Bergman's 1968 *Vargtimmen* (*The Hour of the Wolf*).

the spectator's immediate experience of the audio-visual display and detailed, systematic thinking about a well-delimited and defined philosophical question or theme that arises against a set of philosophically significant background assumptions, or what is in French called *une problématique*.

The first gap is not insurmountable, but it does require us to go outside the cinematic display, strictly speaking, and refer to relations between that display and other items—starting with the thoughts and attitudes and intentions of those who were responsible for making the film. For example, we might suppose that, although Bergman's attitude towards the story in *Persona* is one of imagining and make-believe (which is what gives the sequence and the film as a whole the status of fiction), he and his collaborators made a work inviting audiences to participate in similar make-believe with ulterior, non-fictional motives: he not only wanted us to entertain such-and-such thoughts; he also wanted us to find them compelling and worthy of conviction. (Or, if he was proceeding ironically, he wanted us to become aware of their absurdity or falsehood.) The film-maker could in this case be credited with having done philosophy by means of a cinematic fiction.

Even in the absence of such an earnest, secondary authorial intention, spectators may, when they grasp the thoughts expressed in the passage Alma reads aloud, imaginatively consider the wisdom of applying these thoughts to themselves, or to what they take to be the world around them. They may then recognize these thoughts as being essentially sound or unsound. The film, as interpreted by such spectators, would have helped them to do some philosophical thinking. This could be a matter of the framing or articulation of thoughts one was already inclined to accept or reject, or of becoming acquainted with some new ideas. This kind of philosophical *application* of a film could be prompted by reading an interpretation by a critic, at which point the contents, as interpreted, are brought to mind and endorsed or rejected.

Note, however, that I have not begun to specify what sorts of information the spectator needs to rely upon in order to grasp and entertain the thoughts in question. As I mentioned above, there is knowledge of the relevant natural language(s), but that is just the beginning of a very long story to be told about the spectator's cognitive and emotive competence.[8] Consider, for example, what is required

---

[8] For background, see Per Persson, *Understanding Cinema: A Psychological Theory of Moving Imagery* (Cambridge: Cambridge University Press, 2003).

to come up with the uncontroversial proposition that Elisabet Vogler expresses her agreement with the thoughts expressed in the passage that Alma reads aloud. Bergman cuts from a shot in which Alma asks her companion whether she believes these ideas are correct, to a shot of Liv Ullman portraying Elisabet, who very subtly nods her head. Various complex perceptual and culturally determined cognitive abilities allow the spectator to see, recognize, and understand this kind of bodily movement as the possible expression of an affirmative response to Alma's question; we must also ask whether such a response is coherent with the rest of what we have at this point been able to surmise about the Vogler character, and in so doing the spectator may or may not converge on the thought that her gesture is sincere and expressive of her settled attitudes.

The second gap I have in view is more formidable, and this is the point where the completeness objection finds its strongest basis. Suppose we grant, in keeping with the line of thought just sketched, that philosophy has been done by means of this sequence of the film. We still want an answer to the question about *what* philosophy has been done. And that is the question about *sufficiently complete* content. In what philosophical context do the fiction's indications, and, in particular, the content of the passage read aloud, find meaning or significance? Is it a debate over the immortality of the soul? The rationality or irrationality of religious faith? As there is reference to a 'proof' of some kind of 'unuttered knowledge', is the context a topic in the theory of knowledge? If so, which problem in epistemology is taken up, and with what result? My point is not that the content of the sequence in question is banal or hopelessly nebulous, but that it could acquire the requisite determinacy and detail only if additional philosophical and other background assumptions were brought into play. The sequence in which a contrast between the opinions of Alma and Elisabet is brought out via the philosophical passage should be understood within the larger context of Bergman's characterizations and themes in *Persona*, which in turn need to be understood within a more general philosophical framework.

My general point about the gaps between an audio-visual display and determinate philosophical content can also be illustrated with reference to a second example from Bergman's work. In *The Seventh Seal*, the knight Antonius Block (played by Max von Sydow) enters a church and sees a hooded figure standing on the other side of the iron grid of a window to another chamber. Mistaking this figure for a priest, he begins to confess, revealing his fears and doubts and his ardent desire for direct and certain knowledge of God, as well as the strategy he intends to use to trick Death in the game of chess they are playing. Behind the grid, however, stands not a sympathetic priest, but the allegorical figure of Death, the knight's opponent in the game. Once the knight has betrayed his secret strategy, Death turns to reveal himself, and the knight realizes his mistake. Alert spectators, however, may have earlier noticed the knight's strategic error, since it was already underscored visually by the very appearance of the iron grid separating the knight and the hooded figure. With its configuration of squares, this iron grid, and the shadows it casts on the adjacent wall, strikingly resemble a chess board (Figures 2.2–2.4). Thus Bergman visually makes the point that the game goes on even when the knight thinks there is a truce. It is also possible to interpret this imagery as amplifying some of the larger points in Bergman's allegorical film. Instead of offering absolution, the ritual of confession is only another moment in the hopeless, strategically rational thinking in which the knight is caught. Throughout the film, his unhappy reasoning is contrasted to the grace enjoyed by the intuitive, visionary juggler, Jof. So far so good, but what are the more general philosophical points being raised here? Is Bergman advocating fideism in theology? Is he broaching, or even endorsing, an existentialist line of thought regarding authenticity and the human being's relation to death? Any deeper or more extensive interpretation of Bergman's use of chessboard imagery depends upon a decision about the relevant philosophical background assumptions and questions. I return to this topic in the third part of this book and discuss what can be learnt from the available evidence about aspects of Bergman's artistic, intellectual, and specifically philosophical background.

More generally, to understand a film, or a sequence from a film, in terms of a specific philosophical *problématique* one must decide, first of all, what issues have been raised, and, secondly, what philosophical assumptions can appropriately be brought to bear on those issues. It is very misleading to suggest that such decisions are guided uniquely by 'input' arising from the audio-visual display alone. Otherwise, it would be very hard to explain the remarkable variety of books purporting to elucidate the philosophical contents of a single film. Obviously it is possible for people to see the same film and work with the same background assumptions yet end up disagreeing about the film's meanings because they reason quite differently about the evidence. Yet, in many cases, divergent interpretations are clearly the product of strikingly

Figure 2.2. Chessboard imagery in *The Seventh Seal*: Max von Sydow as Antonius Block and Bengt Ekerot as Death.

Figure 2.3.

Figure 2.4.

divergent assumptions about the relevant background in relation to which the audio-visual display is to be understood. One critic uses Freud, another one Jung, and a third Kierkegaard: is it any surprise that the claims made in their published interpretations disagree over the philosophical content of the films?

RESPONDING TO THE RATIONALITY OBJECTION

What follows if we allow that Hegel is right about the relative effectiveness or completeness of art as a means to knowledge (and possibly other ends as well)? Must we agree with Hegel that it follows that it is a mistake to use art in such ways? One way to try to justify a disagreement with Hegel on this score is to assail what may be taken as Hegel's underlying assumption about optimality, which might be restated as the thesis that it is only appropriate or rational to value a work of art as a means to some end, such as philosophical knowledge, if we have good reason to believe that it is the very best available means to that end, or at least equally good as any other available means.

One might be tempted to object that Hegel's premiss is simply mistaken, and should be rejected as a dreary appeal to an inappropriately high standard of instrumental rationality. Yet we must be careful here. If we in fact believe a better (for example, more efficient) means to our goal is available, would it not indeed be irrational to pass it by? To propose an analogy: if you know you can quickly, easily, and very effectively tighten a screw with a screwdriver that is ready to hand, or laboriously and imperfectly tighten it with a coin, would it not be irrational to prefer the coin (assuming that all other conditions are equal)? Why choose the coin unless you thought it more convenient or at least 'good enough' for your present purpose? The upshot, then, is that Hegel's assumptions about rationality and completeness are sound; rejecting those assumptions is not a good way to try to undermine the rationality objection. If we are to formulate an adequate response to the rationality objection, we must say something more about the specific manner in which the cinematic art form can advance, or be used to advance, philosophical goals, and this in a way that does not come into conflict with some standard assumptions about rationality that we have good, independent grounds for accepting.

My response to the Hegel-inspired rationality challenge begins by conceding that the challenge would be insurmountable if the only choice to be made were between the following two options: on the one hand, finding philosophical knowledge or understanding 'in the film', and, on the other, employing the more traditional methods and tools of philosophical enquiry, which include linguistically mediated thinking, verbal discussion, and written argumentation. As I have already suggested, this concession is informed by the view that a linguistically mediated philosophical context must be established if we are to present an interpretation of an audio-visual display's philosophical content.

What must be rejected, then, is the idea that we must make a choice between doing philosophy with film and doing philosophy with the linguistic and conceptual tools with which philosophy has been done prior to the advent of the cinema. There is no reason to limit the role of cinema to an elusive philosophical insight to be found uniquely 'in' the film (where the film is understood as a type of audio-visual display). Nor must we even restrict ourselves to the idea that the contribution to philosophy is to be found uniquely in a verbal *interpretation* of the film that is more or less adequately grounded in the spectator's experience. An alternative to these overly restricted options is the idea that explorations of films' illustrative and heuristic values can be rational when undertaken alongside and in conjunction with other means of pursuing philosophical goals, such as the more traditional ones just evoked.

To return to the simple analogy evoked above, our choice is not between just the screwdriver or the coin; another option is to use a combination of both tools. There could be a situation where using the coin is the easiest and best way to get the task going; later on, when the screw is almost entirely in, it becomes necessary to pick up the screwdriver and use it to tighten the screw firmly. Note that, in such a situation, it could be correct to say that the job could never be done 'completely' without using the screwdriver. This is compatible with the idea that the job gets done best by using first the coin, then the screwdriver. Alternatively, one might have a case where there is no significant difference, in terms of efficiency or completeness, between just using the screwdriver and using the two different devices in turn. Either choice would be rational.

The relevant choice is not between only doing philosophy with film, and conducting philosophical research uniquely by more familiar (that is, largely verbal) means. Explorations of films' illustrative and heuristic values are rational when undertaken in conjunction with other means of pursuing philosophical goals, and, as I have suggested above, the most effective versions of such explorations are those that draw fully on those other means, by bringing in and reflecting over sophisticated philosophical background assumptions. In short, enquiries into films' epistemic values can be a rational strategy in so far as they provide a useful complement to the overarching project of philosophical pedagogy and research.

This rather abstract conclusion leaves some important questions dangling. One key question can be called the question of expressive agency, which is, more simply put, a matter of asking who is ultimately responsible for the meanings or significance of the cinematic work. Two very general ways of responding to that question need to be kept in mind.

In one type of response to the question of expressive agency, it is the ingenious commentator who is taken as being responsible for a philo-sophical content associated with an audio-visual display. The content of the interpretation is a blend of references to elements of a philo-sophically inflected fictional story and to contemporary philosophical publications unknown to the actual film-makers. This blend is clearly the result of the interpreter's own particular manner of drawing these elements together into a coherent discourse having its own purposes and rhetorical design. The question is not what ideas the film-maker(s) did or did not have in mind or express in a film; the point, rather, is that certain aspects of a film can be helpful in *illustrating* or bringing to mind philosophical problems and positions. With this goal in view, the interpreter takes some features of the audio-visual display and builds a background and interpretative context in which it finds philosophical relevance.

An example of this kind of philosophically motivated reading of a film is a case where a philosophical commentator outlines Søren Kierkegaard's discussion of the aesthetic, moral, and religious 'stages' of life and broaches questions about their nature and relations; the commentator then describes how aspects of a film's characterizations exemplify these stages and help to provide a vivid illustration of their relations. Kierkegaard's ideas, or at least the commentator's particular manner of interpreting them, come to the fore. In such a context, it should be apparent to the reader of such a commentary, at least as long as the commentator is forthcoming about the nature of the operation, that a set of philosophical ideas are being applied to story events that have been selected and described by the interpreter.[9] No matter how strongly the philosophical *problématique* can be seen as resonating with the events in the story as described, there should be an awareness that this is one possible 'application' or 'reading' amongst others. The fact that the story in a fiction film can be seen as illustrating a philosophical thesis does not, of course, provide any sort of evidentiary support for that thesis; it may, however, facilitate understanding of, and reflection over, an abstract philosophical idea. Such illustrations are especially effective in helping students to engage imaginatively with conceptual problems and to take abstract philosophical questions seriously.

The second kind of answer to the question of expressive agency is quite different. Here the claim is that it is the film-maker(s) or cinematic author(s) who are responsible for the expression of philosophical ideas. If the commentator of such a film is successful, he or she manages

---

[9] See, e.g., Guido Aristarco, 'Bergman et Kierkegaard', *Études cinématographiques*, 46–7 (1966), 15–30; the Italian philosopher appears to reason that, because Bergman and Kierkegaard belong to the same 'Scandinavian' tradition, distinctions from *Either–Or* are central to Bergman's characterizations.

to recognize and describe some of this philosophical content of the cinematic work. This sort of interpretation in turn helps others to appreciate and engage with the philosophically significant achievement of a cinematic author. This line of thought rests upon assumptions about expression and (cinematic) authorship that require careful elucidation, as it is sometimes thought that the collective nature of most film-making is inimical to the application of 'traditional' or 'literary' conceptions of authorship and authorial expression. In my next two chapters I shall set forth and defend an account of this kind of approach in greater detail. In Chapters 5 and 6 I exemplify this approach in a discussion of works by Ingmar Bergman.

PART TWO

AN INTENTIONALIST APPROACH
TO FILM AS PHILOSOPHY

3
Types of Authorship in the Cinema

In the previous chapter I contended that the cinema can contribute to philosophical enquiry in part because some film-makers employ the cinematic medium, along with other means, to express philosophical ideas. A film-maker's vivid and stirring evocation of philosophical questions and positions can motivate and guide philosophical reflection. Two objections, however, may be anticipated. It may be complained, first of all, that it is inappropriate to work with a notion of individual authorship, either because that notion is held to be indefensible in general, or because it is thought to be inapplicable to cinematic works, at least with regard to large-scale commercial film production. A second objection grants that cinematic authorship obtains in some cases, yet rejects the idea that films can or should be interpreted or understood in terms of the thoughts or ideas someone *expresses* in them. How, it is fair to ask, can that sort of intentionalist assumption be articulated and justified? What about the intentional fallacy? I discuss the first sort of objection in this chapter and turn to the second type of objection in Chapter 4. My arguments will be supplemented and grounded in Chapters 5 and 6 by means of a more detailed exploration of some of Ingmar Bergman's philosophically oriented cinematic fictions.

CINEMATIC AUTHORSHIP RETRIED

At the end of the first part of his 1998 book *Analysing Musical Multimedia,* the distinguished musicologist Nicholas Cook comments: 'A basic fact about most multimedia is that it is the work of more than one author. But critics and analysts seem to go out of their way to avoid recognizing this.'[1] Cook goes on in this context to assail what

[1] Nicholas Cook, *Analysing Musical Multimedia* (Oxford: Clarendon Press, 1998), 128–9. Subsequent citations in what follows are to the same passage in this book. Cook's

he characterizes as 'the Romantic conception of authorship', said to consist in an unjustifiably strong link between notions of artistic value, individual creative genius, and the work's 'structural unity'. This faulty conception of authorship is in turn linked to what Cook calls the 'erasure' of the 'inherently dialogic nature of opera and of all multimedia', and Cook declares that one of his primary aims in discussing multimedia is to 'reverse this erasure'. A key move in this regard is an emphasis on 'contest', which is set forth as 'the paradigmatic model of multimedia'. Contest, Cook suggests, 'deconstructs media identities, fracturing the familiar hierarchies of music and other arts into disjoined chunks or associative chains'.

Cook's discussion of authorship resonates with a lot of the post-structuralist theorizing on the topic of authorship, so engaging with his comments is a good way to develop a position within this part of the ongoing debate over conceptions of authorship.[2] Cook's comments helpfully raise at least three key issues: the relation between authorship and value, the relation between authorship and the unity of works and/or life works, and the question of whether authorship must be exclusively or even primarily a matter of individual creative work.

To begin with the latter topic, I am in agreement with Cook and many others who observe that there is a crucial distinction to be drawn between authorship as such and individual authorship and art-making. As I shall explain in greater detail below, I think it important to recognize cases of individual authorship as well as joint or collective authorship. Just as there is collective or joint action in everyday contexts (for example, a group of people can work together to launch a boat or move a heavy table), so can people collaborate on an expressive or artistic undertaking. With regard to the more general question of whom, if anyone, should be classified as the author of a work to which many persons have contributed in one way or another, it should be noted that I am far from suggesting that an answer to that difficult question follows

claims about multimedia are meant to apply to any film including a recorded soundtrack that uses music.

   [2] For an insightful survey, see Aaron Meskin, 'Authorship', in Paisley Livingston and Carl Plantinga, eds., *The Routledge Companion to Philosophy and Film* (London: Routledge, 2009), 12–28; for additional background, see, for a start, B. K. Grant, ed., *Auteurs and Authorship: A Film Reader* (Oxford: Wiley-Blackwell, 2008), William Irwin, ed., *The Death and Resurrection of the Author?* (Westport, CN: Greenwood, 2002), and Carla Benedetti, *The Empty Cage: Inquiry into the Mysterious Disappearance of the Author*, trans. William J. Hartley (Ithaca, NY: Cornell University Press, 1995).

immediately from even the most successful account of collective action.[3] By this I mean to say simply that it is one thing to have a reasonably accurate model of different forms of collective action, and something else to be able to identify the relevance of different types of processes and contributions and thereby to settle on a justifiable conception of either individual or group authorship.

With regard to the question of the relation between authorship and artistic and other sorts of value, I am in general opposed to honorific concepts of authorship and contend that, if the term labels a useful concept in aesthetics, that concept should be classificatory and not essentially axiological. In other words, the notion of authorship should cover what logically separate value schemes evaluate as good, bad, and indifferent cases. Perhaps it is useful in some contexts to employ a heavily evaluative term like 'Auteur' in an honorific way, but I deem such usage secondary to a basic classificatory notion of authorship.

My proposal regarding authorship is, however, informed by observations concerning a link between intentional agency and some of the kinds of value we find in works. Part of our interest in works derives from our concern for the goals these works realize, and some of these goals must be intentionally realized by the works' makers. Part of what we admire in works is the skill with which worthwhile goals have been realized; likewise, part of what we tend to criticize and condemn in works is incompetence in the employment of means and media, as well as poor judgement in the choice of ends. One reason why authorship is important to us is this link between certain kinds of values and intentional activity, and my proposal for the use of the term 'author' is attuned to this fact. Artists are sometimes praised and blamed for inept use of artistic means, but they are also judged for the quality of the attitudes their works convey. One of the goals that the making of a work can realize with differing degrees of skill is the intentional conveying of ideas and attitudes, and, in a broad range of cases, the content of a work indeed includes the attitudes of the person or group of persons who have created the work.

With regard to the question of the relation between authorship and the unity, or, as Cook puts it, the 'structural unity' of works, several distinct issues need to be kept in mind. I am in agreement with

---

[3] This paragraph was initially conceived in response to remarks sent to me by Sondra Bacharach in preparation for an American Society for Aesthetics 'author meets critics' panel held in Milwaukee, Wisconsin, in 2006.

Cook if the target of his criticism is the assumption that authorship is conceptually equivalent to the creation of a structurally unified work by an individual genius. That thesis is false, if only because some authors make mediocre works that lack certain kinds of unity. Cook may also be targeting the assumption that only the maker of a large, strongly unified life work or *œuvre complet* truly qualifies as an author.[4] Here again I agree, as this is an overly honorific and restrictive usage of the term 'author'.

The question of the relationship between authorship and unity leads, however, to another important topic. If something, such as an audio-visual display, a textual inscription, or a sequence of sounds, is to be a work at all (as opposed, for example, to a part of a work, an unfinished fragment, or something else entirely), it must have 'unity' in the sense of having been individuated or marked off as a whole. An artist who has spent the day in the studio without finishing anything may very well say that she has done a lot of work that day or that she was working on something, but not that her result for the day was *a* work. A cluster of disparate graffiti found on some wall (or collection of walls) is not an individuated work in this sense—on the assumption that each of the individual slogans or 'entries' was intentionally created by different persons not in any way acting in concert with each other. No single person or group of collaborating persons has made the item and constituted it as a finished unity having some kind of intended expressive or artistic qualities and functions. To be the author of a work is to produce something having such a unity.

It is telling that norms pertaining to appreciation correspond to this same basic idea about the constitution of a work. Thus, reading some but not all of the graffiti that could be found here and there would not be a matter of ignoring some of the evidence relevant to the 'meaning of a work'. Such a case contrasts significantly with one where a critic makes a claim about the meaning of a novel while ignoring counter-evidence to be found in some of the chapters in that same novel. Clearly a work can lack unity in various senses (for example, a novel could lack overall stylistic unity or could be philosophically incoherent), but, if it is a work at all, some person or group of responsible persons must have

⁴ Such an assumption is operative, for example, in several of the contributions to Torben Grodal, Bente Larsen, and Iben Thorving Laursen, eds, *Visual Authorship: Creativity and Intentionality in Media* (Copenhagen: Museum Tusculanum, 2005); see also the papers in Virginia Wright Wexman, ed., *Film and Authorship* (New Brunswick, NJ: Rutgers University Press, 2003).

marked it off as constituting a unitary work (in the sense of a single item or whole). It is significant that critics often interpret the text of an incomplete work, such as the sprawling mess of documents associated with Marcel Proust's *À la recherche du temps perdu*, as an attempt to create a unified and complete work. A work in this latter sense can, of course, be part of an even greater whole, as when a discrete novel is part of a trilogy, as is the case with Theodor Dreiser's *The Financer*, which belongs to his *Trilogy of Desire*.

If, as I have just argued, the completion and unity of a work require a decision or choice with regard to what is and is not to be included as part of the work, then the author of a work must exercise the requisite control or authority, at least with regard to this crucial element in the constitution of the work.[5] This point is reflected in prevalent judgements about what does and does not count as the integral audio-visual display of a given cinematic work: if all that we have seen is an audio-visual display that has been drastically mutilated by a censor who operated without the artist's consent, we hardly think that we have experienced the work-as-authored.

Consider, more generally, an all-too-prevalent category of cases. Artists A and B are at work on a project. Yet C, who is in a position to make threats that A and B have good reason to find credible, intervenes and successfully coerces A and B into abandoning their shared plans and producing something along the lines indicated by C. When we look at the results, we ought not to think that A and B were, to the fullest possible extent, the authors. Consider as well a case where A and B both do things that contribute to the artistic qualities of a work. Yet A is 'in charge', and, for financial, legal, or other reasons, B could never oppose A's decisions (and perhaps would not even dare to make any counter-proposals). Instead, B does what A asks B to do. There is some kind of collaboration here, but it would be strange, to say the least, to call this joint authorship, since A 'calls the shots'. More generally, it would be out of step with the basic interests evoked above to opt for a conceptual framework in which those persons who have the least control and decision-making power in a collective process are identified as the authors of whatever works result from that process.

Coercion comes in degrees, and, to the extent that it is severe, vitiates authorship. Authorship is, then, a scalar concept with respect

[5] For more on this topic, see my 'When a Work is Finished: A Response to Darren Hudson Hick', *Journal of Aesthetics and Art Criticism*, 66 (2008), 393–5.

to coercion. The reason why this is the case is that control, which is precisely what is affected by coercion, is a constituent of the relevant concept of authorship. It is a mistake to think that this notion of control is arbitrarily 'tacked on' to the concept of authorship I am defending, as C. Paul Sellors appears to believe; in fact, as long as authorship is deemed to be a matter of intentional activity (in the form of the intentional making of works), control, which is a constituent of the latter, remains a basic component of this concept of authorship.[6] It is important to point out, however, that the relevant sense of control is compatible with the spontaneous and non-deliberative elements of artistic production; it is, however, inimical to the total absence of intention formation. When we say that A, as opposed to B, is 'in control' of the production of a work, that does not mean that A has to be rational or deliberate or careful. Yet, if anyone intentionally fashions or selects the artistically relevant features of the work, it is A and not B (in other words, the relevant sense of 'control' here is not to be confused with some ideal of deliberate self-control).

Some of Ingmar Bergman's comments about the creation of his films may help to flesh out this last point. Bergman often claimed that many of his films found their point of departure in images that had spontaneously emerged in his mind and somehow captivated his attention. As he dwelt on such an image, his imaginings would continue to develop and become more complex. For example, an image of two women comparing their hands became associated with some basic characters, story elements, and 'situations', and eventually led to the writing of drafts for the film *Persona*. Bergman refers to this process as the 'javelin of intuition', and adds that, for a film to be made, the intuitive moment must be followed by 'common sense' and craftsmanship. In one interview, he commented on the latter as follows:

One can say that during 27 years as a director I have built myself a ship in which I can sail through the problems of direction. I have constructed a practical machine, a method that I use from time to time. But, naturally, this method must be suited under all circumstances to the difficult themes I deal with in my films. But in principle I have a carefully worked-out system.[7]

---

[6] C. Paul Sellors, 'Collective Authorship in Film', *Journal of Aesthetics and Art Criticism*, 65 (2007), 263–71, at 266. In support of the link between intentional action and control, I have repeatedly cited the arguments given in Alfred R. Mele and Paul K. Moser, 'Intentional Action', *Noûs*, 28 (1994), 39–68.

[7] Ingmar Bergman, interviewed by Stig Björkman, Apr. 1972; http://zakka.dk/euroscreenwriters/interviews/ingmar_bergman_01.htm

An emphasis on control in the form of decision-making in the context of collective work was articulated by V. F. Perkins in his discussion of the conditions under which the director of a film can be identified as the author of the work—the thought being that sometimes, but not always, the director is in fact the author. Perkins wrote, in this regard, that 'the director's authority is a matter not of total creation but of sufficient control'.[8] An interest in control is not a theoretical prejudice imposed by this (and many other) commentators on the world of film-making and the arts more generally. There are many cases where film-makers complain about the lack of control and struggle to keep producers and other figures from interfering with their artistic work and decisions. And sometimes artists actually express their appreciation for the freedom and control they may be lucky enough to enjoy. In this vein Bergman wrote the following remarks:

I have the support of a producer who has confidence in me and in whom I have confidence. This producer is crazy enough to believe more in a creative artist's sense of responsibility than advance calculations of box-office gains and losses . . . The minute I lose this freedom I will stop being a film-maker because anyone else is better than I am at the art of making compromises. My only relevance in the world of film is my creative freedom; one can then ask to what extent my creativity has artistic value or not, but that is of secondary importance.[9]

To mention one other example, Mike Nichols makes the following comment about the importance of authorial control to the art of cinema:

There is no democracy in this kind of work. I have to have final authority—not because I'm so terrific but because the picture has to be informed by *one* vision.[10]

In my view Nichols overstates his case: some films are not informed by one vision. I do not argue that all films, or all good films, are the product of one dominant expressive personality; my claim, rather, is that

---

[8] V. F. Perkins, *Film as Film: Understanding and Judging Movies* (Harmondsworth: Penguin, 1972), 184.
[9] This passage was included in a draft of Bergman's essay *Varje film är min sista film* (*Each Film is my Last*) (Stockholm: Svenskfilmindustri, 1959); he initially wrote that the question whether his creativity had artistic value was a matter of 'complete indifference' to him, but he crossed this out, no doubt because he realized it was not true.
[10] Mike Nichols, cited in H. Wayne Schuth, *Mike Nichols* (Boston: Twayne, 1978), 24.

authorship, be it successful or unsuccessful given one's artistic values, requires sufficient control over the production of a work presented as the artist's (or artists') own.

AUTHORSHIP AND EXPRESSION

Sufficient control, while necessary, is clearly not sufficient to authorship. Someone who is uncoerced and exercises perfect control over the process of doing some laundry does some useful work, but is not the author of *a work*. Similarly, someone who controls the printing of a manuscript of a novel is not the author of that novel. Helpful scribes and typists, no matter how skilful, are not the authors. This is the case because only some types of goals of intentional action, when realized, qualify the controlling agent as the author of a work. The goal of creating a work of art is one such goal.[11] Yet some authors are not artists: someone is rightly called the author of a scientific paper or an instructional video, but that does not make that person an artist. In light of this fact, the intentional realization of another type of goal in a work—namely, expression—should be recognized as also being sufficient to authorship. The term 'expression' is used here in the Wayne A. Davis-inspired sense of intentionally making an utterance or work that provides some indication that some psychological state or attitude, broadly defined, obtains in the author.[12] Indications can be misleading. Expression, then, need not be sincere or veridical: an opportunistic person can successfully author a work that promotes ideas that are not his or her own; yet, as a meaningful item presented as the person's accomplishment, the work is an indication of the author's attitudes. Not all expression is intentional, of course, as there are unintentional expressive qualities (for example, of faces and gestures); yet the making of a work is an intentional action, and the author's goal is to endow that work with expressive features.

In the case of some genres or categories of works, expression is a necessary condition on authorship of a work in that category. For example, it is impossible to author a philosophy paper that does not express any attitudes (for example beliefs, which includes beliefs about

---

[11] Ordinary usage is inconsistent here and should not be taken as decisive. It is common to refer to the author of a song or a poem, but not of a painting.

[12] Wayne A. Davis, *Meaning, Expression, and Thought* (Cambridge: Cambridge University Press, 2002), ch. 3.

what other philosophers have believed). Expression is not, however, necessary to the authorship of all categories of works. Perhaps there are perfectly inexpressive films, and some of these could even be works of art having an author or group of joint authors. Such works could be philosophically important at least in so far as their very existence has unintended implications for philosophical generalizations about the art of film. Such cases are not, however, my focus in this book, as the topic of cinema as philosophy draws our attention to the broad range of cases where the work is intended to convey general beliefs and other attitudes (such as evaluative judgements or preferences). And, indeed, many films, including artistic ones, are designed to express the maker's attitudes about general topics. Some films, including works of fiction, are overtly polemical, and it is clear that the author or joint authors of the work have crafted the work so as to promote certain beliefs.

My proposal, then, is that the word 'authorship' is best used in the context of aesthetics and elsewhere to classify accomplishments that we evaluate as instances of expressive or artistic behaviour in various media, where authorship also involves exercising sufficient control over the making of the work as a whole. In many cases in which works of art are created, artistic and expressive goals overlap: many (but not all) works of art have not only various non-expressive artistic properties, but also expressive ones in the sense that they have been crafted with the aim of indicating the attitudes of the author. And when a work has expressive content, the author of that work is the person (or persons) who, by virtue of making (and supervising the making of) the work, thereby should be taken as the source of the attitudes expressed.

The proposed usage of 'author' and its cognates is informed by action-theoretical insights, but its ultimate motivation resides in our interests. People are often interested in expressing their attitudes and feelings in an utterance or work and in this accomplishment being recognized by an audience. Audiences often have a corresponding interest in trying to find out what the maker of a work was trying to convey; or, again, they may be fascinated by the artist and take an interest in the work as a possible source of insight into his or her personality. Accordingly, interpreters often have an interest in the *manner* in which a text or other artistic structure has been created. They are interested, for example, in knowing whether the text has been produced freely or under coercion, for works that are freely created are more likely to be indicative of the maker's attitudes and skill. The people who appreciate and interpret a film often want to know whether a particular author had decided that the work was finished and ready to be shown to the public, or whether the film-maker's activity was interfered with or interrupted by other parties or other causes. The public may also be interested in other aspects of the process of composition or artistic production, starting with the types and levels of skill involved. Although such things may be uncommon, a text or performance or artefact that has the appearance of having been produced in a haphazard or frenzied manner could in fact be produced by someone acting calmly and conclusively on a carefully deliberated scheme; and, contrariwise, episodes of uncontrolled or wanton activity could happen to yield an orderly and neatly composed text that has every appearance of having been finished according to some plan. In the context of a discussion of the use of film to express philosophical ideas and arguments, the relevance of an expression-based conception of authorship is obvious: many spectators are interested in what ideas an author (or group of people working together as joint authors) have tried to express or convey in a film.

INDIVIDUAL AND JOINT AUTHORSHIP

As stated above, the conception of authorship on offer here, with its joint conditions of sufficient control and expressive or artistic design, is not meant to enthrone a purely individualistic notion of film-making. On the contrary, it is my view that the following different schematic types of cases are of interest:

1. *Individual authorship.* In some cases an individual film-maker can be singled out as the author of a cinematic work by virtue of having personally performed the relevant, intentional, film-making activities. The author in such cases is the sole maker of the audio-visual display, which serves as the expression of the author's attitudes (be it sincerely or insincerely, accurately or inaccurately).

2. *Individual authorship in the context of a collective film-making process.* Many people are involved in the making of the audio-visual display, but there is one person who has sufficient control in the sense of decision-making authority and responsibility with regard to the making and overall design of the work. In such cases the author supervises and guides the contributions made by others and decides which results will be used in the function

of his or her preferences regarding the final design of the work. Although various collaborators make artistic contributions, only the author is responsible for the work as a finished whole, and the work is to be taken as a fallible expression of that person's attitudes. That other parties have, under the author's supervision, made artistic contributions to the work does not entail that these persons are also to be taken as expressing their own attitudes in the work.

3. *Joint authorship amongst equals.* Two or more persons work together on an equal footing and share responsibility for the final product. If the work is expressive, the attitudes expressed are to be taken as attitudes they share.

4. *Joint authorship amongst equals.* As in (3), yet the joint authors supervise the work of other contributors and decide which contributions will be used.

Additional remarks about joint authorship may be in order here, especially in the light of Cook's broad claims about 'contest'. A closer look at collective authorship might put in question his claim that *contest* ought to be taken as 'the paradigmatic model' of multimedia, for the broad reason that the conceptual landscape need not be mapped out in terms of an opposition between harmonious individual authorship and conflictual activity resulting in disjointed 'chunks and chains'. No doubt there are aesthetically and artistically valuable effects emerging from highly or even totally uncoordinated activity—and this in keeping with the eighteenth-century 'fable of the bees' idea of an unsociable sociability whereby good effects result from uncoordinated strivings. Yet there is a more important range of artistic values linked to skilful cooperative endeavour ensuing in the production of individuated works. My proposal is that joint authorship is to be contrasted to cases of group or collective art-making in which excessive conflict and the absence of certain conditions on genuine collaboration vitiates the very action of authorship.[13]

Clearly persons who work together do not always agree about everything, so successful joint authorship must allow for conflict and some uncoordinated activity. But there is a threshold here. Minimally, joint authors must share the aim of contributing to the making of an

[13] For additional argumentation on this topic, see my *Art and Intention: A Philosophical Study* (Oxford: Clarendon Press, 2005), ch. 3.

utterance or work for which they will jointly take credit (and blame). Acting on that intention, the joint authors share in the making of relevant decisions, and exercise control over the shape of the final product; and they must intend to realize their shared goal by acting in part in accordance with, and because of what Michael E. Bratman has called 'meshing sub-plans'.[14] The relevant condition here is that the ways and means that the contributing agents have settled on are compatible in the sense that it is not impossible that they could be simultaneously realized. Shared, compatible plans that are the object of mutual belief are precisely what are lacking in cases of chaotic collective art-making in which there is no genuine collaboration or joint authorship.

In many cases where two or more persons jointly author an utterance or work, they intentionally generate or select the text, artefact, performance, or structure that is the work's publicly observable component; in so doing, they act on meshing sub-plans and exercise shared control and decision-making authority over the results; furthermore, in making the work or utterance, they together take credit for it as a whole. If the direct or indirect expression of beliefs or attitudes is part of the work's overall design, the joint authors are collectively to be taken as the expressive parties.

There are less straightforward, hybrid cases as well. For example, each film-maker who agrees to make a film that will be part of a collective *film à sketches* (or omnibus film) believes and has good reason to believe that the other contributors intend to act in accordance with the rules and schemes that govern their individual efforts, and they may even entertain some higher-order beliefs regarding those first-order mutual beliefs. For example, it could be agreed that each director will contribute a fictional film that has a particular setting (for example, Paris) as well as a given theme (young love). Parameters are also established with regard to such factors as the length of the film, and there could also be stylistic and technical guidelines (type of camera and film, use of colour or black and white, and so on). In this way, there are a number of shared and compatible intentions, while other decisions are entirely up to the individual directors as long as they do not come into conflict with the shared guidelines. Thus, if there is a sense in which the different directors have co-authored an omnibus film, each of them can be recognized as the individual author of a short film that has been included in the

---

[14] Michael E. Bratman, *Faces of Intention: Selected Essays on Intention and Agency* (Cambridge: Cambridge University Press, 1999), 98–103.

overall work. We can say that an omnibus film of this very general sort combines joint and individual authorship, as there is clearly a sense in which the omnibus film has been jointly authored, but it is also appropriate to recognize and appreciate the individual authorship of the short films brought together within the larger work.[15]

Although I contend that there are cases of individual authorship in contexts where the production of the work involves extensive collaboration, it is important to acknowledge that this is not the most common scenario in large-scale commercial film-making. It is rare for one individual to write the script and supervise just about every artistically relevant aspect of the film production-process, either generating or selecting strategies and solutions to the artistic problems that need to be solved. An example is Charlie Chaplin's making of *The Gold Rush* (1925). Not only did he write, direct, and play the leading role, but he closely supervised just about everything else. More commonly, much of the work is delegated to specialists, each of whom may have a team — and in some cases a very large team or cluster of interrelated teams — working under his or her supervision. In cases of strong individual authorship, it is the director who exercises uncoerced decision-making authority over the results proposed by any collaborators who happen to be employed. For example, a team specializing in casting has the task of finding a shortlist of actors who might be chosen for the leading role, but it is the author–director who makes the final decision as to which one will be employed. Obviously if the choice of the 'star' was a top-down decision made by producers or some corporate committee long before the hiring of a director, this fact attenuates the extent to which the latter is the individual author of the final film — authorship is, once more, a matter of degree with regard to coercion.

Reference to Bergman's testimony may again be helpful here. Bergman acknowledged the interactive, 'give-and-take' nature of the making of his films, but he also insisted on his own leadership and responsibility, and the term 'foreman' has been used to characterize this aspect of his role as director.[16] With regard to the nature of collaboration, he

[15] I discuss another puzzling case in my 'Artistic Nesting in *The Five Obstructions*', in Mette Hjort, ed., *Dekalog 1: On* The Five Obstructions (London: Wallflower Press, 2008), 57–75.

[16] See Vilgot Sjöman, *L 136: diary with Ingmar Bergman*, trans. Alan Blair (Ann Arbor: Karoma, 1978), 67: 'Sometimes he resembles a foreman who shows the building plans to his co-workers. Sometimes he resembles the schoolteacher who tells the class to open their textbooks to page fifteen.' For interesting comments on how Bergman's angry

commented as follows: 'All I think is, someone must decide the route to be taken. Then one must try to agree on it, and then it's up to the director to see we follow that route together; that the agreements we've made are kept to.'[17] In another statement, Bergman compared the role of the film director to that of an organist. The director has an enormous organ to play and the score is the screenplay, which, if he is to be the author to the greatest degree, he has himself written. The organ has many pedals, pipes, and 'voices', which in the case of cinema are called lens, film stock, set-builders, actors, composers, editors, make-up crew, and so on. If the organist forgets this, he is foolish and probably not a very good organist. If the 'voices' forget it, they should be taken out and replaced, Bergman adds. Bergman allows, then, that film-making is a collective process in which people depend heavily on each other's skills. Yet he insists on the importance of the script and on the director's control of the overall process.[18]

AUTHORS AND ACTORS

My argument for the possibility of individual authorship within a context of collaborative film-making has focused on cases where the author in question is someone who writes the script, directs the shooting and editing of the film, and is actively engaging in a wide range of other actions and decisions involved in the making of the film. Yet it is possible to object that, even when such conditions have been satisfied, the notion of individual authorship is still inapplicable. Such an objection has been made forcefully by Berys Gaut, for whom (artistic) authorship is a matter of the making of artistic or other sorts of works.[19] Anyone who endows

attacks on co-workers helped him maintain control on the set, see Harriet Andersson, *Samtal med Jan Lumholdt* (Stockholm: Alfabeta Pocket, 2006), 70–1. Yet she also comments that he got everything he wanted because people who cooperated with him were spoilt. Here she uses a Swedish folk saying to the effect that his enormous success had a beneficial trickle-down effect on everyone else involved: 'det regnar på prästen så stänker det på klockaren. Och då blir vi väldigt nerstänkta av allt möjligt' (p. 94).

[17] *Bergman on Bergman: Interviews with Stig Björkman, Torsten Manns, and Jonas Sima*, trans. Paul Britten Austin (New York: Simon & Schuster, 1973), 35, 252.

[18] Ingmar Bergman, unpublished TS, 'Page from a Non-Existent Diary' (1950–60).

[19] Berys Gaut, 'Film Authorship and Collaboration', in Murray Smith and Richard Allen, eds, *Film Theory and Philosophy* (Oxford: Clarendon Press, 1997), 149–72; *A Philosophy of Cinematic Art* (Cambridge: Cambridge University Press, 2010), ch. 3. I am very grateful to Berys for allowing me to read a draft of his chapter on authorship; our

a work with artistic or other work-constitutive properties deserves to be recognized as one of that work's multiple authors. Gaut argues that, unless the film-maker is the only actor in the film, he or she cannot be that film's sole author because the other performer or performers depicted on screen (or whose voices are used on the soundtrack) contribute artistically to the work. This would be the case even in a situation where the director guided and supervised the actor's performance and allowed no departures from the indications of the script, for the actor's particular manner of embodying the role or speaking the lines has artistic qualities that are not the director's creation. Since the performer makes an artistic difference, he or she is one of film's multiple authors. If there are multiple authors contributing to a film, that film is not individually authored; yet a multiply-authored work could, Gaut allows, have a 'dominant and coordinating collaborator'. Gaut uses the expression 'mainstream film' to refer to any film that includes at least one on-screen performance by an actor who is not the film-maker. Given his other assumptions, it follows that mainstream films, as defined, have multiple (that is, at least two) authors.

Gaut and I are in agreement on many important substantive issues concerning authorship in film, beginning with the idea that it is ill-advised to 'set aside the facts' and imagine or construct an individual persona who is conceived of as the single and sovereign maker of a film. We also agree that, as a matter of fact, most films are not individually authored, and that the artistic contributions made by a variety of persons merit appreciation. Unlike Gaut, however, I propose that, in some cases where more than one person has directly contributed to the making of a work, the word 'author' is aptly applied to a person who has played the role of the dominant coordinating collaborator in the creation of the work, provided, that is, that the work has been made by this person with the aim of expressing his or her attitudes (or, in the absence of any expressive content, with the aim of endowing the work with artistic qualities).

To illustrate my proposal, I shall hazard a few remarks about Harriet Andersson's role in the making of Ingmar Bergman's 1953 *Sommaren med Monika* (literally 'The Summer with Monika'), a success that was a major boost both to her career as a film actress and to Bergman's career as a director and author. To deny that Andersson made an enormous

subsequent email communications have helped me revise the current chapter and have helped me improve my thinking on these issues.

Figure 3.1. Harriet Andersson as Monika in *Summer with Monika.*

Figure 3.2.

artistic difference to the film would be a serious error. Bergman himself called Andersson a 'cinematographic genius' and contended that, when she stared directly into the lens of the camera during one shot, she made a major innovation in the history of cinema.[20] As Alain Bergala points out, this last claim is not true, as there are counter-examples, one of which can be found in Jean Renoir's *Partie de Campagne* (1936).[21] What is more, Andersson herself reports that it was Bergman who, in an apparently uncharacteristic moment of improvisation, told her at the last minute to stare straight into the lens.[22] Yet, even if it was Andersson who spontaneously came up with this provocative and highly appropriate gesture, it was up to Bergman to decide whether to use the resulting shot in the film. It was Bergman who decided to change the lighting and camera position quite dramatically as the shot continues (Figures 3.1–3.2). The dramatic point and expressive power of Monika's defiant stare largely derive, in any case, from a characterization and story for which Bergman, and not Andersson, was responsible. (Bergman's appropriation and reworking of a story by Per Anders Fogelström is another story that need not be delved into here.)

In my view, Andersson certainly deserves to be credited for her superb performance, but she is the author neither of the part she played in the story, nor of the film of which it is a part, because she did not play the right sort of controlling and expressive roles in the making of the work. Obviously her activities and implicit plans 'meshed' successfully with the director's, but this fact does not elevate her to the status of joint author in the absence of sufficient control, and an expressive intention and role, in the making of the work. In her performance for the film in question, Andersson certainly does a marvellous job of expressing the attitudes of Monika (thereby contributing to the artistic quality of the work), but in contributing to the intentional production of the cinematic work by portraying the character of Monika, Andersson was not even indirectly expressing her own attitudes in the film.

It is true that some performers of fictional roles in films have taken up an authorial function by pursuing the goal of having the views and actions of the fictional persona they portray serve as an expression of general attitudes that they themselves endorse (for example, John

Wayne in *The Green Berets*), but even this does not suffice for them to be counted as authors of the film *as a whole* unless other conditions are satisfied—such as the actor simultaneously working as the controlling 'foreman' during the making of the film. Those conditions have to do, then, with the actor exercising sufficient control, and acting on expressive intentions in the making of the work as a whole (where 'as a whole' means that the content of the film is to be taken as relevant to attributions of attitudes to the person who was the controlling agent in the making of the film).

Here I touch upon an issue raised by V. F. Perkins in his chapter on authorship in film, the idea being that, whereas a number of persons may make artistically relevant contributions to a film, such contributors are in general not responsible for intentionally designing or selecting the *relations* between these different elements. I think Perkins is on the right track here. In a range of traditions, the discourses of appreciation and aesthetic theory have included many terms that refer to artistic and aesthetic relations and organizational properties, such as 'proportion'. David Hume, for example, worries that, when a critic experiences a work, the 'genuine sentiment of beauty' may not be formulated because 'the relation of the parts is not discerned'.[23] In the case of L. B. Alberti, the term *leggiandria* was used to designate an important higher-order relation between three other categories of relational properties called *numero*, *finimento*, and *collocatione*.[24] Given a prevalent and relatively uncontroversial idea about the importance of certain types of relational properties amongst a work of art's artistic and expressive properties (starting with the classical desideratum of unity in complexity, and moving on from there to a host of rhetorical and stylistic patterns), the appreciation of a work *qua* work of art or *qua* expressive utterance leads us inevitably from the various parts and elements to relations between these parts, and, ultimately, to the person (or persons) who can be understood as potentially being responsible for the work's design, which is taken as including such relations between the parts.

To illustrate my claim about the relationship between authorship and cinematic acting, Andersson is not the only performer in the film who is shown staring in the direction of the implicit spectator, as a similar

---

[23] David Hume, 'Of the Standard of Taste', in Eugene F. Miller, ed., *Essays Moral, Political, and Literary* (Indianapolis: Liberty Fund, 1985), 226–52, at 238.
[24] Leone Batista Alberti, cited in Władysław Tatarkiewicz, *History of Aesthetics*, vol. iii, ed. D. Petsch (Mouton: The Hague, 1974), 95.

Figure 3.3. Lars Ekborg as Harry in *Summer with Monika.*

Figure 3.4. Harry remembers Monika.

shot of Lars Ekborg, who plays Monika's abandoned lover Harry, is included towards the end of the film (Figure 3.3). The contrast between the attitudes and plights of the two characters is beautifully underscored by the world of difference between the meanings of these two otherwise similar moments. Monika's stare is defiant in her refusal of the role of the dutiful wife and mother: she will be damned if she is going to hang around and cope with the drudgery of housekeeping and child-rearing while there is still fun to be had. The abandoned Harry is quite literally left holding the baby it will be his responsibility to care for; his affection for the child is evident, yet the shot of his gaze dissolves into a montage of flashbacks evoking his memories of his deeply erotic and romantic days with Monika out in the skerries (Figure 3.4). This contrast between the two scenes helps convey an expressive content that is not attributable to either performer taken singly, but it is attributable to the controlling author of the work. Andersson's brilliant portrayal of Monika is not to be taken as indicative of her attitudes towards irresponsible young mothers, whereas *Summer with Monika* can be appropriately sifted for Bergman's treatment of its various themes. Painful ambivalence about parenthood and about traditional gender roles is a central theme for the Swedish author, and spectators who are not attuned to this dimension of the film's content miss something important. It is telling, perhaps, that expert and informed commentators in fact explicitly refer to and discuss *Bergman's* use of the close-ups in which the actors stare directly into the camera, not Harriet Andersson's or Lars Ekborg's putative authorship of these individual scenes or of the movie of which they are interrelated parts.[25]

It may be helpful to conclude this discussion by pointing out that I do not think anyone owns the word 'author' or that there is any single, correct concept of authorship codified by ordinary usage. Nor do I believe there is any one dominant 'literary' concept of authorship that extends across the various literary cultures. The notion of cinematic authorship that I have presented, with its dual emphasis on control and overall expressive/artistic intentional design in the making of a work, finds its motivation in an interest in certain types of cinematic achievements, such as Bergman's creation of a series of

---

[25] Important examples include Per Persson, *Understanding Cinema: A Psychological Theory of Moving Imagery* (Cambridge: Cambridge University Press, 2003), 140, and Maaret Koskinen, 'Närbild och narrativ (dis)kontinuitet: Nedslag i Ingmar Bergmans närbilder', *Aura*, 1 (1995), 58–63, esp. 61–2.

philosophically probing works. The proposal is not meant to preclude or overshadow other kinds of cinematic achievements, which include those arising from non-hierarchical forms of artistic collaboration. An interest in authorial expressivity should not be allowed to detract from our appreciation of film acting and other kinds of artistic contributions to cinematic works.

It may be objected at this point that it is only an outmoded and long debunked critical approach that traces a 'hermeneutic circle' back and forth between the author's life and his or her fictional works, referring to real person's intentions to interpret the fiction, and mistaking the fiction as a more or less disfigured representation of the author's actual experience and personality. In response, it is crucial to distinguish between the types of intentionalism that are and are not at stake in my remarks about cinema as philosophy, and that is the task of the next chapter.

4

Partial Intentionalism

Even if one grants the assumption that some films should be recognized as the result of either individual or joint authorship, the question may still be raised whether the author's (or authors') intentions and decisions have anything to do with the determination of the work's actual meanings. Are we not in danger of committing the dreaded 'intentional fallacy' the moment we start interpreting a movie in terms of the author's putative intentions? In this chapter I respond to that question by defending a version of intentionalism that withstands the anti-intentionalist's challenges and takes on board some of the insights motivating anti-intentionalist theories of interpretation.

INTENTIONS AND INTENTIONALISMS

Intentionalism in the philosophy of art interpretation is in general a thesis about intention's determination of the meaning *or* the value of works of art. Intentionalism can also be characterized as a family of principles that are supposed to describe apt interpretation or appreciation—namely, those in which authorial intention is the target of some if not all attributions of meaning or value. It is coherent to be an intentionalist about the meaning of works without also being an intentionalist about their value, and vice versa. Yet there are hybrid, axiological and semantic intentionalist theses, such as the idea that appreciation and interpretation should be attuned to a type of artistic excellence partly realized through the artist's skilful accomplishment of semantic intentions.

Saying just what intentions are is an important part of the intentionalist's (and the anti-intentionalist's) brief. This is a topic I have taken up at greater length elsewhere.[1] Briefly, I follow Alfred R. Mele in

---

[1] See my *Art and Intention: A Philosophical Study* (Oxford: Clarendon Press, 2005), especially ch. 1. Cf. Alfred R. Mele, *Springs of Action* (New York: Oxford University Press, 1992).

identifying intentions as an executive attitude towards a plan regarding the intending party's own future actions. One can have a plan for doing something in mind without intending to act on that plan: the executive attitude involves being settled on acting on the plan when the time comes. And, in the absence of a plan, there can be no intending. As I deem it impossible for me to exercise a decisive influence on the weather in Hong Kong next December, I cannot rationally intend to act on any plans along those lines. I can, however, hope or wish for good weather in December. I could also frame and settle on a plan to fly to Bali if there is bad weather in Hong Kong at that time of the year.

Jerrold Levinson has voiced his disagreement with this position (which he labels an 'unpromising strategy') and contends that there are intentions that do not range over the intending agent's own future actions.[2] Such intentions, he proposes, are 'normative attitudes as regards the actions of others', and he adds that some of these intentions have a 'crucial role in art-making'.[3] He supports this claim by sketching a list of such intentions: 'intending something to be taken as a sculpture; intending performers of one's string quartet to use minimal vibrato; intending one's latest work to be seen as a clear departure in style; and intending those of insufficient culture to give one's film, which bristles cinematic allusions, a miss'.[4] This list, Levinson adds, could be extended indefinitely.

I am sceptical about such challenges to the prevalent thesis that all intentions are attitudes ranging over the actions of the intending agent. There are countless examples of intentions involving the aim of acting on some plan of action, and no uncontroversial contrast cases. When we set out to make attributions of intention, clarity is advanced by the policy of looking for the action-plan involving the intending party's own future actions, as such actions are crucial to the very difference between intending and wishing. That bit of methodological advice is applicable to the items in Levinson's list. While I concur that this list may at first glance appear to evoke the sorts of things that could play a crucial role in art-making, the corresponding items that would actually play such a role do so only because they involve the artist's effective intentions to do something. With Levinson's point about the 'crucial role in art-making' in view, I would rewrite the list as follows: intending to make a sculptural

[2] Jerrold Levinson, 'Artful Intentions: Paisley Livingston, *Art and Intention: A Philosophical Study*', *Journal of Aesthetics and Art Criticism*, 65 (2007), 299–305.
[3] Ibid. 303.   [4] Ibid.

work and so intending to get one's hands into the clay; deciding that minimal vibrato is what one wants and so intending to write a score that clearly indicates the use of minimal vibrato; intending to experiment with a new style so as to make one's latest work in a style that diverges quite obviously from that of one's earlier works; intending to write and direct a film that will occasion none of the pleasures typically enjoyed and expected by filmgoers having scant knowledge of the history of cinema.

There are, of course, many different actions a film-maker can perform with the aim of getting some group of people to refrain from attending screenings of his or her film, such as making the film so forbiddingly gloomy or abstruse as to generate bad rumours about the film. It would be puzzling, to say the least, to allow that a director who does not intend to do *any* of those things nonetheless *intends* that those of insufficient cinematic culture give the film a miss. Replace 'intends' with 'hopes' in the last phrase and the problem vanishes. Someone can hope, wish, want, or expect some people to refrain from seeing a particular film, but to intend to bring this result about requires settling on a plan believed by the intending party to have some chance of indirectly or directly bringing this state of affairs about. Otherwise, the important distinction between intending that *p* and wishing or hoping that *p* collapses. Such a distinction matters to debates over intentionalism. Wishing and hoping may play some kind of role in art-making, but not of the *crucial* sort played by intentions, which have a closer link to intentional action and related deliberations and policies. Anyone who is committed to the reality and importance of the distinction between intending and hoping should adopt a concept of intending that squares with this attitude, not one that leads to the effacement of the distinction in question. Some of the normative attitudes as regards the actions of others are not intentions, then; those that are intentions are so because they involve the artist's own plan to perform some action (which could be a mental action, such as performing a calculation in one's head).

The next step in the defence of partial intentionalism is to mark it off from the other kinds of intentionalisms. A first key point in this regard is that partial intentionalism is a species of actualist intentionalism in the sense that it is about the actual intentions of the actual author. This distinguishes the view from a range of others. For example, *fictionalist intentionalism* instructs interpreters to attribute the meanings of a text (or visual representation or other art object) to an imagined or make-believe author or artist.[5] A *conditionalist intentionalism* invites the interpreter to describe the meanings that the author of the text (or the director of the film) *could have* intended, as opposed to those that this person actually intended. The imagining of 'possible' intentions (and corresponding actual meanings) should be guided by some more or less precise indication of the constraints within which such imaginings are to be developed. For example, the intentions in question must square with the audio-visual display and be psychologically or intellectually possible given what is known about the actual film director. For example, it is no good imagining how *Ladri di biciclette* (*Bicycle Thieves*) (1948, dir. Vittorio De Sica) was meant as a comment on *Shiqi sui de dan che* (*Beijing Bicycle*) (2001, dir. Wang Xiaoshuai), because De Sica could not have had any such intention. But Wang 'could have had' De Sica's work in mind (even if he did not), so the conditionalist can build an interpretation using that idea. That, at least, is how this approach is supposed to work, but there are many problems and unanswered questions. Since this kind of conditionalist intentionalism pertains to multiple unrealized possibilities as well as actual intentions, its proponents need to tell us how we choose between them. Distinct intentions could be singly possible yet jointly incompatible. Another problem is that of figuring how to decide which intentions could and could not have been had by the author, since not all cases are as obvious as the anachronistic and non-anachronistic examples evoked above. How do we determine which thoughts about what could have been intended (but was not actually intended) are in some sense true or justified, and which ones are not?

The kinds of problems that I have quickly evoked in the previous paragraph crop up in the proposal made by Thomas E. Wartenberg in his *plaidoyer* for the philosophical significance of fiction films. Although Wartenberg is happy to say that films can 'do philosophy', he is careful to acknowledge that the core philosophical activities, such as making claims, clarifying arguments, and proposing counter-examples, are actions that only agents, or groups of agents, can perform. That is why the phrase 'films do philosophy' is really only a 'shorthand expression for stating that the film's makers are the ones who are actually doing philosophy in/on/through film'.[6] Wartenberg correctly

---

[5] Alexander Nehamas, 'What an Author Is', *Journal of Philosophy*, 83 (1986), 685–91.

[6] Thomas E. Wartenberg, *Thinking on Screen: Film as Philosophy* (London: Routledge, 2008), 12.

points out that we often have recourse to a similar shorthand when we attribute various intellectual operations to written texts. For example, we commonly say things like '*The Meditations* makes more than one argument for the existence of God', as though an English translation of a text by Descartes could really make philosophical assertions.

With regard to the problem of deciding what we must say when we wish to eschew the use of shorthand and speak literally and accurately, Wartenberg introduces a distinction between two kinds of interpretations of a work of art, which he respectively labels 'audience-oriented' and 'creator-oriented'. When a philosopher freely pegs her own theorizing onto characterizations or story events associated with some fictional film, this is a matter of an 'audience-oriented' interpretation. Wartenberg takes his distance from the idea that such interpretative raids on movies are a good way to explore the cinema's philosophical value and significance, and to that end states categorically that 'only creator-oriented interpretations of a film can justify the claim that the film itself is philosophical'. This is in my view a worthwhile point, yet I have to report my disagreement with Wartenberg's manner of developing this thought. In the same context, he adverts to the existence of a type of art interpretation that is defined by its 'attempt to reconstruct the meaning that the creator of the work of art could have intended the work to have'.[7] Wartenberg proposes that a creator-oriented interpretation has to be an interpretation that 'a work's creator could have intended it to have'.[8]

As Robert Stecker has argued in another context, the expression 'S could have intended y' is ambiguous between at least two very different kinds of meanings.[9] One reading is epistemic and has to do with a conjecture about somebody's actual intention in a situation where the evidence is imperfect. The second reading reflects no such epistemic limitation and instead refers to a metaphysical possibility: whereas S intended y, S's counterpart (or a version of S in a possible world) intended not y, but x. Wartenberg gives his readers no explicit indications regarding this potential ambiguity, but at least some of what he writes can be taken to suggest that he favours the epistemic reading. There is, after all, a big difference between author-oriented interpretations and 'counterpart-oriented' ones, and only the epistemic

[7] Thomas E. Wartenberg, *Thinking on Screen*, 26.   [8] Ibid. 91.
[9] Robert Stecker, *Interpretation and Construction: Art, Speech, and the Law* (Oxford: Blackwell, 2003), 73–4.

reading can be squared with Wartenberg's key contention that, when he says that a film philosophizes, this 'is really a shorthand expression for stating that the film's makers are the ones who are actually doing philosophy'.[10]

Wartenberg's loosely framed constraint gives the philosophically minded interpreter very little guidance with regard to what does and does not count as a suitably 'creator-oriented' reading of a movie, especially when the interpreter attempts to apply this approach in the absence of any indications concerning the kinds of evidence with which the conjectural possibilities must be compatible. Suppose a philosopher sets out to develop a philosophical, creator-oriented reading of a film by Wong Kar-wai, such as the work distributed in English with the title *Ashes of Time*. In keeping with Wartenberg's principle, the interpreter's goal is to come up with a philosophical reading that the director 'could have intended' a spectator to hit upon. Suppose as well that this particular philosopher has very limited knowledge of the intellectual sources and artistic intentions of the Hong Kong *auteur*. For such an interpreter, a given reading, such as one inspired by American-style deconstruction, falls easily within the domain of what the film-maker 'could have intended'; so would another interpretation that is deeply incompatible with the deconstructive reading. At least some of these 'possibly' intended interpretations would fall by the wayside should the interpreter gather additional evidence about Wong and his context (starting, for example, with an understanding of the Cantonese titles of the films, none of which was translated literally for the purposes of English-language distribution). Wong's interview statement to the effect that his films 'have nothing to do with deconstruction' might be another helpful indication. Yet how much evidence, and of what kind and quality, must the interpreter possess before he or she successfully produces a 'creator-oriented' reading that genuinely elucidates the cinematic philosophizing *actually* done by the film-maker? (If the answer is 'total and reliable evidence', then the counterfactual intention is understood along metaphysical and not epistemic lines.)

Wartenberg's various philosophically oriented interpretations of particular films provide additional indications concerning the approach he has in mind. He seems to assume that decisions about the philosophical theme central to a given film are relatively unproblematic as long as the interpreter is sufficiently well informed about the history of ideas

10 Wartenberg, *Thinking on Screen*, 12.

and remains attentive to the film in question. It is fairly obvious, for example, that Michel Gondry's 2004 film *Eternal Sunshine of the Spotless Mind* raises questions about the wisdom of having recourse to a dangerous and fallible technology that selectively targets and erases segments of a person's memory, such as everything connected with an unhappy love affair. Wartenberg reasons that, should it turn out that consequentialist moral reasoning would entail that the use of such technology could be justifiable (which is far from obvious in my view), the film-maker's negative depiction of the technology could be taken as evoking a possible counter-example to consequentialism. Yet, in the absence of any internal or external evidence to the effect that any particular version of consequentialism is the film-maker's polemical target, how is the interpreter to motivate reference to any such doctrine in an analysis of the film? Here is where Wartenberg's 'conditional intentionalism' plays a crucial role, for he writes that all that is necessary 'for a creator-oriented interpretation to be acceptable in this regard is that the creator might have been acquainted with the philosophical ideas, etc., because of, for example, their general circulation within a culture', and in the same context he adds that it must be 'plausible' that the director was actually responding to the positions or ideas contained in a philosophical work if material from that work is to be applied in an interpretation of the film.[11] Thus, although there is no evidence that Gondry, the scriptwriter, or other key persons working on the film actually read or thought about J. S. Mill's *Utilitarianism* or related works in moral philosophy, Wartenberg contends that, since utilitarian ideas were pervasive in the film-makers' context, we can infer that they could have been known to the film-makers. This is in turn taken as supporting an interpretation that draws upon such philosophical texts.

My basic objection to these interpretative principles is that they warrant any number of incompatible readings and so do not sufficiently determine a coherent result. If this is correct, then Wartenberg's proposed principle of interpretation does not support his otherwise admirable desire to respond to what he calls 'the imposition objection'—the complaint that it is not the cinematic works that have philosophical merit because the philosophizing is something imposed on the films by philosophically minded interpreters. My objection to Wartenberg's principles of interpretation can be illustrated with

---

11 Wartenberg, *Thinking on Screen*, 91.

reference to one of his own examples. In making *Eternal Sunshine of the Spotless Mind*, Gondry and his collaborators worked in a context where Nietzsche-inspired error theory, a variety of rival psychoanalytic and psychological doctrines, and several distinct and competing versions of utilitarianism were in circulation, and it is plausible to say that the director 'might have' been acquainted with any of these ideas, which would in turn warrant interpreters to bring in the specific contents of a wide range of theories in interpretations of the events in the fiction. Commentators have in fact shown themselves to have great skill in applying a wide range of theories to particular films, and there is no reason to think that Gondry's work is an exception to that rule. Wartenberg himself cites an earlier paper on the same film by Christopher Grau, who drew upon other sources, including Iris Murdoch, Robert Nozick, and Immanuel Kant. Unless such diverse (and in some cases contradictory) doctrines were 'imposed' on the film, it would have to follow that the film's philosophical content was itself contradictory. Although some theorists are ready to bite this bullet, Wartenberg is unlikely to accept the conclusion that the philosophizing 'done by the film-maker' embraces a multiplicity of incompatible assertions. (I once heard him raise a similar objection to Arthur Danto's attempt to unpack the philosophical content of Andy Warhol's *Brillo Box*: the objection was not that one could not give the work a philosophical spin, but that there were too many incompatible ways of doing so. In other words, what embarrasses the commentator who is mindful of the 'imposition objection' is his own interpretative *richesse*). In sum, the interpreter's initial selection of philosophical topics and related texts and sources is insufficiently motivated in the absence of evidence pertaining to the film-maker's actual sources and attitudes.

It might be objected here that another account of interpretation—namely, hypothetical intentionalism as articulated and defended by Levinson and others—in fact rescues the interpreter from the imposition objection. As I and various other philosophers have presented detailed criticisms of hypothetical intentionalism elsewhere, I shall not open up a lengthy parenthesis on the topic here, but a few remarks may be useful.[12] Briefly, as I understand it (and there is a serious 'moving-target'

---

[12] See my *Art and Intention*, ch. 5, Stecker, *Interpretation and Construction*, Noël Carroll, 'Interpretation and Intention: The Debate between Hypothetical and Actual Intentionalism', *Metaphilosophy*, 31 (2000), 75–95, and 'Andy Kaufman and

problem in discussions of the various ideas associated with the label 'hypothetical intentionalism'), a key aspect of the approach is the idea that the interpreter must read the text (or other artistic structure) in terms of what can be known about the context in which it was actually created. The theory does not say just how much research the interpreter has to do into the life, works, and socio-cultural context of the actual author. The idea seems to be that the interpretation has to be in line with *almost* all the evidence—almost because the theory also rules that one kind of evidence should *not* be considered to be decisive, namely, any information, no matter how reliable, that pertains to the author's specifically 'semantic' intentions, or, in other words, what the author intended the work to mean. Statements made in letters and diaries, for example, are explicitly ruled out. With regard to that kind of intention, the interpreter is free to set aside the facts and to 'hypothesize', or, more accurately, to imagine what an author very much like the actual author could have meant, the one additional constraint being that the interpretation should maximize the artistic value of the work. So, if the author is known to have a boring or otherwise inferior semantic intention, it is correct to substitute in more interesting intentions, which are then said to be those of a 'hypothetical' author. Clearly, this opens the path for the importation and imposition of philosophically interesting views, but in some cases it also blocks the path to any claims that the interpreter's results are a matter of an account of the author's actual philosophizing, since contradictory evidence about the latter was set aside on non-epistemic grounds (that is, not because the author's statement of intention was deemed insincere or otherwise misleading). One point that is especially unclear about this family of interpretative principles is just how verisimilar the portrait of the artist has to be: is the interpreter required to conduct extensive research into the author's life and attitudes prior to constructing the 'hypothesis' about the author, or are the text-centred methods of the New Criticism basically deemed good enough? And how many different, incompatible portraits of the author-and-work can be hypothesized within the broad constraints prescribed by hypothetical intentionalism? The absence of any principled response to such basic questions may be one reason why this philosophy of interpretation finds no counterparts in extensive

the Philosophy of Interpretation', in Michael Krausz, ed., *Is There a Single Right Interpretation?* (University Park, PA: Pennsylvania State University Press, 2002), 319–44.

'practical criticism' or detailed studies of the work of specific artists or authors.

One way to rescue 'creator-oriented' interpretation from the kinds of problems I have been evoking in the last few paragraphs is to espouse an *actualist intentionalism*, which is based on the idea that it is the actual author's intentions that are ideally to be identified in the interpretation of at least some of the meanings of a work, at least in cases where those intentions have been successfully acted upon. In cases of collaborative authorship, the relevant intentions would be the joint intentions, and related individual intentions, of the actual persons involved in the making of the work.

Actualist intentionalism comes in different strengths. A moderate or partial intentionalist thesis holds that intentions determine some, but not all, of the semantic properties of at least some works of art. This is arguably the approach we tend to adopt in our basic day-to-day interpretations of each other's verbal and written utterances. We acknowledge that people do not always mean what they say and say what they mean, but we are on the lookout for happy cases where they do, and, when we find them, we conclude that the utterance meaning and speaker's meaning coincide (not logically, but as a matter of fact). In other cases, there is a gap between the speaker's intended meaning and what the words actually said mean. Consider the kind of example that is often given in introductory discussions of pragmatics: with the intention of issuing an invitation to come into his office, a teacher says to the student: 'the door is open'. While the conventional meaning of the sentence certainly factors into the meaning of the utterance, it is not equivalent to it; in another context, the same phrase could be used to enjoin someone to close the door, or it could be used figuratively to encourage the listener to envision various possible courses of action.[13] Similarly, motion picture shots have depictive contents; when such shots are combined, rhetorical patterns such as parallelism and contrast emerge. As in the case of sentence types, such as 'the door is open', a sequence of moving pictures can be put to a variety of uses in the making of a particular utterance, the meaning and force of which are not determined by the content of the audio-visual display alone.

[13] See, for a start, Kent Bach and Robert M. Harnish, *Linguistic Communication and Speech Acts* (Cambridge, MA: MIT Press, 1979). For a speech-act theoretical approach to cinema, see Trevor Ponech, *What is Non-Fiction Cinema?: On the Very Idea of Motion Picture Communication* (Boulder, CO: Westview Press, 1999).

THE UTTERANCE MODEL AND IMPLIED
MEANINGS

As I have just indicated, intentionalists of various kinds tend to think about the meaning of works of art along the same lines as one thinks about the meaning of an utterance, and one anti-intentionalist objection is that it is inappropriate to apply this 'utterance model' to works of art.[14] In response, it should be noted first of all that 'utterance' is generally taken in a broad, Grice-inspired sense, according to which an utterance is anything that has a certain kind of expressive function or, in Grice's terms, 'non-natural meaning'. A puppet show or physical gesture, then, could be an utterance, as could a deliberately created and displayed audio-visual representation.

Yet the pertinence of an utterance model, even in this broad sense, is sometimes contested. A first reason is that, while it usually makes perfect sense to ask what the meaning of an utterance is, it may sound ill-conceived or even foolhardy to ask for *the* overall or total meaning of sprawling works like Marcel Proust's *À la recherche du temps perdu*, Rainer Werner Fassbinder's *Berlin Alexanderplatz* (1980), and Michael Cimino's fragmentary *Heaven's Gate* (1981). This could be because literary, cinematic, and other artistic works are not utterances in any case and so are just not the sort of thing to have such a meaning. In response, it may be agreed that it is hard to spell out the meaning of imposing and complex artistic achievements (especially fragmentary ones), but this does not suffice to establish the more general thesis that most or even all artworks are not utterances. As long as we accept a classificatory and non-honorific concept of works, we can identify short and simple works, the utterance meaning of which is not so hard to identify. Also, there are some very long non-artistic utterances the meaning of which it would be difficult if not impossible to elucidate completely, but that does not entail that these discourses are not utterances, as long as we understand the term 'utterance' as referring to expressive or communicative acts

---

[14] Deborah Knight usefully raised this objection to me. For background, see Peter V. Lamarque, 'Objects of Interpretation', *Metaphilosophy*, 31 (2000), 96–124; Stein Haugom Olsen, 'Interpretation and Intention', *British Journal of Aesthetics*, 17 (1977), 210–18. My views on this topic are largely in harmony with those of Robert Stecker in his 'Moderate Actualist Intentionalism Defended', *Journal of Aesthetics and Art Criticism*, 64 (2006), 429–38.

indicative of attitudes. So the distinction between utterances having meanings, and the sorts of things that do not have meanings of this kind, does not map neatly onto the distinction between things having a meaning that can and cannot be readily paraphrased or elucidated. The meaning can be too complex to allow of an exhaustive restatement, which does not imply that more partial elucidations, in keeping with our cognitive limitations, cannot be provided.

Another reason given in support of the thesis that works are not utterances is that the utterance model of meaning equates the meaning of an utterance with the speaker's or author's meaning. Assuming that the meanings of a work of art are not reducible to the author's semantic intentions, it follows that the utterance model is inappropriate. In response, one may reply that one reason why a concept of utterance meaning is attractive as a way of understanding works of art is that it offers an alternative to both a narrow conventionalism and an absolute intentionalism. Utterance meaning is not equivalent to the speaker's or author's meaning, but emerges in a relation between utterer's meaning, conventional or linguistic meaning, and contextual factors. Utterances have plenty of unintended meanings, such as symptomatic meanings discovered by statistical analysis of lexical frequencies.[15] One does not have to reject the utterance model in a swerve away from absolute intentionalism.

A third main reason given in support of the thesis that works are not utterances is that works, unlike utterances, should be understood as having an interest and relevance independent of the situation in which they were initially produced.[16] On one theory, to read a text as literature, for example, is to detach it from its context of origin. In response to this line of thought, intentionalists may advert to the many reasons why features of the context of creation are crucial to adequate appreciation of a work's aesthetic, artistic, and artistically relevant semantic properties. This is not the place for a book-length argument in favour of contextualism in aesthetics, but one point can be made quite briefly, and other reasons emerge below. Before one sets out to read 'the text' as a work of literature (or 'the display' as a

[15] See, e.g., Cindy K. Chung and James W. Pennebaker, 'Assessing Quality of Life through Natural Language Use: Implications of Computerized Text Analysis', in William R. Lenderking and Dennis A. Revicki, eds., *Advancing Health Outcomes Research Methods and Clinical Applications* (McLean, VA: Degnon Associates, 2005), 79–94.

[16] John M. Ellis, *Theory of Literary Criticism: A Logical Analysis* (Berkeley and Los Angeles: University of California Press, 1974).

work of cinema), one needs to know whether what one has available is the complete text or display, as opposed to some fragment thereof. Yet we cannot even determine that a given stretch of images is the total audio-visual display of a finished cinematic work or not if we have no knowledge of the context and process of its making, as the very distinction between complete works and incomplete ones depends on the circumstances and decisions of the relevant maker(s).[17] To mention but one example, Federico Fellini's 1969 *Fellini-Satyricon* deliberately cuts off abruptly in imitation of the fragmentary work by Petronius on which the script of the film was very loosely based. While it makes sense to regret the loss of the complete text of the Latin satire, conjectures about the missing ending of Fellini's film are simply misinformed. There are, of course, mutilated prints of a film in circulation, and the very standard of correctness in relation to which a given print is judged defective sends us back to the film-maker's final intentions.

Another reason why people try to drive a wedge between the utterance model and the interpretation of films is that they believe there are too many differences between the process whereby someone produces a verbal utterance and the process whereby a feature-length film gets made. In other words, film-makers are not the author of a film in the same way a person is the author of an everyday statement. I have responded to this type of objection in the previous chapter. It would be absurd to deny that there are important differences between writing a short story and writing and directing a feature-length fiction film, but it is possible for an author to express his or her attitudes in both cases.

Even if this broad defence of the applicability of the utterance model is accepted, it may still be asked under what conditions the intended meanings are actually those that belong to the work or utterance. While it is a truism to say that intention, or at least intended meaning, is crucial to what the *speaker* means, it is not so obvious that the identification of the speaker's or writer's or performer's meaning is essential to the determination of the meaning of the ensuing *utterance or work*. The key question here can be framed as follows: assuming that some speaker or writer says or writes something that means some proposition or thought, p, in order to imply some q, under what condition does the *utterance* actually mean q?

---

[17] See my 'When a Work is Finished: A Response to Darren Hudson Hick', *Journal of Aesthetics and Art Criticism* 66 (2008), 393–5, and 'Counting Fragments, and Frenhofer's Paradox', *British Journal of Aesthetics* 39 (1999), 14–23.

One influential approach to this problem is the Gricean attempt to anchor the justification of a claim about implicature (or implied meanings) in a norm arising from cooperative rationality. Grice's central conjecture in this vein was that the following imperative guides conversational exchanges: 'Make your contribution such as required, at the stage at which it occurs, by the accepted purpose or direction of the talk exchange in which you are engaged.'[18] Grice further claimed that it is a 'well-recognized empirical fact' that this *ceteris paribus* principle, and some related maxims said to be derivable from it, apply to all talk exchanges that do not consist of wholly disconnected remarks. In an effort to argue that the principle is grounded in rationality, Grice contends that persons participating in conversational exchanges share such purposes as exchanging information. Only if conversation is conducted in accordance with the cooperative principle can such shared purposes be realized. Given knowledge of this fact, it is rational to behave in accordance with the cooperative principle and to expect others to do so as well. Given assumptions about shared conversational ends, effective means to those ends, and rationality, the cooperative principle and presumption are rational. And indeed, on one salient reading of Grice's imperative, the cooperative principle includes a norm of rationality within it, since it is *rational* to make one's contribution fit the purpose of the conversation.

With regard to the question of the success conditions on the expression of implicit meaning in an utterance, the upshot of the Gricean approach is that intended meanings are those of the utterance just in case they are ones that would be attributed to the writer or speaker by interpreters rationally working with the cooperative principle. In other words, the speaker who says *p* in order to imply *q* successfully produces an utterance with that implicature just in case the audience can derive *q* from the cooperative principle and the other relevant information, which includes contextual factors and linguistic conventions.

One problem with this approach, however, is that it is wrong to assume that authors and their audience are always engaged in conversation, or even in a (primarily) cooperative endeavour.[19] Instead,

[18] Herbert Paul Grice, 'Logic and Conversation', in *Studies in the Way of Words* (Cambridge, MA: Harvard University Press, 1989), 22–40, at 26.

[19] Asa Kasher, 'Conversational Maxims and Rationality', in Asa Kasher, ed., *Language in Focus: Foundations, Methods, and Systems* (Dordrecht: Reidel, 1976), 197–211; Wayne A. Davis, *Implicature: Intention, Convention, and Principle in the Failure of Gricean Theory* (Cambridge: Cambridge University Press, 1998).

what is decisive in the determination of meaning is not what the audience *presumes* about the artist's cooperative rationality, but the artist's actual performance or accomplishment, which may or may not be cooperative or communicative.

Another strategy is to frame the question as an empirical problem: the intention to imply some thought, p, with utterance U is successfully realized just in case the audience understands U as meaning p. Such a formulation is, however, far too simple, as it offers no indication concerning which audience's judgements are supposed to be decisive. One might prefer a probabilistic formulation involving the likelihood of a target response amongst the members of some target audience. The upshot would be that, if the audience in question fails to make a given inference (with sufficient frequency), then the author has failed to realize the intention in question. If, on the other hand, the target audience does make the inference (with sufficient frequency), then the intended meanings are part of the utterance's meaning. It may be objected to this approach, however, that some actual audience might perform incompetently and fail to register the implicit meaning of a work. Another objection points to the possibility of cases where the audience's 'uptake' in fact corresponds to authorial intention but does so only in a wayward or haphazard manner. If the audience's uptake is to be decisive, it must be warranted or justified.

Another proposal for the needed success condition that takes this problem into account has been set forth by Robert Stecker, who writes:

An utterance does mean what a speaker intends if the intention is apt to be recognized in part because of the conventional meaning of the words used, or of a context that extends those meanings. I will say an intention is successful if it is apt to be recognized on the basis just mentioned, and otherwise unsuccessful or failed.[20]

This success condition is partly couched in terms of an audience's tendency to recognize the intention, but what is decisive is not the vagaries of actual reception, but the grounds upon which the recognition of intention is to be based. These grounds involve the sorts of factors that anti-intentionalists have tended to identify as determinative of the meaning of a work or text—namely, the conventional meanings of its sentences and the ways in which these meanings are inflected by non-intentional contextual factors. Stecker's success condition thus provides

---

[20] Stecker, *Interpretation and Construction*, 14.

an intention-independent standard of success—that is, one that does not itself rely on an intention-determined textual meaning.

One respect in which this proposal remains sketchy is the nature of the conditions under which a context can and cannot 'extend' the conventional linguistic meanings of a text. Stecker has observed that extensions of conventions must be not only contextually supported but also 'permissible'.[21] Stecker admits that the interplay between the various factors contributing to the meaning of an utterance is complex, and he does not try to provide a detailed mapping of the conditions under which the extension of conventions is permissible. More recently, he has suggested that intentions are successful as long as they are compatible with the text's conventional meanings and there is some publicly accessible evidence that would allow an informed audience to recognize this intention. Stecker proposes that there is no limit to the evidence that can be appealed to in discovering the intention in the work, the key condition being that the intention must be able to be recognized by an audience and grounded in conventions and their extension. Part of his motivation for this view is the basic thought that art is communicative, which runs contrary to the idea that there could be successful intentions in the absence of an audience having evidence that the author had such intentions. While it is clear that much art derives from communicative intentions or has a communicative function, it is unclear to this author how it could be established that all works of art are communicative in this sense.

THE MESHING CONDITION

My own proposed solution to the problem under discussion runs as follows: the intention to mean *q* by saying or otherwise representing *p* is successful just in case the intention to imply *q* *meshes* sufficiently with what is written, spoken, or otherwise put on display. As various commentators have correctly remarked, this meshing condition is vague. I have no proposal for a sharpening of the meshing condition or any method or explicit procedure for its application. I contend that many

[21] Robert Stecker, *Aesthetics and the Philosophy of Art: An Introduction* (Lanham, MA: Rowman & Littlefield, 2005), 130–3. See also his 'Intention and Interpretation', *Journal of Literary Theory*, 2:1 (2008), 1–16.

particular cases can be readily classified as either satisfying or failing to satisfy this meshing condition.

Talk of meshing is metaphorical, and may seem to evoke only simple images, such as a gearbox that either grinds or runs smoothly. Like many English terms to do with fishing, the word 'mesh' was borrowed from the Dutch. A mesh is a net, and the meshes of a net can be either too fine or too large, depending on what one is trying to capture. The net I have in mind is supposed to capture utterance or work meaning, including that part which is not said, but implied. Meshing is a relation between an intention and the various sorts of actions and accomplishments to which it can give rise, such as the making of a text, picture, or audio-visual display.

The meshing condition covers implicative relations that fall short of logical entailment, so the ideal standard of deductive closure is the wrong model for thinking about meshing. A sequence of sentences can be logically compatible in the sense that the thoughts they express are not contradictory if conjoined, yet incoherent in the sense of not exhibiting sufficient conceptual links or rhetorical relations. Consider an example of a 'scalar' implicature. If I say 'some politicians are honest', the sentence does not *entail* my thought that many politicians are dishonest; I can without contradiction add: 'indeed most or even all of them are'. Yet saying 'some politicians are honest' meshes well with the intention to imply that many of them are dishonest. If I say 'some politicians are honest', it is not likely that I am thinking that all or most of them are; and, if I did have the latter thought, it is unlikely that I would try to express it by saying 'some politicians are honest'. This sort of reciprocal raising of likelihood is what C. I. Lewis called 'congruence', and this is a good symptom of a relation of meshing between intentions and rhetorical patterns.

The meshing condition applies to the relation between the content of the intention and the text's or structure's conventionally determined meanings as well as the explicit and implied ideational relations that give a work its coherence, such as rhetorical connections between its various parts.[22] The meshing of intention and structure requires a high degree of coherence between the content of the intention and the display's rhetorical patterns. This requirement is satisfied when the intended ideas are integrated with such internal semantic relations as contrast,

[22] Nicholas Asher and Alex Lascarides, *Logics of Conversation* (Cambridge: Cambridge University Press, 2003).

parallelism, and exemplification. Suppose, for example, that a cinematic author's intention in making a short fictional film was to express the thought that wealth corrupts, and this intention is matched by an audio-visual display that depicts story events developing a contrast between a protagonist's condition before and after his sudden acquisition of a large fortune. The virtues of a simple, honest fisherman's life are exemplified in a host of narrative details and are further articulated by means of parallels to the similar lives of other characters in the village; these descriptions stand in stark contrast to the vices and misfortunes that follow from the initially joyous windfall. The rhetorical relations between the film's segments serve to elaborate this more general contrast, which in turn instantiates the intended explanation of the events of the story. It is implied, but nowhere overtly stated in the movie, that the disastrous changes in the lives of the fisherman and his companions are the result of wealth's inevitably baleful influence.

The ideational connections constitutive of meshing can take many forms, but, as some discourse theorists have hypothesized, many of them involve such basic categories of thought as part–whole relations, cause and effect, similarity and difference, and spatio-temporal links or contiguity. It is important to note that, as the attribution of such ideational connections and rhetorical structures can be independent of reference to corresponding authorial intentions, they thereby provide an independent source of evidence of the successful realization of intended meaning in the utterance. The meshing condition does not require that the intention regarding implicit content correspond to or bear a strong conceptual association with each and every feature of the text, display, or structure. In cases where the meshing condition is satisfied, competent interpreters are likely to find that the intentions readily integrate with the meanings of the display and with the rhetorical structures and other patterns of coherence established by that display's conventional meanings. In contrasting cases, even an astute and well-informed interpreter is likely to find that coherence breaks down. Sometimes an author intends to introduce an implicit, explanatory rationale for a large sequence of imagined story events, but the intentions in question were too impoverished, or too imperfectly thought through and acted upon, to provide anything like a consistent and reasonably detailed fleshing-out of the story elements and rhetorical structures conveyed by the text or display, so it would be a mistake for anyone to identify the work's meaning along those intended lines.

In *Art and Intention*, I illustrated another sort of failure of coherence in a fairly detailed interpretation of the film *Meeting Venus* (1991, dir. István Szabó), where there is ample evidence of a failure to integrate intentions with the rhetorical structures of the audio-visual display. Other examples can be mentioned. One such case is *Twelve Angry Men* (1957, dir. Sidney Lumet). While the film quite poignantly plots the triumph of deliberative reason over prejudice and dogma, a closer and more critical look pinpoints details that may be taken as undermining that overarching design. For example, the dogmatic bully who is eager to reach a vengeful verdict has to be physically threatened before rational arguments can be heard, and the triumphant *raisonneur* (elegantly played by Henry Fonda) must resort to an array of rhetorical and even theatrical devices in order to get his points across. The interpreter of the film might press this point and contend that the intentions and rhetorical features of the audio-display do not fully mesh. Although the intended point of the film is that reason, and not coercion and rhetoric, prevails in the courtroom, aspects of the rhetorical content of the film belie this thesis. Another example of a case where a philosophically rewarding interpretation of a film describes both intended meanings and unintended meanings or significance is *Gattaca* (1997, dir. Andrew Niccol), which, as philosopher Neven Sesardic contends in his analysis of the film, invites the spectator to admire a character whose behaviour is shown to be irrational and questionable because it wilfully endangers the lives of others.[23]

I shall conclude this chapter by providing a more detailed discussion of an example that illustrates the application of the meshing condition introduced above.

DAY OF WRATH AND MESHING INTENTIONS

Carl Theodor Dreyer's 1943 film *Vredens Dag* (*Day of Wrath*) was based on *Anne Pettersdotter*, a play written by the Norwegian author Hans Wiers-Jenssen (1866–1925). This play was first performed in Norway in 1908 and enjoyed a significant but relatively short-lived international success. The play was based loosely on the case of the

---

23 Neven Sesardic, 'Gattaca', in Paisley Livingston and Carl Plantinga, eds., *The Routledge Companion to Philosophy and Film* (London: Routledge, 2009), 641–9

actual condemnation and burning of Anne Pettersdotter, the widow of an influential protestant pastor, in Bergen in 1590.

The action of the film is set in seventeenth-century Denmark. Anne (portrayed by Lisbeth Movin), the young wife of an elderly pastor (Absalon, portrayed by Thorkild Roose), has an affair with his son, who is roughly her age. She is subsequently accused of witchcraft and is condemned to be burnt at the stake. Among the many interesting questions that this fascinating film raises is whether it is true in the story that Anne genuinely is a witch—in the sense of someone who uses demonic powers to try to realize evil goals. In many films in the gothic and ghost story genres, such as *The Exorcist* or the several films based on the Harry Potter novels, this kind of question is raised and quickly answered by providing the viewer with direct audio-visual evidence of beings and events strictly incompatible with a naturalist explanation. Any interpreter who responds appropriately to what is explicitly presented in such films recognizes that magical or supernatural events are part of the story. *Day of Wrath*, however, is not that kind of film. As the film unfolds, the possibility of actual witchcraft is raised, and evidence on both sides of the question emerges. Statements made by several of the central characters, including Anne, indicate that they fully believe in such things as demonic possession and the kinds of supernatural causation associated with witchcraft. This does not in itself tip the scales in favour of a supernaturalist interpretation, however, since such beliefs are wholly in keeping with Dreyer's notorious attempts to achieve a high degree of historical verisimilitude. The spectator is also given reason to think that the characters' beliefs in demonic powers are ill-founded and extremely harmful. Thus two salient interpretative options emerge: either witchcraft is real in the story or it is not. It would be unsatisfactory to say that both of them should be deemed simultaneously correct, as it would be deeply incoherent to proclaim Anne wholly innocent of witchcraft *and* someone who intentionally employs real demonic powers. That kind of contradiction can be ruled out because it cannot be squared with the uncontroversial assumption that this is a film designed to convey a coherent story.

Some very well-informed film scholars have contended that the question about the reality of supernatural causation is not really fundamental to the film.[24] Since I am in agreement with the thought that

---

[24] Raymond Carney, *Speaking the Language of Desire: The Films of Carl Dreyer* (Cambridge: Cambridge University Press, 1989), 134. A similar point is made by

an interpretative question can turn out not to be fundamental (or even appropriate) to a given film, even when there are appearances to the contrary, I should provide good reasons for my contention that the witchcraft question is indeed central. At the end of the film, Anne has been condemned of witchcraft. Her lover, Martin (Preben Lerdorff Rye), has abandoned her to side with the accusers. She will be burnt, and, as the spectator has witnessed a horrific witch-burning earlier in the film, he or she has a vivid sense of what this means (Figures 4.1–4.4). If Anne only wrongly believes she is a witch, her burning must be understood as a gruesome and unjust error. If, on the contrary, Anne really is a witch who has used demonic powers to seduce Martin and to kill her husband, then the condemnation cannot be contested. Someone might argue that, even though Anne is in league with the devil, she ought not to be punished so brutally and still deserves the spectator's sympathy, but this position corresponds to a sensibility that is not genuinely attuned to a belief system according to which there exists a supernatural evil that can quite literally become incarnated in people, an evil that can either be resisted and driven out, or lead oneself and others to eternal damnation. To put the point more bluntly: it is only coherent to declare the witchcraft question unimportant to our understanding of the film if one does not take the theological options seriously to begin with, which is a singularly anachronistic perspective to take on this historical subject. In short, if we want to be able to say what happened in the film, and how the story ended, we need an answer to the question about the reality of supernaturalism. Any number of basic facts about the film's characterizations, which are fundamental to our understanding of the film as telling a coherent story, depend on that answer.

With this rough sketch of the interpretative question in place, we can ask what grounds there can be in principle for arriving at a correct answer to it. In other words, what is the relevant evidence? According to the partial intentionalist position that I defend, Dreyer's intentions with regard to the story he was telling are relevant and indeed decisive, provided that the intentions *mesh sufficiently* with the relevant features

Edvin Kau, who argues that Dreyer's thematics should not be limited to the question of whether there is witchcraft or not in the story. Instead, we should attend to his masterful cinematic critique of a life-repressing ideology and system of spiritual control. See his *Dreyers filmkunst* (Copenhagen: Akademisk, 1989), 281.

Figure 4.1. Herlofs Marte is burnt in *Day of Wrath*.

Figure 4.2.

Figure 4.3.

Figure 4.4.

of the audio-visual display, where those features are, among others, the rhetorical structures constituted by the characterizations, dialogues, *mise-en-scène*, montage, and other expressive and artistic devices. So, if the meshing condition is to be applied, the intentionalist must have answers to two questions: (1) what were the cinematic author's relevant intentions, and (2) what are the rhetorical structures constitutive of the audio-visual discourse's coherence? Note that the answer to (1) is, like all historical matters, an empirical issue about which there could never be absolute certainty or scepticism-proof knowledge. All the evidence we have about Dreyer could be systematically misleading, or, more plausibly, it could simply fall short of unambiguously yielding one clear and compelling answer to the question about his intentions with regard to the content of the story. (Note that this is different from saying that, although he was effectively the author of this film, his intentions shifted, or that he somehow had no determinate ideas or intentions about what story he meant to tell in this film.)

Here, then, are some of the options the interpreter of this film faces:

1. ignorance of the facts about the film's authorship, including the author's relevant intentions, which would entail ignorance of the work's story content;

2. justified belief, or even knowledge, of the authorial intentions, and either

    2.1. supernaturalist intentions that either

        2.1.1. mesh with the audio-visual display (Anne is a witch), or

        2.1.2. fail to mesh (Dreyer meant Anne to be a witch but failed); or

    2.2. naturalist intentions that

        2.2.1. mesh with the audio-visual display (Anne is not a witch), or

        2.2.2. fail to mesh (Dreyer wanted to make a naturalist work but inadvertently made an audio-visual display that conclusively shows her to be a witch);

2.3. hesitation intentions (the film was designed to be perfectly ambiguous between these two interpretations), that either

2.3.1. mesh with the audio-visual display (the work is ambiguous), or

2.3.2. fail to mesh (Dreyer inadvertently tipped the scales).

Like the Dreyer scholar Maurice Drouzy, I am inclined to believe that the best option is 2.2.1.[25] In what follows I shall sketch an argument in support of this option, my primary concern being to provide a reasonably complex illustration of the application of the meshing condition (and not an exhaustive and systematic interpretation of the film as a whole, which would be a book-length errand).

Support for an interpretative option may derive from both internal and external evidence, where 'internal' refers to the meaningful features of the audio-visual display, and 'external' refers to evidence pertaining to the context in which the film was made and what we can learn about the author and his intentions. As internal evidence can be relevant to our understanding of external evidence, and vice versa, the interpretative process is one of reciprocal adjustment leading ideally to a reflexive equilibrium based upon an integration of the totality of relevant evidence. How, then, does one apply a principle that requires that intentions 'mesh' with the rhetorical patterns of the audio-visual display? There is no method or set of rules to be followed. The interpreter has to sift and make sense of the audio-visual evidence with an eye to such typical rhetorical patterns as contrast, parallelism, exemplification, generalization, explication, and elaboration.

Such rhetorical patterns are quite salient in a carefully designed film such as *Day of Wrath*. As David Bordwell has established in great detail, parallelism and contrast are employed at a variety of levels, including the use of light and shadows within the cinematic frame, patterns of editing and camera movement, sets and decors, and the selective distribution of sounds, music, and voices. The priest Absalon and his stern, domineering mother are associated throughout the film with gloomy, bare interiors and a repressive religious order. Anne is associated, on the contrary, with life, love, joy, pleasure, a spirit of rebelliousness, and natural beauty glimpsed when Anne and Martin

[25] Maurice Drouzy, *Carl Th. Dreyer né Nilsson* (Paris: Cerf, 1982), 288–9.

momentarily escape into the countryside to enjoy their love for each other. As Bordwell puts it:

The mise-en-scène defines the social as the realm of the chamber—the rectory (with its bars and grids in the décor), the cellarlike torture chamber, Absalon's sacristy, Laurentius's home . . . The growing love between Anne and Martin is presented as the response to social constraint, an outburst of natural energy . . . the allure of the realm of nature is strongly marked by the light streaming into the rectory, revealing the leafy trees outside the window. Characters in the film are defined in terms of such causes.[26]

Although Dreyer refuses to provide simplistic characterizations that neatly contrast entirely good and entirely evil persons, the rhetorical design casts Anne as a far more sympathetic figure than the person who accuses her of using witchcraft to kill her elderly husband. Merete, the pastor's mother (portrayed by Sigrid Neiiendam), is from the outset shown to be an overbearing and possessive mother-in-law who wants power and control over her son and all other affairs in the house. She is the kind of person who will not even let her daughter-in-law keep the keys to the household cupboards. Although her accusations are sincere and in some sense informed by pious intentions, the woman is self-righteous, unforgiving, and motivated by her desire for rigid order and control. For Dreyer's target, twentieth-century Danish audience, she is anything but a sympathetic character. For this same audience, Martin commits a terrible injustice when he breaks his promise to Anne and abandons her to side with his accusatory grandmother.

The external evidence also supports the hypothesis of a basic polarity associated with the contrast between oppressive accusers and the romantic victims of the vestiges of medieval persecution in Renaissance Europe. Dreyer said in an interview that one 'understands her [Anne's] terror when she believes herself also a witch'.[27] What Dreyer could have said but did *not* say was that Anne learns, finds out, or comes to know that she really is a witch. The thought that Anne is not a witch, but a victim of an unjust accusation, corresponds to the idea that Dreyer had a strong interest in making a film that condemns the persecution of innocent victims. It strikes me as entirely plausible to

[26] David Bordwell, *The Films of Carl-Theodor Dreyer* (Berkeley and Los Angeles: University of California Press, 1981), 123–4.
[27] From an interview in *Social Demokraten*, 17 Nov. 1943, cited in Jean Drum and Dale D. Drum, *My Only Great Passion: The Life and Films of Carl Th. Dreyer* (Lanham, MA: Scarecrow, 2000), 191.

think that Dreyer worked with the ambition of having his audiences generalize such anti-scapegoating reflections, particularly with regard to relevant affairs in the film's initial context of reception, Nazi-occupied Denmark. This oft-stated point has been challenged on the grounds that Dreyer could hardly have been interested in using a cinematic allegory to make a largely redundant and ineffectual attack on the Nazis.[28] Yet it can be responded that his intention very likely covered a critique both of Nazi persecution and of scapegoating and persecution more generally. Another key attitude expressed in the film, which is directly linked to the witchcraft question, concerns the romantic love Anne experiences with Martin, which is positively contrasted to the oppressive and unsatisfactory marriage that she was forced into as a young woman. Dreyer celebrates the young lovers' temporary escape from the confines of the prison-like interiors of the pastor's house in two lyrical sequences that can hardly be squared with an interpretation in which these expressions of love are really only manifestations of some kind of magical devilry or satanic temptation (Figures 4.5–4.6). Sympathy for Anne could hardly be maintained, however, were it true in the story that her behaviour is in fact one of Satan's worldly manifestations. Nor could sympathy for Anne as victim be maintained if the spectator concluded that the evidence in the world of the fiction was perfectly ambiguous between the rival claims of accusation and defence.

Arguments over the meaning of *Day of Wrath* sometimes make reference to the play on which the script was based. This is indeed a relevant source of evidence, but it must be handled with care and can hardly be taken as decisive, if only because the play itself requires interpretation, and its meanings may not be those of a film that is not simply a 'filmed version' of a theatrical work. Yet while the script does diverge significantly from the text of the play, many key elements of both the characterizations and action are adopted, and as I shall suggest below, some of the key assumptions were carried forward.

---

[28] Carney, *Speaking the Language of Desire*, 137, n. 14. Carney says that such an interpretation 'narrows a profound exploration of the limits of social and ethical understandings of life into a tendentious political allegory. It makes a work that speaks to the situation of all viewers seem to address only a particular historical aberration.' Carney does not defend the implicit premiss that it would be somehow incoherent or even impossible on Dreyer's part to intend jointly (*a*) to invite the audience to make-believe that Anne is an innocent victim of witchcraft persecution, and (*b*) to invite spectators to recall that Nazism perpetrates an analogous form of persecution.

Figure 4.5. Anne Pettersdotter (Lisbeth Movin) and Martin Pederssøn (Preben Lerdorff Rye) in *Day of Wrath*.

Figure 4.6.

It can be fairly easily established that the texts of the play do not support the idea that Wiers-Jenssen was trying to tell a story in which Anne was actually possessed by the devil. Wiers-Jenssen was the founder and editor of the *Norwegian Journal for Psychical Research* and authored two books on psychic phenomena. He drew directly upon his ideas about psychical powers in trying to explain what he with scare quotes refers to as 'witchcraft' (both within the play and more generally). This is made explicit at a key point in the texts. Anne has been told that her mother was a witch who had special powers, including the ability to 'call' people and make them do her bidding. Anne wonders whether she has inherited such powers, and, in her longing for Martin, tries to 'call' him with her thoughts. She has a special feeling when she indeed manages to perform the internal act of calling on Martin, and this feeling leads her to exclaim aloud 'I can do it' even before he actually comes to her. When Martin indeed appears, she takes this as evidence that she does enjoy some special powers. What Wiers-Jenssen writes in his stage indications at this point is that she 'brings about the phenomenon "witches" referred to as "to call" (long-distance hypnotic influence)' (Og mens hun star sån, frembringer hun det fænomen, 'heksene' benævnte 'at kalde' (Hypnotisk fjernvirkning)).[29] The scare quotes are Wiers-Jenssen's: there are not any real witches, just women with special spiritual powers—powers, moreover, that do not derive from some malevolent external source. In the first manuscript of the play, Wiers-Jenssen added that, when Martin in fact goes to Anne at this moment in the action, there should be no appearance of any somnambulism, because 'he is only a man who has been weakened by a long-repressed passion'.[30] In other words, even if Anne did have some special hypnotic ability, this is not what caused Martin to come to her. As Wiers-Jenssen thought psychic powers could be investigated and understood by a new science of psychic phenomena, we can say that he favoured a 'naturalistic' approach to the events mislabelled as 'witchcraft', provided, that is, that we recognize that he had a way of tracing the boundary between natural and supernatural that diverges from that of our current natural science.

Day of Wrath was modelled, then, on a drama in which beliefs in demonic possession and witchcraft are meant to be understood as

---

[29] Hans Wiers-Jenssen, *Anne Pettersdotter* (Oslo: Forening for Norsk Bokkunst, 1962), 47.

[30] Øyvind Anker, 'Anne Pedersdotter på scenen', in ibid. 81–100, at 87.

a misrepresentation of the special psychic powers possessed by some persons; these powers are not, however, 'demonic' or a manifestation of some supernatural evil, even if the agents themselves misunderstand them as such as a result of social influence and unsympathetic attributions. I contend that the guiding intention of Dreyer and his colleagues was to respect this central premiss of the play on which the film was based.

Another, rival interpretation needs to be discussed—namely, the ambiguity or 'hesitation' reading evoked above. For such an interpretation to succeed, the spectator's temporal experience of the film, especially with regard to the progressive presentation of evidence pertaining to characterization and action, must involve a tension or conflict between two or more rival interpretations that at different moments appear to be correct. For example, when Anne is shown to acquire the conviction that she is a witch, this at least temporarily lends some support to the thought that this may indeed turn out to be a story in which some persons actually have and use demonic powers. Yet at different moments in the film, the attentive spectator is pulled in the opposite direction. For example, during the sequence in which an old woman accused of witchcraft is tortured and her confession is dictated to her, there is hardly

Figure 4.7. Torture scene in *Day of Wrath*.

any evidence that she has any genuine demonic powers. What we see instead is a pathetic old woman being tortured by the men who govern an authoritarian religious community (Figure 4.7). The content of the 'confession' is literally dictated by one of the interrogators Similarly, the scene in which Anne 'calls' or attempts to call Martin to her is ambiguous between coincidence and causation. Just after Anne makes her inner incantation, she exclaims 'I can do it', and precisely at this moment Martin appears in the upper-left corner of the frame, behind Anne's back (Figures 4.8–4.12).

The basic thought, then, is that, at the end of the film, any attempt to sort out and weigh the evidence falls short of providing adequate grounds for ruling in favour of any one of the rival hypotheses about the work's implicit content. There can be no retroactive decision to the effect that some of the earlier inferences about this content were correct while others were not. Thus there emerges a second-order hypothesis that this stand-off between first-order inferences is the best option. A coherent interpretation can be achieved, then, if it is determined either that the author intended to leave some of the key questions in suspense, or, not having any such intention, incompetently produced an audio-visual display that partially lends itself to two or more incompatible readings.

Figure 4.8. Anne 'calls' Martin and he then appears.

Figure 4.9.

Figure 4.10.

Figure 4.11.

Figure 4.12.

It is important to note, however, that an interpretative decision in favour of such a second-order hypothesis entails that the spectator ought to adopt an attitude of deep uncertainty with regard to the first-order interpretative questions. We do not know whether Anne is an evil witch or not. Any emotional responses to her based on either assumption are simply unfounded. Similarly, we know little or nothing about Martin's real character. Perhaps he is a weak person who succumbs to his passion but then betrays his lover in fear; on the other hand, he could be a young man who temporarily gives in to evil temptation but then successfully wrests himself free from its baleful influence and guides his steps courageously onto the path to salvation. Thus we see that this kind of second-order reading has some strange implications that may not at first be obvious. In so far as emotional responses to the events in the story depend on inferences about what is actually happening (which is an uncontroversial assumption), the ambiguity hypothesis rules against the spectator concluding in the end that any such responses he or she experienced along the way were correct. If Anne really could be a witch, but we know that we can never find out, sympathy felt for her along the way would have been deeply erroneous. According to such a second-order, ambiguity reading, the spectator should in the end be deeply puzzled and quite clueless as to how to feel when Anne stands condemned and in tears because the man she loves has abandoned her to side with her accusers. We should have no idea what to feel about Martin's action. In short, the 'ambiguity' reading is a deeply sceptical hypothesis that, if taken seriously, leads the spectator into a kind of suspension of affective response. Since this is unlikely to correspond to anyone's actual experience during a first viewing of the film, it must be concluded that, on such a reading, Dreyer's work is a deeply deceptive affair that tricks the audience into having various responses and then expects the reflective viewer to put them all in doubt.

As I have argued above, the evidence pertaining to *Day of Wrath* does not in fact warrant this sort of sceptical attitude. The evidence that is supposed to weigh heavily in favour of the witchcraft hypothesis is, when examined more carefully, far too slight to counterbalance the many contrasting indications. Consider, for example, the very best evidence that can be identified in support of both the witchcraft and ambiguity interpretations. Anne and Martin are alone while Absalon is returning from his long and difficult day at a friend's deathbed. A shot of Anne flirting with Martin and taking him by the hand is followed by a shot of Absalon struggling against the heavy wind on the heath.

Figure 4.13. Anne admits to thinking of Absalon's death.

Figure 4.14. Absalon (Thorkild Roose) reports that he senses the hand of death on the heath.

Figure 4.15. Anne tells Absalon she has wished him dead hundreds of times; he rises and falls dead.

Figure 4.16.

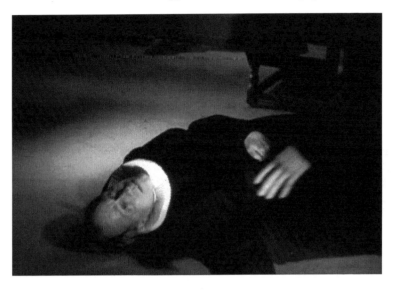

Figure 4.17.

Dreyer then cuts from a shot in which Anne confesses to Martin that she has indeed thought about how much better things would be if Absalon were dead, to a shot in which Absalon reports, when a powerful gust of wind strikes him on the way home, that it is 'as if death brushed past his sleeve' (Figures 4.13–4.14). Finally, Anne tells Absalon to his face that she had repeatedly wished him dead, and the man rises, visibly stricken, and collapses (Figures 4.15–4.17). Here the cinematic rhetoric would seem designed to lead the spectator to draw inferences to supernatural causation. Why would Dreyer make these rhetorical choices if he really wanted spectators to conclude that Anne is just an innocent victim? My response to this crucial question is to say that Dreyer's rhetorical design was to make the erroneous witchcraft inference available and even somewhat tempting to the spectator so as to make possible a better understanding of the ease with which such accusations arise. It is one thing to know that a given inference should be classified as an error (to embrace, for example, the abstract proposition that scapegoating is wrong), but something else to experience what it is like to be led to make such a mistake, and it is the latter knowledge that Dreyer's editing is clearly designed to get across. In other words, these rhetorical elements in the film are meant to function like a practical lesson in the fallacy of *post hoc ergo propter hoc*: Absalon thinks about death when the powerful wind strikes him on the heath; Anne was thinking about Absalon's death just prior to that moment, *therefore* Anne was the cause. Yet Absalon is a frail old man who has spent a strenuous day at his dying friend's bedside. The wind is so strong it makes it difficult for him to walk. Why should he not think of death at such a moment? In his confrontation with Anne, he is profoundly shocked when his acknowledgement of the wrong he has done Anne leads her to tell him that she has become involved with his son and has therefore wished hundreds of times that he was dead. A naturalist explanation of his sudden demise lies well within the bounds of medical and psychological possibility (in the play, we are told early on that he has a very weak heart.) Such a perspective stands in contrast to the rival explanation whereby it is true in the story that Anne's demonic powers have suddenly taken effect, but completely vanish after this one satanic event.

In conclusion, I hope to have shown in this relatively brief discussion of a very complex film how the meshing condition on authorial intentions can be applied. Many cases are far more simple and allow a fairly smooth application of this broad interpretative principle. And, as is to be expected with regard to all empirical, historical issues, in other cases the evidence is simply lacking and the questions about both intentions and their success cannot be answered. In such cases, spectators may nonetheless float hypotheses about the work's implicit meanings, some of which could be philosophically significant.

In the next two chapters I explore a case where the evidence is rather more abundant and promising. As in all empirical or fact-oriented investigations, the possibility of error remains. Yet I hope to show how an interpretative strategy of an intentionalist stripe can be a promising avenue for those who are interested in exploring the cinema's philosophical potential.

PART THREE

ON INGMAR BERGMAN
AND PHILOSOPHY

5

Bergman, Kaila, and the Faces of Irrationality

Ingmar Bergman (1918–2007) is notorious for having been a 'gloomy' film-maker and has often been vaguely associated with existentialism. The many published interpretations of his films draw on a number of strikingly different theoretical backgrounds, including the work of the Danish philosopher and theologian Søren Kierkegaard, Jean-Paul Sartre, Albert Camus and other existentialists, the I Ching, Freudian psychoanalysis, Jungian psychology and archetype theory, Ludwig Wittgenstein, Denis de Rougement, and Lutheran theology.[1]

While Bergman's films can, of course, be interpreted by applying notions drawn from these and various other jointly incompatible theoretical sources, it has never been established that Bergman's artistic projects were actually inspired or informed by them. Bergman declared that he was always an avid reader, but he made no claim to having systematically engaged with theoretical and philosophical works. With reference to attempts to read some Ludwig Wittgenstein or Jacques

---

[1] See, for a start, Richard Aloysius Blake in his *The Lutheran Milieu of the Films of Ingmar Bergman* (New York: Arno Press, 1978); C. B. Ketcham, *The Influence of Existentialism on Ingmar Bergman: An Analysis of the Theological Ideas Shaping a Filmmaker's Art* (Lewiston, NY: Edwin Mellen Press, 1986); R. E. Lauder, *God, Death, Art, and Love: The Philosophical Vision of Ingmar Bergman* (New York: Paulist Press, 1989), and 'Ingmar Bergman: The Filmmaker as Philosopher', *Philosophy and Theology*, 2 (1987), 44–56; Gordon A. Lee, 'Perceiving Ingmar Bergman's *The Silence* through the I Ching', Ph.D. diss, San Jose State, 1995; Bernt Ostermann, 'De Stora Frågornas sorti och Antonius Block', *Finsk tidskrift*, 3 (1989), 177–86; Hans-Helmuth Schneider, *Rollen und Räume: Anfragen an das Christentum in Filmen Ingmar Bergmans* (Frankfurt am Main: Lang, 1993); Irving Singer, *Ingmar Bergman, Cinematic Philosopher: Reflections on his Creativity* (Cambridge, MA: MIT, 2007); Richard Sonnenschein, 'The Problem of Evil in Ingmar Bergman's *The Seventh Seal*', *West Virginia Philological Papers*, 27 (1981), 137–43; and Amos D. Winberly, 'Bergman and the Existentialists: A Study in Subjectivity', Ph.D. diss., University of Texas at Austin, 1979. For more, see Birgitta Steene's indispensable *Ingmar Bergman: A Reference Guide* (Amsterdam: Amsterdam University Press, 2005).

Lacan, he commented that 'after two pages of confusion and anger' he asked himself whether the problem lay with his own inability to understand these texts, or some other reason.[2] Given the notorious obscurity of both Wittgenstein's and Lacan's writings, there is no good reason to assume that the problem was entirely Bergman's.

There is evidence, moreover, of one major exception to Bergman's tendency to prefer reading literary rather than theoretical works. Although it is not widely known, Bergman read and was strongly influenced by the Finnish philosopher and psychologist Eino Kaila (1890–1958). Here is one of Bergman's remarkable statements on this topic, which he made at the very end of his preface to the published screenplay of *Smultronstället* (*Wild Strawberries*) in 1957:

Philosophically, there is a book which was a tremendous experience for me: Eino Kaila's *Psychology of the Personality*. His thesis that man lives strictly according to his needs—negative and positive—was shattering to me, but terribly true. And I built on this ground.[3]

Only a few Bergman scholars have even mentioned this statement, and no one has ever systematically investigated its significance for Bergman's work.[4] One reason why very few people have followed up on this rather striking statement of Bergman's is that the book to which it refers was written in Finnish and has never been translated into any major languages. Originally entitled *Persoonallisuus*, this treatise in philosophical

[2] Ingmar Bergman, *Femte akten* (Stockholm: Norstedts, 1994), 10. References to major philosophers are extremely scarce in Bergman's various statements and interviews. In a talk entitled 'My Danish Angels', he once told a Danish audience that he had read Kierkegaard's *Sickness unto Death* when he was 16 years old; *Morgenavisen*, 18 Nov. 1989; cited in Steene, *Ingmar Bergman: A Reference Guide*, 117. I have not found any evidence that the content of this especially difficult work by Kierkegaard surfaced anywhere in Bergman's work.

[3] Ingmar Bergman, *Wild Strawberries: A Film by Ingmar Bergman*, trans. Lars Malmström and David Kushner (London: Lorimer, 1960), 12. Bergman made a similar statement in an interview with Arne Ericcson broadcast on Swedish radio on 6 Feb. 1960. I thank Paul Duncan for bringing a transcript of this interview to my attention.

[4] Three of the most knowledgeable Bergman researchers I know—Birgitta Steene, Maaret Koskinen, and Erik Hedling—confirm this conclusion about the absence of investigations into the Bergman–Kaila connection. Very brief mention of Kaila is made by Vernon Young, *Cinema Borealis: Ingmar Bergman and the Swedish Ethos* (New York: Avon, 1971), 167, and by Hubert I. Cohen, *Ingmar Bergman: The Art of Confession* (New York: Twayne, 1993), 439; Richard Blake also quotes Bergman's line about Kaila, but says that the reasons for it are 'mysterious'; he also wrongly states that the Swedish translation of Kaila's 1934 book first appeared in 1950 (*The Lutheran Milieu*, 18–19). In Chapter 6 I discuss the two slightly longer references to Kaila that I have been able to find in the Bergman literature.

psychology was first published in 1934; a Swedish translation appeared one year later, and a Danish translation was first published in 1946.[5] As none of Bergman's screenplays was published in Sweden until 1963, his 1957 remark in an English-language edition of the script of *Wild Strawberries* remained relatively unnoticed amongst Bergman's Swedish audience. Nor did his interview statement on the radio in 1960 seem to make a strong impression. In a Scandinavian context, Bergman was hardly the first artist to credit Kaila for philosophical inspiration. The award-winning and highly influential modernist writer Willy Kryklund is a salient example, for he has long been something of a cult figure in the Swedish intellectual milieu and made explicit references to Kaila's influence.[6] This point is significant in the light of many film scholars' assumption that Bergman can be unproblematically situated in a very general 'European' existentialist tradition or movement.[7]

In order to explore this philosophical 'ground' on which Bergman says he built, I shall devote the next few pages to a survey of some of Kaila's views. While I do not propose to try to reduce Ingmar Bergman's fictions to simple illustrations of Kaila's ideas, I think it important to recognize the extent to which the characterizations and rhetorical design of Bergman's cinematic works mesh powerfully with some of Kaila's central psychological premises. As I argued in Chapter 4, when an

---

[5] Eino Kaila, *Persoonallisuus* (Helsinki: Otava, 1934); *Personlighetens psykologi*, trans. Jan Gästrin, introduction by John Landquist (Stockholm: Natur och Kultur, 1935; 2nd rev. edn., 1939); *Personlighedens psykologi*, trans. Sunna and Franz From (Copenhagen: Villadsen and Christensen, 1946; 2nd edn., 1966). I am in no position to assess the accuracy of the Swedish translation: it is, in any case, what Bergman claims to have read. In this and the following chapter page numbers given in the text refer to the first edition of Gästrin's Swedish translation. It should be noted that there are differences between the first and second, revised editions of the Swedish translation: Kaila reordered sections in some of his chapters and did some rewriting designed to emphasize his systems-theoretical perspective. All of the passages I cite are the same in the first and second editions.

[6] I am indebted to Mikael Pettersson, Staffan Carlshamre, and Birgitta Steene for informative conversations on this topic.

[7] e.g. Blake, *The Lutheran Milieu*, 19: 'Bergman is not a systematic philosopher, yet his work clearly stands in the tradition of the existentialist movement in Europe.' It is far from clear, to me at least, that such a unique tradition can be rigorously identified or that Bergman belongs to any such thing, at least if such belonging involves having read and understood the works constitutive of the tradition in question. It is a non-trivial question, of course, how philosophical traditions are to be correctly identified and attributed to specific authors and works. It strikes me as telling that, with the exception of a staging of Albert Camus's *Caligula*, Bergman never chose to stage any of the great existentialist dramas, such as Jean-Paul Sartre's *Huis Clos*. For background and detailed documentation, see Steene, *Ingmar Bergman: A Reference Guide*, 816–825.

author's intentions are sufficiently integrated with the relevant features of the text or image (and, in the case of cinema, the audio-visual display), the intentions help to determine the content of the work. (This is not meant to rule out, by the way, the unintended meaning and significance of the works.) In some cases, Kaila's ideas function as premises, but Bergman's development of characters and events constitute explorations of implications and questions that are not in any simple way contained in those premises. Also, I shall argue in Chapter 6 that on at least one key topic Bergman's philosophical position diverges from Kaila's. So there is no question here of a 'reduction' of Bergman's complex cinematic works to simple illustrations of Kaila's tenets. Nor do I wish to overlook the rather major differences between writing philosophical prose in order to defend theoretical claims and making works of cinematic fiction.

I shall, however, in this and the following chapter, present quite a lot of evidence in defence of the hypothesis that some of Kaila's ideas inform and orient important aspects of Bergman's cinematic achievement. One of Bergman's statements in an interview can provide a context for this argument. When asked about the meaning or point of his 1980 film *Aus dem Leben der Marionetten* (*From the Life of the Marionettes*), Bergman responded that it is a film about manipulation. Yet he then said that he never gives commentaries on his films. He has always been surprised by directors who do so and finds it 'comic' and puzzling. He then explains that this is not because the film-maker has no ideas. On the contrary, Bergman goes on to say. When working on a film it is necessary 'to know precisely what one wants. It has to be entirely clear for us that at a given place we think this and that at another place we feel that, and that a given thought releases a given feeling.' Such things, Bergman remarks, must be 'clear as day' for those making the film. But he does not think it is a good idea to give people 'the answers' (*facit*); this takes away some of the suggestiveness, excitement, and joy involved in experiencing a film.[8] Such statements help us understand how it is consistent to believe that a director has specific ideas to express, uses the devices of the audio-visual medium to do so, but is reluctant to make detailed pronouncements about or paraphrases of those ideas.

---

[8] Ingmar Bergman interview by Arne Ruth Knut-Göran Källberg, 'Ingmar Bergman berättar om sin nya TV-film "Ur marionetternas liv"', *Expressen*, 15 Mar. 1989, Kultursidan, p. 4: 'Det tycker jag inte man ska ta ifrån människor genom att tillhanda hålla facit.'

KAILA AND THE PRIMACY OF MOTIVATIONAL FORCES

Son of Archbishop Erkki Kaila (originally Erik Johansson), Eino Sakari Kaila had a brief career as a dramaturge for the National Theatre of Finland but then devoted himself to science and philosophy. He became a docent in Psychology at the University of Helsinki in 1919, but moved to Åbo in 1921 to take a position as Professor of Philosophy. He subsequently returned to Helsinki in 1930 to a professorship in theoretical philosophy. He became associated with members of the Vienna Circle and conducted empirical work in Vienna on infants' reactions to the human face. Kaila's interest in research in brain and behavioural sciences led to the publication of *Persoonallisus*, the book that Bergman found shattering yet terribly true.

Kaila's treatise is an overview of psychological topics that creatively blends elements from Gestalt psychology, empirical psychology, theoretical biology, and systems theory, as well as the insights of various literary and philosophical authors, including Hobbes, Nietzsche, and La Rochefoucauld. Although there are some Freudian elements in Kaila's work, he was sharply critical of various psychoanalytic tenets and classified Freud's mode of thought as an outdated 'mechanistic associationist psychology' (p. 231). This is important, since some interpreters have been too quick to read Freudianism into Bergman's life, characterizations, and stories, and it might be thought that his reference to Kaila lends some support to this interpretative strategy. I return to this issue below.

Kaila's central thesis is the claim that there is only one effective psychic force, which he refers to using the Finnish word *tarve*.[9] This term is, like the Swedish and Danish *behov*, ambiguous between the English words 'need' and 'desire'. In what follows I will translate it as either 'want', 'need', or 'desire'. Kaila lays great emphasis on the conflict between basic appetites and what he calls the 'spiritual' and 'high spiritual' desires, such as a desire for religious purity or salvation. Kaila explains that he conceives of a want as a 'driving inner force in an organism' (p. 21). Living systems have a tendency to move, or at least to attempt to move, from a state of disequilibrium

[9] Many thanks to Professor Bo Pettersson for help with Kaila's Finnish.

to a preferred state of equilibrium, and a want or desire is a 'state of tension' corresponding to such a disequilibrium. To a given want corresponds a 'direction' or behavioural tendency, which targets a return to equilibrium. Kaila contends that wants are the key to the explanation and understanding of behaviour: 'Spiritual as well as animal life are dominated by wants' (p. 12). 'All psychic life, all life processes are subjected to their pressure and must be understood with them as our point of departure' (p. 22).

Kaila rejects a rationalist conception of the mind and focuses on the decisive influence of motivational forces on cognition and belief. One of his main preoccupations in this regard can be introduced by referring to the fable of the fox and the grapes, which Kaila discusses at several key points in his book. As the fable goes, when the fox cannot reach the grapes he wants, he ends up thinking they are sour. Kaila comments that, by denying the value of something valuable yet unattainable, the creature is spared the negative feelings of humiliation and low self-esteem, but this at the cost of an unjustifiable and irrational change of belief (p. 15). Kaila calls this a form of *inauthenticity*. This theme in Kaila's book finds a hyperbolic expression in such pronouncements as the following: 'One can say that human beings, and especially cultured human beings, have a natural *inclination to see life incorrectly*' (p. 153). 'Human thought and representational processes are dominated by non-theoretical desires; thought is generally a matter of *wishful thinking* [*önskedrömmande*]' (p. 293; emphasis in original).

One might be inclined to object that a sweeping conclusion about the prevalence of motivated or 'hot' irrationality is unfounded; it certainly does not follow from the claim that motivational forces play a pervasive role in the determination of human behaviour. And, indeed, it may be added that the most reliable way to satisfy one's desires is to have a clear-headed and reasonably accurate belief about the best means to one's ends, and to act intentionally or deliberately in keeping with such beliefs. To put this point more bluntly, garden-variety rationality serves, rather than hinders, the business of need and desire satisfaction to which Kaila grants such great importance. None of these points is lost on Kaila, yet he thinks the picture is more complicated, and this for several reasons: first of all, he insists that desire often influences the fixation of belief in an irrational manner; secondly, he claims that human desires are often conflicting and incompatible, and hence not susceptible to a rational ordering and deliberative control; thirdly, he argues that the satisfaction of desire is not only, and perhaps not even most often, brought about through rational, intentional action; actual human motivational dynamics often do not correspond to the philosophical ideal of a reasoning process in which desires, and beliefs about the means to their satisfaction, rationally conjoin to yield decisions and corresponding intentions. (It is somewhat ironic that one of Kaila's most famous students was Georg Henrik von Wright, who devoted a number of pages to a careful rational reconstruction of the 'practical syllogism' whereby actions, or at least the intention to act, is rationally derived from beliefs and desires.[10])

Kaila does not deny that rational intention formation is part of human psychology, but lays far greater rhetorical emphasis on the discussion of irrational desire satisfaction. In this context, Kaila focuses on unreasonable displacements of motivation. When a desire cannot be readily acted on or satisfied, it may be replaced by a desire for some surrogate object. The transition from the desire for an initial object to the desire for some surrogate is not supported by a justifiable instrumental belief, and, indeed, it often rests upon a very unreasonable belief triggered by a perceived similarity between two objectives. This perceived similarity or 'analogy' (as Kaila puts it) supports the specious belief that the first objective can actually be met by pursuing the second one, and this in spite of glaring and significant differences between the two objectives. Such a belief may itself be the product of a prior episode of motivated irrationality, such as wishful thinking or sour grapes. Kaila contrasts such instances of inauthentic desire formation to cases where a desire is well grounded in either an intrinsically valuable experience or a well-established means–end connection.

One of Kaila's examples of irrational motivation, which must have strongly impressed Bergman, is the sadistic punishment of children, by means of which a parent's frustrated desires find an 'outlet' (p. 300). According to Kaila, a sadistic desire to punish a child is inauthentic because it finds its actual, but unrecognized, basis in another desire or in the aggressive person's own tension. The cognitive blind spot in this process is the inability to understand the distortion at work in the emergence of the surrogate desire. Acting on this surrogate desire may yield some measure of satisfaction, but such actions do not represent an authentic solution and generate new problems in turn. The punished child may want to strike back; when this desire is inhibited, it may in

---

[10] G. H. von Wright, *Explanation and Understanding* (Ithaca, NY: Cornell University Press, 1971).

turn be replaced by a series of surrogate objects in a perpetuation of the cycle.

As I mentioned earlier, Kaila's combined emphasis on motivational forces and the decisive functions of the unconscious mind could lead some to think that what Ingmar Bergman and others were likely to have found in Kaila's book was a primer in psychoanalytic doctrine, but this would be a serious misrepresentation. Kaila's emphasis on unconscious drives does recall Freud's claim to have brought about a 'Copernican' revolution in psychology precisely along these lines. Yet Kaila uses the same rhetoric of a Copernican revolution to evoke a different set of breakthrough principles—namely, the above-mentioned idea of a non-additive holistic approach to living systems, and the idea that the meaningful content of psychic states is derived from their relation to needs, desires, and their satisfaction. Kaila explicitly rejects Freudian orthodoxy and accuses psychoanalysis of being mechanistic, especially with regard to the thesis that developmental episodes and structures are decisive in the formation of the personality. Kaila also refuses to acknowledge Freud as the discoverer of 'the unconscious', and adds that whether a psychological factor is conscious or unconscious is not the key issue. The real force of a mental item is not a function of whether it is conscious or unconscious, and there is a distinction between having *knowledge* of a need and 'feeling' it, focusing on it, or being aware of it. Kaila's alternative is to say that the expressions of needs are immediately and originally meaningful, and that this assumption renders the postulation of a special psychic unconscious superfluous (p. 231). Kaila also believes there is a distinction to be drawn between experience and conscious experience. One could experience seeing something without having an acute, conscious awareness of doing so, he claims. He rejects Freud's overarching emphasis on sexuality, just as he rejects Nietzsche's emphasis on the 'will to power'. Kaila also contests Freud's central contentions about the interpretation of dreams, allowing that dreams can have an escape-valve function, but denying that their effective content is always latent, repressed, and wishful. Dreams and the neurological function of dreaming, he protests, are just not that simple. He accuses psychoanalysis more generally of accepting the mechanistic idea that habit and the association of ideas constitute genuine psychic forces. Finally, in Kaila's work there is no positive mention of, or explanatory reliance on, Freud's idea of the Oedipal or Electra complexes, castration anxiety, or penis envy, and there is no attempt at a Freud-inspired 'explanation' of homosexuality or any other erotic inclinations.

Yet Kaila does claim to have found something of value in Freud's work—namely, the adoption of a dynamic or energetic model in which psychological events are to be explained in terms of psychic energies or forces. However, what Kaila grants to psychoanalysis with one hand gets taken back with the other. Kaila writes:

The service done by psychoanalysis is in no way the 'discovery' of the 'psychic unconscious', but the *discovery of the dynamics of the life of the mind*, or in other words, the 'discovery' of the fact that wants are the only psychic forces—which fact we have always been perfectly aware of in our practical knowledge of ourselves and in our accumulated wisdom about life.   (pp. 237–8)

In the light of such two-handed remarks, it is hard to see how anyone who read and was excited by Kaila's book could have come away from it with the idea that psychoanalytic doctrine has any great importance, since, according to Kaila, what is genuinely original and most characteristic in psychoanalysis is incorrect, while what is correct is not original.

Kaila believed it to be the task of a truly scientific and naturalistic psychology to discover the laws that govern the inner dynamics of psychic life, which would at bottom amount to a plotting of the systemic patterns whereby motivational forces arise and find an outlet or discharge through various types of behaviour. These laws would not, he proposes, be simple, and they would certainly not permit a reduction of the variety of human desires or needs to one underlying impulse. Kaila makes no systematic presentation of the laws of human motivation, but he does identify a number of piecemeal theses, which he presents as offering deep insight into the human personality, or the mental life, construed as a biological life form tied to the central nervous system. In this vein he espouses what he relates, with no great rigour, as David Katz's 'law of avidity'. This is presented as an experimentally confirmed finding to the effect that human desires become harder and harder to satisfy with each new success, as the organism's internal standard of satisfaction tends to change in function of the results obtained. In other words, if the fox is fortunate and can jump high enough to get hold of the grapes, they may be sweet the first time around, but, later, new desires will arise and the fox will no longer be content to satisfy his hunger with such ordinary grapes. Eventually the fox will discover some new, attractive fruit that is well out of reach, and it may turn out that this encounter with an unattainable object of desire will lead to a new instance of 'sour-grapes' irrationality.

So much for a brief presentation of some of the central claims in Kaila's treatise; some other aspects of his work will surface below.

INGMAR BERGMAN AND KAILA: IN SUPPORT OF THE INFLUENCE HYPOTHESIS

Although Bergman declared in print and on the radio that Kaila was foundational for his work, his remarks could be misleading for any number of reasons. So the hypothesis that Kaila's book actually informed any of Bergman's artistic projects requires independent support.

Even if we set aside Bergman's testimony, it remains highly likely that the young Ingmar Bergman found Kaila's positions shattering and convincing. Some of Kaila's main themes correspond quite well to important aspects of Bergman's own experience, such as childhood humiliations and ritualized punishments, as well as his own powerful ambitions, sexual desires, and notorious outbursts of anger. Bergman's artistic *œuvre* manifests a lifelong interest in, and condemnation of, the spontaneous, ritual, and artistic forms of scapegoating and humiliation. Kaila's discussion of ritualized punishment as a form of irrational scapegoating directed at a surrogate object must have been of special significance, at least if Bergman's own subsequent and recurrent autobiographical and fictional evocations of this type of behaviour is any indication. Kaila's discussion of 'surrogate reactions' and irrational desire satisfaction based on unacknowledged 'analogies' includes a discussion of the lifelong impact on a child whose nanny punished him by locking him inside a closet (pp. 306–7). Spectators of either the theatrical or the televised versions of Bergman's *Fanny and Alexander* (1982) will know that the brutal punishment of Alexander (portrayed by Bertil Guve) constitutes a central event in the drama. Bergman relates his own experience of such punishment in his autobiographical *Laterna Magica*, and cites this very narrative at length in his second autobiographical tome, *Images*.[11]

---

[11] Ingmar Bergman, *Bilder* (Stockholm: Norstedts, 1990), 38–41; *Laterna Magica* (Stockholm: Norstedts, 1987), 13–14. There has been some discussion concerning the accuracy of Bergman's references to his own ritualized punishment as a child, and at least one commentator contends that Bergman's accusations are ill-founded (Hans Nystedt in

Another related moment in Bergman's work is a scene from his 1968 *The Hour of the Wolf*, a film in which Bergman presents a fragmentary portrait of a deeply troubled artist, Jan (portrayed by Max von Sydow). During a bout with insomnia, Jan tells his wife Alma (played by Liv Ullmann) about how he was ritually punished as a child. This narrative carries a special significance in the film. One reason the artist tells his wife about these painful childhood experiences is that she has confessed to reading his diaries without his consent and has voiced her distress over their morbid contents. He wants to try to explain to her why he is tormented by thoughts of aggressive behaviour—his own and that of the demons who are after him.[12] The spectator is meant to understand, along with Alma, that there is an implicit, causal connection between the artist's angst and the childhood humiliation he recounts. This does not mean that there is nothing mysterious about the artist's psychosis, but it is important to understand that this narrative registering the impact of repeated childhood humiliations can be contrasted to vague talk about Nordic 'gloom'. This is a point that surfaces in any number of Bergman's other productions. For example, in the script of the 1969 film *En passion* (*A Passion*), Andreas complains that 'the word freedom is a drug that the humiliated get by on' and that no one knows what it really means. Punishment and humiliation take away one's possibility of truly living. And, in a line that Bergman deleted, perhaps because he reflected that it was hyperbolic, Andreas added that it was better in the time when people were publicly flogged, as this was at least an open and comprehensible barbarism.[13]

In sum, an important reason why Kaila could very well have exercised a real influence on Bergman was that ideas Bergman found forcefully stated in Kaila's book corresponded to his own experience, independent

his *Ingmar Bergman och kristen tro* (Stockholm: Verbum, 1989)). I take no stance on this topic, but will add that Bergman's fictions and interview statements are more charitably read as targeting the more general phenomenon of child abuse and not merely his own case. Characters such as Andreas in *A Passion* speak rather eloquently about humiliation and punishment in general, and not merely about their own experience.

[12] In this regard, the film is an improvement on the script, where the punishment narrative is not a response to the wife's confession that she has secretly read her companion's diary.

[13] Here and elsewhere in this chapter and the next I make reference to Bergman's scripts and unpublished texts, sometimes citing material that he obviously decided not to include in the final version of a film or essay. For the rationale behind the use of such evidence, see my 'Pentimento', in Paisley Livingston and Berys Gaut, eds., *The Creation of Art* (New York: Cambridge University Press, 2003), 89–115.

thinking, and personal inclinations. I give additional reasons in support of this conjecture below.[14] Another reason why there is a strong resonance between Kaila's philosophy and Bergman's works is that these two figures drew on common, anterior sources. Kaila's positive references to Friedrich Nietzsche were in harmony with Bergman's own prior thinking, at least if we can rely on his own report concerning his youthful interest in Nietzsche.[15] More importantly, perhaps, Bergman must have noted that at least some of Kaila's notions about human behaviour were already vividly expressed by such revered literary masters as August Strindberg and William Shakespeare (as Maaret Koskinen pointed out to me, Bergman had by 1957 staged various works by both of these authors). Although Kaila's book is a philosophical treatise written by a professional philosopher and psychologist, Kaila cites Strindberg and many other authors and claims that their works express important psychological insights. Bergman may have found Kaila's treatise congenial in part for this reason.

Additional support for the influence hypothesis may be found in a series of remarkable parallels between some of Kaila's topics and the film scripts that Bergman authored during the decade following the publication of his remark about 'building' on the ground of his experience of Kaila's book. Kaila contends that one of the best ways to gain insight into the workings of normal human personalities is to study cases where the psychic system malfunctions and breaks down. Kaila devotes a number of paragraphs to a description of the schizophrenic's experience in an effort to underscore the many ways in which mental illness can strongly influence both the perceptual and the affective states of the subject. The very landscape takes on a new appearance, he remarks, and the psychotic subject experiences a world full of secrets, a world on the verge of collapse. It is quite possible that Bergman found here some motivation for his cinematic adaptation of a story about a schizophrenic in *Såsom i en spegel* (*Through a Glass Darkly*) (1961).

---

[14] I am not arguing, by the way, for a static image of Ingmar Bergman's life and work. I would suggest, for example, that the Kaila resonance was less pronounced and consistent during the last two decades of Bergman's life. We know, for example, that there was an at least momentary flirtation with the thought of Arthur Janov. Bergman was in any case a complex and multi-faceted figure, and it is no doubt wisest to conclude with Harriet Andersson that it is really quite difficult to understand how the different facets fit together as a whole; see Harriet Andersson, *Samtal med Jan Lumholdt* (Stockholm: Alfabeta Pocket, 2006), 71: 'Det går inte riktigt att begripa sig på honom.'

[15] Bergman, *Laterna magica*, 133.

In this film, Harriet Andersson portrays a young schizophrenic who succumbs to terrifying hallucinations.

Kaila discusses various mental disorders at some length, including cases where the most general sense of 'reality' is weakened to such an extent that the patient perceives her surroundings as a kind of theatrical set. Kaila discusses how such basic distinctions as image/thing, name/object, and dream/reality can collapse. For Kaila, the collapse of such distinctions is characteristic of magical thinking. Bergman often explores this terrain in his films. A good example is his (1958) *Ansiktet* (literally, 'The Face', but distributed in English both as *The Face* and as *The Magician*), a film in which the crone played by Naima Wifstrand easily casts her magic spell over the servants and children who interact with her in the kitchen. Yet the actions and characterization in this film also correspond to Kaila's insistence on the idea that even the most civilized and modern personality can easily revert to primitive thinking when in the grip of affect. Kaila claims that the animistic tendency to mistake purely natural events for the workings of spirits can manifest itself when the rational, educated person experiences a crisis of sufficient magnitude, which is precisely what happens when Bergman's magician (portrayed by Max von Sydow) uses tricks to terrify the rationalist Dr Vergérus (Gunnar Björnstrand) in *The Face*.

Kaila gives a very specific example of a way in which an intelligent and cultured person can be seen irrationally to confound a representation and its referent: tearing a picture in two, someone vents emotions related to the actual person, taking it out on a piece of paper (p. 170). A Kaila-esque moment of this sort figures in *Persona* when nurse Alma hands the sophisticated actress, Elisabet Vogler, a picture of her son; in response, the actress tears the picture in two (Figures 5.1–5.3). One of the drafts of the script for this film includes a passage in which the nurse reports on this incident to the doctor and comments that Volger's manner of performing this gesture was so beautiful that it seemed like a scene in a theatrical performance; the nurse adds that Volger too seemed to experience it this way. That Bergman deleted this passage could have various grounds, but one reason may have been that it could have been taken as diminishing the irrational and emotive nature of the gesture. In the film, the Volger character has a very disturbed look in her eyes when she tears the picture in two. She has just interrupted the nurse's reading of her husband's letter by suddenly grasping the letter and tearing it apart. Her breathing is heavy. When the nurse hands her the picture, saying that the boy looks 'awfully sweet', Vogler takes

Figure 5.1. Elisabet Vogler tears the photograph of her son in two in *Persona*.

Figure 5.2.

Figure 5.3.

the picture, gazes at it for a second, and with a pained but decisive expression tears it in two. This disturbing gesture is accompanied by the dissonant, descending musical motif that recurs throughout the film at moments of distress and mystery.[16]

Another central Kaila motif is the contrast and potential conflict between different sorts of needs and desires. Kaila contrasts animal sexuality to the 'high [or deep] spiritual needs' manifested in romantic love (p. 371), a contrast played out rather vividly in Bergman's characterizations in *Sommarnattens Leende* (*The Smiles of a Summer Night*) (1955): just as Kaila compares human courtship with the displays put on by competing birds, so does Bergman instruct the coachman to strut and leap about like a rooster as he chases after the servant girl. The young theology student, Henrik, struggles to resist his desire for the attractive servant girl whose charms distract him from his pious meditations. He is ludicrously presented as being buffeted back and forth between his desire to satisfy his lust and his desire to read passages

---

[16] The rather brilliant music for this film was composed by Lars Johan Werle. For background, see Ingemar von Heijne, *Lars Johan Werle* (Stockholm: Atlantis, 2007).

from Luther's shorter catechism to the charming young woman. In a more serious tone, a Kaila-esque conflict between 'high' and 'low' desires surfaces in Bergman's 1963 *Tystnaden* (*The Silence*). Esther (Ingrid Thulin) says she is 'humiliated' by her sister Anna's (Gunnel Lindblom) promiscuity, whereas Anna is angered by her sister's high-minded and accusatory attitude about her sexual activities. Esther is indeed more intellectual than her sister, but Bergman emphasizes her frustrated sexuality, which is expressed even in her longing for her sister's company.

Another passage in Kaila's book may well have provided inspiration for a Bergman script. I have in mind the section (pp. 365–71) devoted to an analysis of the social and motivational dynamics at work in a character's shifting states of awareness. Kaila's example is the conceited pastor depicted in 'Huru jag blev väckt' ('How I was awakened'), a story by the Finnish writer Juhani Aho. Bergman, of course, had his own independent motivation and ideas for writing the script for his 1962 film *Nattvardsgästerna* (literally 'The Communicants', but distributed as *Winter Light*), yet these may have found reinforcement or a catalyst in Kaila's comments on a pastor's highly problematic relation to his own faith and that of the others.

To mention another possible influence, Kaila devotes a number of paragraphs to discussions of the various senses of the word 'persona'. He begins his book by questioning the value of a single-minded focus on the persona, where this is understood as a being having self-awareness. Kaila (p. 373) also takes up Arthur Schopenhauer's discussion of the rift between the 'persona' and the genuine personality, or, in other words, between the socially presented mask and the real self. It is the clown, adds Kaila (p. 374), who in festive and theatrical events is allowed to strip away the persona or mask to reveal 'human inauthenticity', a gesture Bergman, who often aligned himself with bedraggled clowns and circus people, never seemed to tire of performing.

While any one of these (and many other) apparent correlations between motifs and ideas in Kaila's book and Bergman's scripts and films could be entirely coincidental, when taken together they lend strong support to the hypothesis that the experience of reading Kaila was indeed a ground upon which the inquisitive and ambitious Bergman built—which is precisely what he declared in 1957. I see no good reason to doubt his word on this topic.

CHARACTERIZING IRRATIONALITY

I shall now try to show in greater detail how some of Bergman's scenes and characterizations mesh beautifully with Kaila's central points about irrational behaviour.

The first scene to be discussed is from *Det sjunde inseglet* (*The Seventh Seal*) (1957) and takes place in a rustic inn (which in the script was called 'Värthuset Förlägenhaten' or the 'Inn of Embarrassment'). I should preface my comments on this film by pointing out that Bergman clearly states that the film was not intended to provide a realistic representation of Sweden in the Middle Ages.[17] (And indeed various anachronisms have been identified, such as the fact that the bubonic plague began around half a century after the end of the last crusade, whereas the Knight and his squire return from their crusade to find Sweden in the grip of the plague.) Such facts are irrelevant, however, to the main goal mentioned by Bergman himself, which was to 'translate' the experience of modern people into a poetic and allegoric form. If this is correct, then what Bergman was after in the scene in the 'Inn of Embarrassment' is an evocation of some typical patterns of behaviour, not a literally accurate representation of specific actions taking place in a particular medieval context. In keeping with Bergman's programmatic declaration, the segment even begins with the Squire's flagrantly anachronistic declaration that Doomsday talk and ghost stories are unfit for *modern* man! And, indeed, the scene is designed to express Bergman's oft-stated emphasis on the destructive place of both spontaneous and ritualized humiliation and scapegoating in human affairs.

Bergman sets the scene by cutting between shots of various persons who make brief pronouncements indicative of their discontent and fear. Business has gone bad, at least in part because of the plague, which is interpreted as a sign that the Day of Judgement is near. Rumours about weird omens and people dying like flies are repeated. The anxiety and

---

[17] Untitled programme note by Ingmar Bergman to *The Seventh Seal*. Here I cite a published, German translation that includes an introductory paragraph not to be found in other versions of this introductory note; see *Das Siebente Siegel, Cinemathek*, 7 (Hamburg: Marion Schroeder Verlag, 1963), n.p.

other negative emotions expressed by these people are soon to find an outlet, when two unhappy characters, the blacksmith and Raval, focus their hostility on Jof, a naive and kindly actor who happens to be sitting near them.

The blacksmith is looking for his wife, who has run away with an actor. Jof protests that he is innocent, but is forced to stand on his head and then to dance like a bear in a brutal imitation of some kind of ancient sacrificial ritual. The crowd jeers and laughs. The terrified actor collapses onto some burning sticks on the floor near the table, a visual detail that will be echoed later in the film in a scene where a young girl accused of witchcraft gets burnt at the stake. The actor is ordered to get up and continue his bear dance. (That this bear dance was considered crucial to the scene by Bergman is evident in the notes he made to himself in his personal shooting script: 'Remember the bear dance', he wrote in big letters.)

The crowd's ugly behaviour is meant to be read as a textbook case of ritualistic aggression directed at a surrogate figure, be it human or animal—precisely the kind of motivated irrationality that Kaila emphasizes. Bergman's script also stresses the role of biased thinking in this crowd dynamic. The blacksmith's wife has run away with an actor; Jof too is an actor, so 'it is logical', as the accuser puts it, to take it out on Jof. Spectators are obviously meant to reflect that this sort of accusation is anything but logical. The accuser here is the drunken thief Raval, who seems to get angry at Jof because he did not want to buy a stolen bracelet from him. Raval has been identified earlier in the film as a theologian from Roskilde who persuaded The Knight and his Squire to join a pointless Crusade to the Holy Land. Bergman's rather harsh characterization of the theologian fits in with the film's hypercritical and anachronistic portrayal of the Church's institutions and practices, such as the shrieking procession of flagellants, and the torturing and burning of a 14-year-old accused of witchcraft. All of these aspects of Bergman's script rest squarely on the foundation of Bergman's experience in reading Kaila's book, where religion—by which he means the Christian religion—is identified as the great 'cathedral of wishful thinking' (p. 381).

FROM THE LIFE OF THE MARIONETTES

As I mentioned above, Kaila challenges the Aristotelian conception of *anthropos* as the rational animal by pointing to prevalent displacements of motivational force in which an initial, authentic object of desire is irrationally replaced by a surrogate. I shall now discuss another of Bergman's explorations of this topic, which lies at the very centre of his stark characterizations in *From the Life of the Marionettes* (1980), a work that Maaret Koskinen has aptly called 'a black gem'.[18] What follows will be best appreciated by readers who have seen this film, but I shall try to provide enough description to make the points comprehensive to those who have not done so or who do not recall the details. At best I shall only scratch the surface of this black, and indeed morbid, gem. In Chapter 6 I attempt to round out my discussion of Bergman's philosophical themes by introducing some less dire elements.

The film begins with a sordid scene in a brothel where Peter Egerman (a successful German businessman portrayed by Robert Aztorn) meets a prostitute named Katarina Krafft (Rita Russek). He does not initially reveal any great desire for her and refuses even to take off his coat, yet something snaps inside him and he attacks her, kills her, and then has anal intercourse with the corpse. The rest of the film is a series of flashbacks that constitute a kind of 'investigation' into this event, culminating in a final report dictated by the psychiatrist, Dr Professor Mogens Jensen (Martin Benrath). In the first of these segments, the psychiatrist presents official testimony to the head of the criminal investigation. He recounts that Peter had called him after the murder, at which point the psychiatrist went to the scene of the crime.

In the next segment, we are shown an earlier encounter between the psychiatrist and Peter. Peter goes to the psychiatrist for help, and, after beating around the bush nervously for a while, confesses that for two years he has been troubled by his desire to kill his wife Katarina (Christine Buchegger). Peter tells the doctor that he wants to hear from him that some kind of hormonal disorder is responsible for these thoughts. He says that 'shrinks' (in German, the term is *Seelenarzt*, which translates literally as 'doctor of the soul') are interested in dreams, but his are banal and meaningless (we find out later that this is a lie). Mogens responds impatiently, and with some anger complains that

---

[18] Bergman wrote the script for this film in Swedish but the film was made in German. As usual, the published screenplay diverges massively from the actual film; most scenes are shortened significantly and their order is altered; and, as usual, the English subtitles to the film are an imperfect crutch; see *Ur Marionetternas liv* (Stockholm: Norstedt, 1980), *Aus dem Leben der Marionetten*, trans. Hans-Joachim Maass (Hamburg: Hoffmann and Campe, 1980); *From the Life of the Marionettes*, trans. Alan Blair (New York: Pantheon, 1980).

Peter does not really believe in the soul and has no reason to come to him for help. When Peter asks for a prescription, the psychiatrist tells him he should take a long walk and have a strong cup of coffee with a couple of shots of cognac. Peter gets up and makes for the door, but then hesitates and says he does not want to leave, so Mogens listens to more of Peter's awkward revelations. When Mogens asks how he kills Katarina in his fantasies, Peter goes into the details (which Bergman chooses to illustrate in a dream-like sequence). The psychiatrist points out that actually cutting his wife's throat would be very messy and that the gory details would not correspond to his fantasy of having an ecstatic, otherworldly experience. He then tells Peter that he can, of course, admit him to a clinic, where he would be pumped so full of drugs that he would lose his identity entirely. He tells Peter he is taking him very seriously, while furtively glancing at his watch. He gives Peter an appointment for another day and indirectly asks him to leave by saying he has another person coming.

As soon as the psychiatrist thinks Peter is out the door, he calls the man's wife. When she shows up, he has changed into more casual clothes and greets her with a kiss and holds her hands. She asks for a drink. Mogens invites her to join him on a six-week-long vacation to Tunisia. She declines, but indicates that she is quite willing to have sex with him on the spot; a few minutes later, she changes her mind. Mogens then gingerly mentions Peter's violent fantasies and recommends that Katarina stay away from Peter for a while; he invites her a second time to go to Tunisia with him. She refuses and suggests that Mogens is simply trying to come between them, which is clearly the case.

In a moment I will discuss some of the other segments, but turn now to the penultimate segment, in which the psychiatrist dictates his final report to the legal authorities. He begins with a self-serving lie designed to cover up his own involvement in these matters, especially his failure to react appropriately to Peter's revelation of his desire to kill his wife. He says that Peter has never come to him with any acute psychiatric disorder. He could, of course, have been sick without knowing it, the doctor adds.

The rest of the psychiatrist's official analysis runs as follows: Peter had a domineering mother and a poor relation to his father, which led to latent homosexuality. Although this inclination remained unconscious, it had a strong, disruptive effect on his relations to his wife and other women. This fact, along with the anguish generated by his transferred agressivity towards the domineering mother, could find no natural outlet in the social world in which Peter was raised, where any kind of emotional outburst was taken to be 'almost obscene'. Peter accordingly became a stranger to his own feelings. Instead of being himself, he adopted 'attitudes' and played socially dictated roles. Self-discipline and social success prevented him from giving his feelings free rein. He became strongly attached to his wife, who was as domineering and strong-willed as his mother. His inexplicable angst, and his angst over this very angst, were ritualized in keeping with an established social model involving the use of alcohol and drugs to provide an acceptable and even recommended outlet. Had Peter remained within this circuit, the disaster would perhaps never have happened, but, once he came into contact with a prostitute, anything became possible. Any small detail could have triggered it: a word, a gesture, a tone of voice. The doctor then adds that Peter 'killed the girl in an emotional short-circuit' (unfortunately, the English subtitles at this point misleadingly read 'emotional blackout'); the German term is *Kurzschluß*, which accurately translates the Swedish word *kortslutning* used by Bergman in the original script). The doctor continues by saying that Peter's pent-up aggressivity was released, setting in motion an avalanche of feelings. 'One only possesses or controls that which one kills,' the doctor proclaims. Applying this same formula, the psychiatrist concludes that Peter is in danger of committing suicide, because only someone who kills himself fully controls himself.

The cinematic presentation in this segment of the film is noteworthy. The initial murder sequence at the beginning of the film is shot in colour; the subsequent flashbacks are all in black and white.[19] The doctor is up late (a clock shows that it is around 1.19 a.m.) and sits in his darkened office speaking into a tape recorder. When the doctor comes to his line about how in the encounter with the prostitute 'everything becomes possible', Bergman cuts to a close-up of Peter's face, and the image takes on colour again, *precisely when the doctor uses the phrase 'emotional short-circuit'*. In an epilogue, still in colour, a mournful Katarina visits the clinic and hears from the nurse about how

[19] According to a statement made by Bergman in an interview published in *Les Cahiers du cinéma* in 1990 (cited by Steene, *Ingmar Bergman: A Reference Guide*, 325), he wanted to make a black-and-white film but 'had' to put in colour in the opening sequence because the producers thought the initial television audience might think there was something wrong with the broadcast if it was in black and white. Bergman not only accepted but made valuable use of this constraint, opting to make a selective and expressive use of colour at both the beginning and end of the work.

Peter passes his days, carefully arranging his bedspread, playing chess with the computer, suffering anxiety attacks, finding comfort in an old teddy bear, 'probably a childhood memory'.

What are we to make of Bergman's characterizations of the murderer and his psychiatrist? In a preface to the published screenplay, Bergman writes that it has become his habit in such prefaces to try to elucidate his reasons for writing the script. Such a task is not easy, because there is the danger of rationalization and a deceptive appearance of wisdom. Yet, in the case of this film, the task is relatively easy, as a single question forms its basis: how can a 'short-circuit reaction' arise in a well-adjusted and well-established person? Bergman goes on to say that none of the persons involved can claim to explain or clarify the drama: 'they are all involved in it and therefore confused'. A parenthesis that was stricken from the German published version of the script reads as follows: '(The psychiatrist who by virtue of his profession should be the closest to understanding is in fact at the greatest distance.)' Bergman then goes on to say that his intention is that anyone who wants to or finds it exciting should draw his or her own conclusions about the answer to his question; those who do not wish to can, he hopes, view it all as entertainment. This last bit is somewhat ironic. On a separate page at the back of his copy of the script, Bergman comments on the completion of the project and writes: 'I have made a disgusting, distressing, unpleasant, grey, strange film. So I have, and I am glad about it!'[20]

Although Bergman may have been tempted to delete the line about the psychiatrist being the most remote from understanding Peter, this was not because he somehow changed his mind and decided that the psychiatrist was not confused and should be taken as his *porte-parole*. If that had been the case, more than the deletion of one parenthesis from the preface would have been required in order to achieve a sufficient meshing of intentions and audio-visual rhetoric. As the French film critic Joseph Marty comments, Bergman is 'ferociously ironic' with regard to the 'psychoanalytic clichés' used by the conniving doctor.[21]

---

[20] This statement is dated 14 Dec. 1979. The text reads: 'Jar har gjort en ruskig, ledsam, obehalig, grå, konstig film! Det har jag och det är jag glad for!'

[21] Joseph Marty, *Ingmar Bergman: Une poétique du désir* (Paris: Cerf, 1991), 184. There are, as is to be expected, commentators who disagree. Hubert I. Cohen writes: 'In his preface to the screenplay of *From the Life of the Marionettes*, Bergman says that Jensen's summary is far from the truth. In spite of this warning, which also can be regarded as Bergman's attempt to distract us from truths about himself, we must listen to Dr Jensen because many of his insights are valid'; see his *Ingmar Bergman: The Art*

How, he asked, can the spectator be expected to take seriously an analysis proffered by such a deeply comprised character? Shortly after the film's opening, Bergman gave an interview in German in which he diverged from his usual, fairly strict observation of his policy of refusing to provide explicit comments on the meanings of his films. He says that this film is about 'manipulation'. The people in the film are manipulated, not just politically, but also humanly, by doctors and television and food and drink, and by powers that they cannot control. When asked whether a particular line delivered by the psychiatrist is Bergman's own 'recipe', the response is unambiguous:

No. It is the recipe of Mogens, the psychiatrist. Mogens has very little to do with me. And I believe we do not like each other. In any case Mogens does not speak for me at all.[22]

(Nein. Das is ein Rezept von Mogens, dem Psychiater. Der Mogens hat sehr wenig mit mir zu tun. Und ich glaube, wir lieben einander nicht. Jedenfalls spricht der Mogens überhaupt nicht für mich.)

Lest it be suspected that such an unambiguous and strident interview statement could turn out to be a misleading, *post hoc* rationalization on the part of the director, it should be pointed out that additional evidence in support of this reading can be found in material indicative of the director's thinking during the making of the film. In Bergman's copy of the shooting script, a variety of notations reveal his unambiguous emotional and intellectual distance from the psychiatrist's behaviour. For example, at one point Bergman comments derisively, on the facing left page (a space usually reserved for technical indications and thoughts

---

of Confession (New York: Twayne, 1993), 342. Cohen concludes finally that the film is a kind of confession in which Bergman confesses and accepts the forces that have crippled and made him unhappy. In *The Passion of Ingmar Bergman* (Durham, NC: Duke University Press, 1987), Frank Gado says that 'Bergman supplies all the facts necessary to understand the only mystery with which the film deals' (p. 487), and 'the film Bergman presents confirms the analysis in all its details. Although the psychiatrist could be said to have missed the truth in not articulating the specifically Oedipal source of Peter's problem with women, the analysis implies it' (p. 490). Gado finds additional 'confirmation' in the supposition that this interpretation broadly applies to 'the' story Bergman has told repeatedly for four decades. In my view this claim is disconfirmed by the careful descriptive work done by Maaret Koskinen in her study on the relevant thematic and psychological continuities and discontinuities in Bergman's authorship; see her *I begynnelsen var ordet: Ingmar Bergman och hans tidiga författarskap* (Stockholm: Wahlström & Widstrand, 2002).

[22] Ingmar Bergman, interview with Joe Hembus, in *Ingmar Bergman: Die großen Kinofilme* (Lübeck: Amt für Kultur der Hansestadt Lübeck, 1988), 211.

about blocking) is: 'Här har du Mogens typiska förnuft!' (Here you have Mogens' typical reason!).

On another page in the shooting script, Bergman reasons about Mogens's reaction to Peter's disquieting revelation of his obsessive thoughts about killing Katarina:

Why does Mogens react in this peculiar manner? He wants to take his distance from the whole affair. He does not believe Peter's horrible confession. That's the whole fact. HE DOES NOT BELIEVE HIM. HE DOES NOT BELIEVE HIM! In any case he doesn't believe he thinks he'll commit a crime. In any case none [unintelligible scribble]. He doesn't believe in Peter's madness. [unintelligible] his signals are double: reason and intuition.

And in another note at the end of the conversation, Bergman comments that the psychiatrist treats Peter with 'a kind of usual tone of ordinary disdain'. The psychiatrist is arrogant and thinks of himself as a man of culture; he has a certain amount of contempt for what he perceives as the limited mentality of people in business. (When Katarina asks him whether he is coming to her fashion show, he says that his wife will go, but he will be too busy preparing an academic lecture he is giving at a conference.) In the script, he comments that Peter and Katarina have a routine and 'unanalytic' habit of cultural consumption; the psychiatrist, on the other hand, is something of an art collector.

Bergman's characterization of the psychiatrist in the film coheres perfectly with the negative comments he has made elsewhere. Although the doctor frames the question about Peter in precisely the terms Bergman uses in his preface, there is no good reason to think that Bergman meant the spectator to swallow the self-interested psychiatrist's rather mechanical application of psychoanalytic clichés to Peter's case. And, indeed, it is only when the doctor drops that language and speaks of how any small detail could have triggered the 'short-circuit' that Bergman depicts Peter with an extreme close-up in colour. To understand better how this visual rhetoric functions in this context, some background remarks are required.

Bergman commented in an interview:

We made *From the Life of the Marionettes* in black and white, the first picture in almost ten years we did that way. We start in colour, and then after about three or four minutes go over to black and white, and then the last two or three minutes are in colour. Perhaps I'm wrong, but to me the great gift of cinematography is the human face. Don't you think so? With a camera you can go into the stomach of a kangaroo. But to look at the human face, I think, is the most fascinating.[23]

Bergman is notorious for his repeated programmatic insistence on the importance of close-ups of human faces.[24] He has gone so far as to call this the 'highest point' of the art of cinema.[25] His most oft-cited remark in this vein is from a 1959 essay, 'Each Film is My Last', and reads as follows:

There are many film-makers who forget that the human face is the point of departure for our work. We can certainly become absorbed in the aesthetics of montage, we can produce wonderful rhythm with objects and still life, we can make astoundingly beautiful nature studies, but proximity to the human face is without a doubt the cinema's most special feature and mark of distinction. We should draw the conclusion from this that the actor is our most precious instrument and that the camera is only a means of registering that instrument's reactions . . . We should realize that the best means of expression the actor has at his or her command is the gaze. [The spectator has a constant desire to experience reactions and tensions in the gaze.] The objectively composed, perfectly directed and played close-up is the director's most powerful means of influencing the audience. It is also the most flagrant proof of his competence or incompetence. The lack or wealth of close-ups shows in an uncompromising way the temperament of the film director and the extent of his interest in people.[26]

So far so good, but we must look more carefully at Bergman's specific use of a close-up of Peter's face in profile as he sits in the clinic at some point after the murder. The close-up in question here, which is a slow zoom culminating in an extreme close-up of Peter's eye (Figure 5.4),

[23] William Wolf, 'Face to Face with Ingmar Bergman', *New York*, 13, 27 Oct. 1980, pp. 33–8; cited at http://www.bergmanorama.com/bib_80.htm.

[24] See, e.g., Birgitta Steene, *Ingmar Bergman* (New York: St Martin's, 1968), 68; Diane M. Borden, 'Bergman's Style and the Facial Icon', *Quarterly Review of Film Studies*, 2 (1977), 42–55; and, for a historical perspective, Maaret Koskinen, 'Närbild och narrative (dis)kontinuitet: Nedslag i Ingmar Bergmans närbilder', *Aura*, 1 (1995), 58–63. Koskinen raises the questions whether Bergman's use of close-ups has not changed during his career, and whether they are always made to serve the continuity of the narrative. With regard to the latter question, she eschews a radical 'fragmentation' thesis.

[25] Ingmar Bergman, unpublished notes for a talk on directing actors held in Stockholm on 18 Sept. 1964: 'den rätt instruerade och rätt spelade närbilden av en skådespelares eller skådespelarskas ansikte'.

[26] Ingmar Bergman, *Varje film är min sista film* (Stockholm: Svenskfilmindustri, 1959). My translation. The sentence given in square brackets is translated from an earlier typescript version of this essay that Bergman presented to the Copenhagen Student Society on 13 Feb. 1959.

draws the spectator's attention to Peter's intense concentration on something outside the frame, the nature of which is unknown to the spectator. What is the focus of the intense concentration of a man who has gone amok and committed what he himself would, in even a moderately reflective moment, consider a senseless and horrible crime? As the doctor continues with his analysis, Bergman cuts from a close-up of Peter's eye in profile to a close-up of the chessboard he has been studying. Peter moves his knight, and the screen on the computer displays a message: 'You missed the mate' (Figures 5.5–5.8). This is ambiguous, of course. One thought on offer here is that the computer's circuits are sufficiently well designed to defeat Peter's efforts at rational calculation. (For spectators capable of making the connection, the game of chess can be read as an allusion to the Knight's struggle with death in *The Seventh Seal* (Figure 5.9).) There is also a cruelly ironic point here that Peter missed killing his wife in killing a mere surrogate. He killed 'Ka', the prostitute, but not Katarina, his wife. Another point that is implicit here is that mere visual scrutiny of Peter's physical appearance and expressivity cannot in fact reveal the depths of his mind. Taken

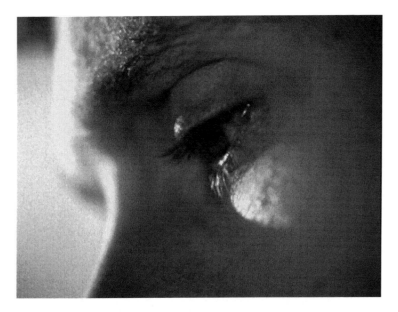

Figure 5.4. 'You missed the mate': Peter Egerman (Robert Atzorn) and the chess computer in *From the Life of the Marionettes*.

Figure 5.5.

Figure 5.6.

Figure 5.7.

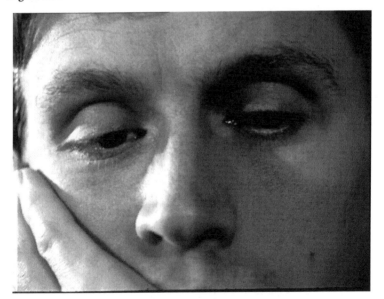

Figure 5.8.

in isolation, the close-up of his face and gaze do not tell us what is really going on. The line about an emotional short-circuit coincides with a close-up of Peter in colour, but we still do not have evidence here that confirms any particular analysis of why the emotional short-circuit took place. Nor can we fully grasp his current condition. In sum, the image hardly confirms the psychiatrist's verbal account of this complex person's condition, such as his rather speculative idea that Peter is likely to attempt suicide in an attempt to master himself. Had Bergman wished to find some visual rhetoric that would valorize and confirm the doctor's discourse in the spectator's mind, he surely could have found something more effective than a sequence in which the viewer suddenly learns that the patient is playing chess with a machine but 'missed the mate'. For example, Bergman could have illustrated the psychiatrist's remarks about Peter's desire for his mother with flashbacks showing Peter interacting with his mother, thereby rhetorically reinforcing the putative explanatory connection between the killing of the prostitute and postulated incestuous desire. Instead of such options, Bergman uses a medium-long shot (Figure 5.10) that shows Peter in his cell, his hands

Figure 5.9. Antonius Block (Max von Sydow) plays chess with death in *The Seventh Seal.*

Figure 5.10. Peter's imprisonment in *From the Life of the Marionettes.*

against the chessboard-like window, the overall impression being one of imprisonment.

To return to my more general point, the evidence we are given to work with in the film does not uniquely call for or warrant an explanation couched in Freudian terms. Even if it were the case that some specific version of psychoanalysis turned out to be true in our actual world (a highly controversial proposition, to say the least), it would not follow that it would be appropriate to apply such a doctrine to the explanation of the fictional character Peter Egerman. When we make up stories, we are not bound to do so wholly in keeping with whatever we take to be the truth of human psychology. That means that, even if Bergman believed in some version of psychoanalysis (which is highly dubious), he would not have to rely on such notions in constructing one of his characters. And, if we are to understand a fictional story as told by someone else, we have to figure out what sort of psychological assumptions were actually relied upon by that person in developing the characters and events in the make-believe. In the case of a film-maker such as Bernardo Bertolucci, those assumptions are indisputably Freudian; it follows that, if someone wants to elucidate the implicit, intended content of *his* fictions, they must work with psychoanalytic premisses.[27] If one has doubts about the plausibility of those premisses, one may be unlikely to think the work has the virtue of verisimilitude; it could nonetheless be deemed instructive in any number of ways and have many artistic virtues, even though it lacked that of being psychologically insightful. In the case of Bergman, there is additional evidence that the film was not designed to support the idea that the Freudian explanation is implicitly true in the story. Many other features of what we see and hear do not cohere very well with such an explanation, and the overall presentation leads in a different direction, which I shall now begin to describe.

The spectator learns that Peter Egerman and his wife Katarina are a childless, egotistical couple who live professionally successful, but hectic, anguished, and conflict-ridden lives. Their relations have degenerated into a series of ugly quarrels in which they taunt each other viciously, sometimes in the presence of friends or one of the lovers with whom they openly betray each other. For example, Katarina ridicules Peter when he makes the mistake of proclaiming that he knows how to satisfy her sexually. She mocks him for wanting to sodomize her one evening but failing to get an erection. When Katarina is later contrite after this quarrel and says she behaved 'hysterically', Peter coldly points out to her that her apology is just another strategy for winning the upper hand; whatever concessions he might go on to make will be remembered and used against him in the next quarrel. He coldly continues to read a book and tells her to leave him alone.

The coldness and brutality of the dialogues between Peter and Katarina are harrowing. And the rare moments when they calm down and actually attempt to come to some understanding of each other end in failure. At one point during a sleepless night Katarina tries to get Peter to tell her why he is so miserable. When he responds by saying 'all ways out are blocked' and 'tedium', she does not follow. When she asks what exactly he means by 'tedium', he says that part of it is that it is tedious to try to explain it to anyone. She then tries to tell him about

---

[27] Bertolucci tells us, for example, that the opening scene in his film *Luna* should be understood as an illustration of Freud's 'primal scene', and, when asked whether the ball of yarn symbolizes the umbilical cord, his response was 'that was intentional'; in Fabien S. Gerard, T. Jefferson Kline, and Bruce Sklarew, eds., *Bernardo Bertolucci: Interviews* (Jackson, MS: University Press of Mississippi, 2000), 136. Similar comments are made about the importance of psychoanalysis as the background to *The Conformist*: 'I substituted Marcello's unconscious—a psychoanalytic explanation, that is—for the presence of destiny in the book [by Alberto Moravia]' (pp. 66–7).

a strange sense of loss that she herself recently experienced, but he does not follow and starts to fall asleep.

An important part of the dramatic structure of the film involves Tim (portrayed by Walter Schmidinger), a gay friend of the couple who works with Katarina in the fashion industry. It is Tim who put Peter in contact with the prostitute, and at one point he confesses that he did this because he was in love with Peter and hoped somehow to come between him and Katarina. Such is Tim's connection to the plot, but, more importantly, there are two lengthy scenes in which Tim speaks about himself, including a bit that Bergman referred to in his private script as 'Tim's big aria'. These speeches are important because they contribute to a rhetorical parallelism by means of which Bergman develops a general psychological perspective that transcends the narrow and mechanistic assumptions employed by the psychiatrist in his official report on Peter. Tim's thoughtful and insightful words are meant to carry at least a certain degree of conviction.[28] What Tim presents is a rather bleak (and thoroughly Kaila-esque) perspective on the limitations of self-knowledge and knowledge of others. This is not a total scepticism, following which it would be impossible to know anything about oneself or others; rather, the position could be more accurately described as a certainty with regard to the need for a depth-psychological explanation, coupled with a strong belief that such an explanation is most often out of reach, precisely as Kaila says. Staring into a mirror (Figure 5.11), Tim says:

I am governed by forces that I do not master. It is as simple as that. What kind of forces? I do not know. Doctors, lovers, pills, drugs, alcohol, work—nothing helps. The forces are hidden. What are they called? I do not know. Perhaps it is just the fact of ageing in itself. Putrefaction. I do not know. Forces that I do not master.

Tim goes on to say that as he looks into the mirror and studies his seemingly familiar face he observes that deep in this combination of flesh, blood, and nerves there are two incompatible things that he does not know how to name. (The English subtitles rather misleadingly have him go on to call them 'people'.) Tim describes a dream of contact, closeness, belonging, self-forgetting, and of all that is living. And, on the other side, he finds violence, piggishness, the horror, the threat of

---

[28] As Maaret Koskinen also observes, Tim figures amongst the list of 'sexually ambivalent' characters in Bergman who figure as bearers of truth, insight, and human sympathy. See her *I begynnelsen var ordet*, p. 67.

death. And often he believes that they have a common origin. But he does not know: 'And how should I be able to know?', he adds. Having said these lines, he turns to Katarina, who seems to have been sleeping through Tim's revelations. He asks her to take his hand and place it on her cheek. (In the script, Tim literally proposes this as 'an experiment', but Bergman cut this line out.) 'Do you feel my hand?', he asks. She nods affirmatively. 'But do you feel that it is me? [*Dass ich es bin?*]', he pursues. She shakes her head to indicate a negative response (Figure 5.12). In the script, Bergman had Tim add 'Now you know what I mean', but he eliminated this line, perhaps to reinforce the impression of the lack of genuine understanding between Tim and Katarina. In one of the many changes that make Katarina a much harder and more violent character than the script indicates, Bergman deleted a reaction in which she becomes tearful and says she believes him.

These and many other elements of Bergman's characterizations in this film mesh perfectly with Kaila-esque assumptions. Behaviour is governed by motivational forces that often take irrational forms. The subject can be perfectly aware of this general fact, but it does not follow that the specific configurations of desires and needs can be fully understood, even

Figure 5.11. Walter Schmidinger as Tim in *From the Life of the Marionettes.*

Figure 5.12. Can you tell it is me? Christine Buchegger as Katarina Egerman in *From the Life of the Marionettes.*

less explained. Yet these constraints on self-knowledge and autonomy are not a matter of a mechanical structuring of personality that takes place during childhood along the lines of the Oedipal complex. Some of the desires that govern behaviour are sexual, others not. Katarina, for example, visibly enjoys exerting her influence and power. She enjoys mocking her husband, for example, when at the last minute she insists on getting drunk in a bar instead of doing as he wants and coming along to a dinner at his mother's house. She enjoys annoying him by making him late. He comments that a lack of punctuality is a symptom of repressed aggressivity, to which she responds rather frankly and proudly that hers is not repressed.

In short, again and again these characters indicate that they are not fully in control and are intermittently aware of it. Yet even during these moments of partial lucidity, the specific nature of these motivational circuits—and short-circuits—escapes them. Peter's enormous frustration with the life he is leading somehow leads to the catastrophic explosion and murder in which 'Ka' the prostitute stands in for Katarina the wife. Precisely how and why this happens remains unknown. Does the fact that the women bear the same first name make any difference? One frustrated desire, or perhaps a whole series of frustrated desires for one thing, are suddenly replaced by a desire to do violence to the surrogate. Neither Peter nor Mogens can say how this happens. Bergman's point is that it does happen, following the circuitous and unforeseeable pathways of the mind. Raising his unanswered question about how a short-circuit reaction can arise in a sophisticated and apparently well-adjusted person, Bergman added in a draft that 'we witness them daily, especially in the mass media, but sometimes in ourselves'. Bergman has at times applied this notion of irrational surrogates in a political context. Pursued by an interviewer about his position on nuclear power, he responded that the debate is a substitute for something completely different, such as a much deeper angst and 'a much deeper need or desire [*behov*] than is at stake in being for or against nuclear power'.[29] Oddly enough, at one point Bergman was going to have Katarina say that Peter was involved in 'unbelievably complicated' negotiations to do with nuclear power, but he deleted this line.

These reflections on Bergman's thoughts about unknowable and potentially very destructive psychological forces lead quite directly to the topic of Bergman's repeated emphasis on 'angst' and the question concerning his understanding of this notion. Bergman makes no reference to Kierkegaard or any of the other authors who have written about this phenomenon. In his papers there is a single definition written out in an uncharacteristically clear hand (with no indication regarding sources or the occasion on which this definition was formulated). The definition reads: 'ångst är en obehaglig upplevelse av en odefinerbar fara. En kansla av att "något" rör vid grundvalarna för din trygghet ja för din existens!' (Angst is an unpleasant experience of an undefinable danger. A feeling that 'something' touches the foundation of your security and indeed of your very existence). If Kaila is correct about the irrational springs of human motivation, angst with regard to the unknown enemy within is only to be expected.

In conclusion, the considerations set forth in this chapter should suffice at the very least to have established the plausibility of the 'Kaila connection'. Yet my discussion of some Kaila-inspired expressions of irrationality in works by Ingmar Bergman leaves us with a rather incomplete picture, first of all because the conception is altogether too bleak and too partial to provide an adequate representation of

---

[29] Ingmar Bergman interview by Källberg, 'Ingmar Bergman berätter'.

Bergman's philosophically relevant works, and secondly because I have not discussed any of the interesting ways in which Bergman's artistry moves beyond the Kaila-esque assumptions. There is also more to be said with regard to Kaila's proposed explanation of the prevalence of distorted self-understanding, as well as the possibility of authentic self-awareness. An at least partial rectification of these shortcomings is the errand of the next chapter, where we will see how Bergman's perspective on moral knowledge takes us beyond Tim's grim 'aria'.

6

Value, Authenticity, and Fantasy in Bergman

As I pointed out in the previous chapter, only a few of the numerous critics who have written about Ingmar Bergman's cinematic *œuvre* have mentioned his testimony regarding his foundational experience of reading Eino Kaila's treatise in philosophical psychology. Some of the critics who have mentioned Bergman's statement on the topic discount it as a mysterious or misleading moment in his authorship. Some of these critics cast doubt on authorship in general and on Bergman's vaunted 'auteur' status in particular, and so are not inclined to take very seriously the 'propaganda' he may have made for himself at some point in his career.

A few commentators have, however, remarked that Bergman indirectly alludes to Kaila in a statement made by one of the characters in *Wild Strawberries*, but the philosophical implications of this allusion remain to be pursued. In my view these implications are quite significant and lead directly to some of the most important issues in Bergman's films, including some interconnected views about the status of moral judgements, issues concerning irrationality and self-knowledge, and the modernist artist's critique of fantasy. I shall first describe the relevant moment in *Wild Strawberries* so as to set the stage for a discussion of these more general issues.

WILD STRAWBERRIES: WHAT THE SCHOOLBOOK SAYS

In a pause on the way to Lund, where Professor Isak Borg (Viktor Sjöström) is to be honoured for his lifelong contribution to science, Borg sits in the car conversing with his daughter-in-law Marianne (Ingrid Thulin). She recounts an important quarrel she has had with the professor's son Evald (Gunnar Björnstrand). In a flashback that illustrates her narrative, we observe that Marianne has taken a drive with Evald down to the seaside. She reveals to him that she is pregnant, fully expecting that he will be displeased. She insists that she is going to have the child. He gets out of the car in anger and protests that he does not want any children. She will have to choose between staying with him and having the baby. Following him out of the car, she says 'Poor Evald' and clutches his arm with both hands. In a line that was later stricken from the script, he was to say: 'Please spare me your pity. I have chosen my position in full awareness and in complete possession of my senses.' In the film he makes a vehement outburst saying it is absurd to live in this terrible world and absurd to bring children into the world thinking they will be better off. She says this is just an excuse, but he angrily responds that he was an unwanted child in a hellish marriage. He says he has no more time to discuss the matter and moves back towards the car. When she calls him a coward, he turns and says that life sickens him. He does not want to take on a responsibility that would require him to live a single day longer than he chooses (Figure 6.1). He adds that she knows that he means it and that he is not just being hysterical, as she initially thought. He returns to the car and she follows him. In another line struck from the script, he tells her to go ahead and have the child. It will be economically difficult, but at least they will be free from each other. In the film, Marianne calmly says: 'I know this is wrong.' This is the moment (Figure 6.2) at which Björnstrand delivers Evald's line that a few Bergman scholars have recognized as carrying an allusion to Kaila: 'There is nothing called right or wrong. One functions according to one's needs: you can read that in a schoolbook.' Marianne pursues: 'And what are our needs?' He tells her she has a hellish need to live and to create life. And his need is 'to be dead, absolutely, totally dead'.

In his brief discussion of this sequence, Frank Gado does not hesitate to identify the fictional 'schoolbook' to which Evald refers with Kaila's philosophical treatise.[1] Gado's main goal in his lengthy book on Bergman is to use psychoanalytical assumptions to provide the key to Bergman's personality. Bergman's works of fiction are then interpreted as more or less symptomatic expressions of the personality structures determined by Bergman's relation to his parents. At one point, Gado

---

[1] Frank Gado, *The Passion of Ingmar Bergman* (Durham, NC: Duke University Press, 1987), 225.

Figure 6.1. Gunnar Björnstrand as Evald Borg in *Wild Strawberries.*

Figure 6.2. Marianne (Ingrid Thulin) and Evald Borg (Gunnar Björnstrand) in *Wild Strawberries.*

goes so far as to say that Bergman has been rehearsing the same fantasies over and over again for four decades, the story in question being the familiar triangular 'family romance'. In the case at hand, this means that Evald's conflictual relationship with Professor Borg in the fiction of *Wild Strawberries* is symptomatic of the film director's ambivalence towards his own father.

Yet there are very good grounds for doubting such reductive interpretations, including one that posits a simple equation between Kaila's philosophical treatise and the book to which the character refers. The line about functioning according to needs certainly echoes Kaila, yet, as Bergman and anyone else who has actually read Kaila's book must know, it is grossly inaccurate to characterize Kaila's difficult treatise as a 'schoolbook' (in Swedish the expression is 'Folkskolans läsebok', a reader used in the state-run primary schools; incidentally, this line is missing from the English subtitles). Obviously Evald is exaggerating, as schoolbooks in Swedish primary schools in the 1950s were hardly designed to teach children that there is no such thing as right and wrong!

There are plenty of other reasons for doubting that Evald is Bergman's spokesman. First of all, it is hard to see why Bergman would want to associate himself directly with Evald's unpleasant and symptomatic outburst. The utterance has no genuine purpose in the character's relationship with his wife. He could hardly imagine that he would persuade her to have an abortion by speaking in this ugly manner, nor is she likely to feel inclined to reward him for begrudgingly coming around to her point of view. His remarks are, on the contrary, quite hurtful and he will need to make up for them later. What the spectator indeed finds out subsequently is that Evald does not consistently believe what he says in this scene, in spite of his conviction that his position is stable and the product of some kind of rational equilibrium. In fact he does not really need or desire to be dead, as he blurted out to Marianne. A few days later he tells his father that he cannot live without Marianne and that he has agreed that they will do as she wants. When his father asks him whether he means that he cannot face the prospect of living alone, Evald corrects him and says he means he cannot live without Marianne. Given this otherwise admirable attachment to Marianne as an individual person, Evald's earlier outburst, including his strong claims about meaning what he says and having deep convictions about life and so on, is shown to have been misleading in spite of the obvious vehemence and sincerity with which it was delivered.

Even if we consider Evald's statements in the quarrel with Marianne in isolation from his subsequent behaviour, his declarations are internally inconsistent and patently unreliable. If, as he proclaims, there is no right or wrong, how could the action of taking on a moral responsibility be possible or in any way binding? Why would agreeing that Marianne should have a child prevent him from committing suicide at some later point should he so desire? It might be surmised that he would think it irresponsible or wrong to abandon his child in this manner, and this thought would be an obstacle to his desire to kill himself. But how does this fairly ordinary reasoning square with the doctrine that there is no right or wrong? If people merely function according to their needs or desires, why could not Evald allow that he could currently act on a desire to let Marianne have the child, but later act on his desire to kill himself? Is he assuming that he will end up desiring to behave correctly or morally in relation to the child? Yet that is not consistent with his claim that he does not believe that anything is right or wrong. Is he simply afraid that becoming a parent will somehow make him change his mind? What would be 'wrong' with that? In any case, this is not what he takes himself to be telling his wife. Evald is clearly confused.

Jesse Kalin is the only other critic I have found who discusses this scene and the Bergman–Kaila connection at any length. His paragraph on the topic deserves to be quoted in full:

Kaila's psychology, so positively cited by Bergman and summarized as 'Each man does what he needs to do', may have these Nietzschean tones of someone who can rise above life and master it in his or her own way. But there has been almost no discussion of how this 'psychology of needs' really applies to Bergman's films, if it does. If anything, it points to what turns out to be a kind of defeated egoism in the character of Evald in *Wild Strawberries*, who seems to quote Kaila in his defense of his refusal to accept Marianne's pregnancy, but in fact only offers the excuse of, as Marianne says, a coward afraid to live (itself a kind of Nietzschean charge without any of the Nietzschean background). While Bergman himself may feel an affinity for Evald and the force of his own 'needs', there is always more, as the context of *Wild Strawberries* and Bergman's films in general makes clear. Egoism may remain a deep strand of human psychology (with a concomitant 'will to power'), but it is not all that there is, either in the films or Bergman's own life.[2]

---

[2] Jesse Kalin, *The Films of Ingmar Bergman* (Cambridge: Cambridge University Press, 2003), 193.

What indeed could Bergman's point have been in embedding the allusion to Kaila's philosophy in a petulant and self-deceived outburst of 'defeated egoism'? It would be a mistake to think that his point was to discredit Kaila's philosophy as a whole by having it be endorsed by a character in what is recognizably an ugly and incoherent outburst. Such a conclusion cannot be squared with the fact that some of Bergman's key psychological ideas, especially with regard to motivation and self-knowledge, are found in Kaila's work (and in the wide range of sources Kaila cites). Yet Bergman's strategy of putting Kaila-esque language in Evald's mouth may have the crucial rhetorical function of suggesting that there is nonetheless a critical distance between Bergman's perspectives and some of Kaila's views. In particular, I have in mind Kaila's statement that a 'scientific conception of the world is only possible to that extent that we are aware of the "subjectivity" of all values' (pp. 186–7). It is far from obvious that what Bergman found worthwhile in Kaila was the idea that nothing is right or wrong, or the idea that 'therefore' the satisfaction of needs or desires is the only standard of conduct. In fact, in his published statement about Kaila (which was cited early in Chapter 5), Bergman persists in referring to 'positive' and 'negative' needs, an evaluative idiom that is not used by Kaila himself and that would in principle be out of place in a consistently nihilistic philosophy. In the context in which Bergman was operating, he hardly needed to turn to Kaila to find that kind of view on the status of values; such a position was notoriously defended by the Professor of Practical Philosophy at Uppsala, Axel Hägerström, and by his followers in the so-called Uppsala school.[3]

BERGMAN AND KAILA ON SELF-KNOWLEDGE

As I argued in the previous chapter, Kaila's main focus in his psychological treatise is on the various forms of human irrationality, with an overarching emphasis on ways in which motivational events and 'forces' vitiate rational cognition. The idea of inauthentic and faulty self-understanding, understood as motivated irrationality of belief, is

---

[3] See, e.g., Axel Hägerström, *Socialfilosofiska Uppsatser* (Stockholm: Bonniers, 1939). Hägerström's position anticipates later, influential Anglo-Saxon expressions of an 'expressivist' theory in meta-ethics: moral judgements are neither true nor false.

central here, and there can be no doubt that this is a topic at the heart of Bergman's thematics. It finds an excellent expression, for example, in a passage from the script to *Wild Strawberries* that unfortunately did not find a place in the actual film. When Isak Borg addresses himself to us in the first person, in his very first sentence he informs us that he has become too old to lie to himself. But he then adds that he cannot be entirely sure, for even his calm attitude towards truth resembles a hidden deceptiveness (*förlugenhet*).

Kaila at times makes sweeping pronouncements about the pervasiveness and indeed the inevitability of 'inauthentic' and faulty self-awareness, and ignorance regarding the mainsprings of human action. Yet this leads to a problem.[4] Whenever someone sets forth and defends a theory saying that *all* thinking is distorted or irrational, one question should quickly come to mind. What are the implications for the theorist's own claims? If thought is just wishful thinking, fantasy, or a form of substitute satisfaction for frustrated desires, as Kaila repeatedly proclaims, what about philosophical thought? What about Kaila's own philosophy? Does consistency require him to allow that his own theorizing is just wishful thinking too? And, if that is so, why should anyone believe it? A thoroughgoing cynicism in philosophy is patently self-defeating, since it has to dethrone philosophy along with the ego and everything else.[5]

Kaila does say that much of philosophy, such as Platonic metaphysics and Christian theology, is indeed an elaborate kind of fantasy. Yet Kaila wants to add that this does not mean that all philosophizing has to be false. Objective, rational thought is possible, but such moments of lucidity only emerge in the relatively few cases where there is some drive compelling us in this direction, a drive that prevails over the

---

[4] Kaila does not discuss this problem in his 1934 treatise, but it does come up in his *Tankens Oro: Tre Samtal om De Ytterska Tingen* (Helsingfors: Söderström, 1944). This intriguing book is organized as a dialogue between two figures, Aristofilos, who presents a late Romantic, quasi-mystical 'life' philosophy, and Eubulos, a hard-nosed positivist who represents Kaila's own later views. The latter discusses the philosophy of quantum mechanics at great length and argues for a 'field-theoretical Gestalt behaviorism', which looks like a kind of neurophilosophy. It is Aristofilos who broaches the idea that when Nietzsche's cynical philosophy gets applied to itself it is self-defeating; Nietzsche would then have to allow that his own favorite ideas are also lies and deception, but that leads to 'chaos' (p. 79).

[5] This is the 'tu quoque' argument, as it is a matter of applying standards to the person who promotes them. For an example of its application, see Clarence Irving Lewis, *Values and Imperatives: Studies in Ethics* (Stanford, CA: Stanford University Press, 1969).

non-theoretical desires that normally turn thinking into wishful thinking or some other form of motivated irrationality (p. 354). Kaila remarks, then, that people engage in objective, factual, rational thinking only in the relatively few cases where they have a need to do so—for example, a genuine researcher doing scientific work. And he elsewhere comments that 'scientific knowledge of humanity only begins to make essential progress when the compulsion to paint a pretty picture of humanity gives way to a striving to achieve the naked truth', and here he credits the 'revelatory psychology' to be found in Schopenhauer and Nietzsche (p. 23). Kaila adds some comments about the particular motives that allowed such figures to gain psychological insight—in Schopenhauer's case, a particularly bitter and powerful desire for recognition. One way in which people can become lucid, Kaila says, is by falling so short of social norms and ideals that they are forced to engage in painful reflection (pp. 371–2). Full lucidity is never acquired, Kaila adds, but life is in some cases a series of 'awakenings' in which light is shed on more and more aspects of one's situation (p. 368).

A very compelling illustration of this line of thought may be found in *Persona*. I shall describe this aspect of the film at some length below in an effort to show how one of Bergman's most powerful works expresses insights concerning inauthentic self-understanding and its partial overcoming.

As she spends more and more time taking care of Elisabet Volger, nurse Alma becomes increasingly fascinated with the silent and mysteriously disturbed actress. Nothing in the audio-visual display of *Persona* informs the viewer how famous Vogler is or what the nurse knows or thinks about her prior to their meeting. When the nurse discusses the assignment prior to her first encounter with the actress, she expresses misgivings, saying that the actress clearly has great mental strength and may need a nurse with more experience. In an early encounter with the patient, the nurse naively states her half-baked views about the 'enormous importance of art in life'. She studies the actress and admires her gestures. In the script, Bergman included a scene in which Alma reads an interview with the actress in a weekly magazine, the heading of which reads: 'The interpreter of the complicated feminine soul, Elisabet Volger, speaks freely from her heart'. Alma carefully studies a close-up of Elisabet, who is quoted as saying: 'My life is based on love and truth.' The interviewer then comments: 'And she means what she says.'

Alma's growing fascination with Elisabet is further developed in a draft of the script (but not in either the published script or the

Figure 6.3. Dagmar Brink as Eva Henning in Hasse Ekman's *Flicka och hyacinter.*

film) in a lengthy section describing an evening at the cinema. Alma watches an old film in which Elisabet Volger plays the leading role. As described in the script, this film-within-the-story reads like a cross between something by Bergman and Antonioni, with a bit of Hasse Ekman's dark, expressionistic style thrown in as well.[6] Surrounded by 'interesting men', the character played by Vogler sleeps with several of them and talks at length about her problematic subjectivity. Like the suicidal character in Ekman's *Flicka och hyacinter* (1950), she walks alone in dark and increasingly deserted streets (Figure 6.3). She meets a lesbian schoolmate and goes dancing with her, but panics when the lesbian wants to kiss her on the mouth. She goes home to find her

---

[6] Readers unfamiliar with the history of Swedish cinema are not likely to find my reference to Hasse Ekman (1915–2004) very illuminating, which is unfortunate. Briefly, Ekman wrote, directed, and acted in dozens of films, and at one point was viewed as a major rival to Bergman. In Swedish there is Leif Furhammar and Jannike Åhlund, *En liten bok om Hasse: Hasse Ekman som filmregissör* (Göteborg: Filmkonst/Filmbiblioteket 4, 1993), which includes a brief foreword by Ingmar Bergman in which he describes how jealous he was of Ekman early in his career. My thanks to Fredrik Gustafsson for tutorials on Ekman.

husband asleep and discovers a love letter he has written to her. When he begins to make love to her, she 'lets it happen'.

While Alma is alone with Elisabet at the doctor's summer house, the distance between the nurse and her patient appears to break down. Elisabet takes Alma's hand and caresses it and appears to be flirting. Alma gazes back at her in appreciation and admiration. The formal address—'Mrs Vogler'—used at the hospital is now replaced by 'Elisabet' and 'dear Elisabet'. Elisabet would appear to be a sympathetic and comprehending listener, so Alma lets down her guard and begins to confide in the actress in increasingly longer monologues. Alma seems to assume that the famous actress is interested in every detail of Alma's life story, but Bergman includes shots that reveal Elisabet's sceptical and bored reactions to Alma's self-indulgent narrative (Figures 6.4–6.5); yet the same sequence includes shots where Elisabet caresses Alma and stands giving Alma a massage while Alma goes on about what a great listener Elisabet is (Figures 6.6–6.7). In this way, Bergman gives the spectator evidence to the effect that Alma does not fully grasp what is going on.

The actresses' smiles, nods, and caresses are systematically misinterpreted by Alma in a wishful and deceptive train of thought in which she imagines an appealing reversal of roles. Instead of sitting admiring images of the actress on screen, Alma can now enjoy having the famous performer as her admiring audience. This wishful and delusive acting-out of an egalitarian fantasy finds its crescendo in a scene where an intoxicated Alma tells the actress how she's reflected over their resemblance. 'You're prettier, but we are alike' (Figure 6.8). Elisabet, she proposes, could in a snap be like her, but, with a bit of effort, Alma could also be her—on the inside.

This vein in Bergman's fascinating film raises several interesting philosophical questions: how is this kind of error possible? Can it be overturned, and if so, under what conditions?[7] To start with the first question, the cinematic presentation of Alma's behaviour gives us no grounds for postulating any mysterious internal partitions whereby the nurse's mind splits into two parts so that the one internal agent can

---

[7] For an incisive and brief overview of contemporary views, see Alfred R. Mele, 'Motivated Irrationality', in Alfred R. Mele and Piers Rawling, eds., *The Oxford Handbook of Rationality* (Oxford: Oxford University Press, 2004), 240–6. In contemporary terms, Kaila's approach to self-deception is what Mele calls an 'anti-agency view', which means he eschews the postulation of partitions and internal agents, and explains self-deception in terms of motivational forces.

Figure 6.4. Elisabet Vogler (Liv Ullmann) listens to sister Alma in *Persona*.

Figure 6.5.

Figure 6.6. Vogler caresses and massages Alma.

Figure 6.7.

Figure 6.8. Alma's exclamation to Elisabet: 'We're alike'.

intentionally lie to the other. This amounts to imposing the model of interpersonal deception on the individual, but faulty and inauthentic self-understanding is not cogently conceptualized as a matter of literally lying or speaking insincerely to oneself. A better model is the Kaila-esque one in which it is the agent's desire for something that impedes a thorough sifting of the evidence. Alma's desire to win Elisabet's admiration guides her attention. Among the things that Alma's desires lead her to overlook is the abstract but crucial fact of her social role and of the socio-cultural distance between herself and the famous actress, who has been temporarily brought into her proximity by the doctor. It could be important to refer here as well to the tension between these social facts and the ambient egalitarian framework of the Swedish welfare state and of modern Scandinavian culture more generally.

Alma's desires also lead her to overlook the possibility that the flattering representations of Elisabet that she has found in the media are marketing devices and may not be especially probing or accurate. Nor can she hope to learn much about Elisabet by studying the roles she acts out in fictional films, even though the vivid close-ups of the actresses' lovely and expressive face may make it seem so. In the film—as opposed to the drafts and script—what an inebriated Alma says she thought about after seeing Elisabet in one of her films was how much they were alike. Bibi Andersson's way of delivering this line is extraordinary, and perfectly expresses the nurse's fantasy. She came home from the cinema and looked in the mirror, she says, drawing her drunken face close to Elisabet's and then: 'but we're alike' (men vi är li—ka!) with a stress and an exaggerated upward tone on the two-syllabic 'lika', followed by an audible gasp of pleasure.

As I indicated above, Elisabet fuels Alma's delusion with deceptive gestures, but there is evidence running in the other direction—evidence that Alma ignores. For example, she has apparently forgotten, or cannot be motivated to recall, her initial remark to the doctor about having noticed a rather 'severe' look in Elisabet's eyes. And how does the nurse happen to discount the disquieting evidence presented by Elisabet's transgressive gesture of tearing the photograph of her young son in two? Is this the gesture of a fully sympathetic listener? One factor that is relevant here is that what the nurse cares about is what Elisabet thinks about her, and as a result she is less interested in how the actress feels about her son and husband.

Another important reason why Alma lacks lucidity about her own manner of thinking about Elisabet—and of thinking about herself in relation to Elisabet, including Elisabet's thoughts and feelings about her—is that her conventional understanding of her gender identity and social role get in the way of a recognition of the nature of her own interest in Elisabet. Trying to get closer to the actress and to be understood and even admired by her is not part of that official story. And Alma's official self-understanding as a woman happily involved with a man overshadows any recognition of her erotic interest in Elisabet, which surfaces in her dream of nocturnal intimacy with the actress (in a passage from a draft of the script, this is an explicit sexual encounter in which the actress takes the initiative, fondles, and climbs on top of the receptive nurse; in the film this erotic dimension of Alma's interest in the actress is more subtle). The next day, when the two women are out on a walk, Alma asks Elisabet 'were you in my room last night?', and Elisabet, puzzled by this curious question, shakes her head. (If the encounter was not just a dream, why does not Alma know it?) Alma walks past her but turns and continues to walk backwards, slowly, gazing longingly at Elisabet.

To sum up, desires and feelings steer attention in ways that can be gratifying but not necessarily truth-indicative. We can call this self-deception. Or perhaps more neutrally, it is a matter of a faulty and irrational process of belief formation in which motivation plays an unknown, vitiating role. Here is one of Kaila's characteristic passages on the topic:

Wants are real forces, the dynamic effects of which are independent of their being the object of knowledge. A want that remains unconscious or unknown can none the less have a great effect. And as one's beliefs about oneself function under the influence of the same psychic forces as everything else in psychic life, we understand that these beliefs can also be erroneous, and that there can emerge *systematic errors of self-understanding*. It is quite common that self-love gives us a *consequentially false representation of ourselves*, because self-assertion drives self-understanding in its own direction. (p. 353)

Kaila adds that one reason why self-understanding can be inadequate is that a genuine awareness of an experience requires knowledge of the forces of which it is an expression, and ordinary introspection does not immediately provide any clarity in this regard. Such knowledge requires a grasp of 'the relations between the experience, other experiences, and behaviour' (pp. 354–5).

With regard to the question concerning the recognition and over-turning of such errors, Bergman provides no theory, but in the film he does provide significant indications, some of which mesh very nicely Kaila's ideas. The blind spot is neither essential nor ineliminable. Alma experiences an awakening, albeit an unkind one. In the Volvo on the way to run errands, she notices that Elisabet's letter to the doctor, which Alma is meant to post, is not sealed. The 'voice' that she discovers for the first time in reading this letter is remote from that of the person she has believed Elisabet to be. The letter is a complete betrayal (as Bergman writes in the script). Elisabet confides her thoughts to the doctor, which stands in painful contrast to the way in which she has concealed her thoughts from Alma. And the most painful thoughts that Elisabet reveals are her thoughts about Alma, including Alma's self-deception, which has been apparent to Elisabet:

She's enjoying herself and is quite taken with me, and is in love with me in an unconscious and charming way. Moreover it is quite amusing to study her. Sometimes she cries over her sins, including an episodic orgy with a totally unknown boy and the subsequent abortion. She complains that her ideas about life don't match her actions.

This is quite sufficient, and Bergman probably did not want to spoil the rhythm of the film by requiring his viewers to read even more lengthy

Figure 6.9. Alma reads Elisabet's letter.

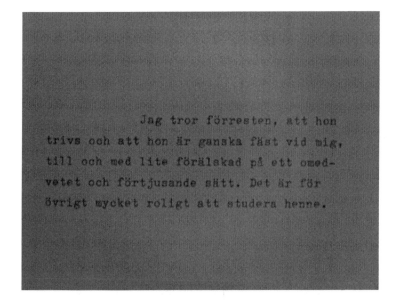

Figure 6.10.

Figure 6.11.

passages from the letter (we are selectively shown close-ups of the typed pages intercut brilliantly with shots of Alma's intense scrutiny of the letter (Figures 6.9–6.11). A slow dripping sound is heard as Alma reads, echoing the doctor's earlier line about 'life seeping in'). When writing the script, Bergman composed a significantly longer and even more revealing missive. He has Elisabet say that she does not long to see her little boy because she knows that he is doing well. She comments further on Alma, saying she has 'a robust, earthly sensuality' that she enjoys. Alma's way of moving both calms and stimulates her. Most importantly, perhaps, in this version Elisabet explicitly tells the doctor that she has got Alma to talk. This is significant, because this is one of the first accusations that Alma hurls at Elisabet in her subsequent outburst of hurt and fury: 'You got me to talk. You got me to tell you things that I have never told anyone. And you passed it on.' Alma, it is true, has in some sense deceived herself, but she had active help from Elisabet.

Having read the letter in the parked Volvo, Alma gets out and reflects for a while. Bergman's initial plan was to have her sit on a rock and muse over the betrayal. At some point in the filming this plan

Figure 6.12. Painful reflection: Bibi Andersson as sister Alma in *Persona*.

was replaced by a better idea. Bergman gives us a medium long-shot of the nurse standing in her black raincoat at the edge of a pond, peering down into her own reflection (Figure 6.12). Self-knowledge, here quite distinct from the satisfying musing of self-love, arises in a reflection overshadowed by the other. At least in some circumstances, inauthentic self-understandings can shatter and be replaced by an active and at least partially successful process of enquiry. That, at least, is one cogent way of understanding the sequences that follow in *Persona*: now that her false image of Elisabet, and of herself in Elisabet's mind, has been shattered, she undertakes to find out the truth about this woman, and, in so doing, learns a great deal about herself.

To sum up, the Kaila thesis of the primacy of motivational forces is not contradicted by the idea of an at least partial lucidity into the mainsprings of the human personality. Instead, different kinds of motivation are identified, including some that advance, rather than hinder, a cognitive exploration of the world. As I shall suggest below, this point has implications for Bergman's perspectives on both art and morality.

BERGMAN AND MORALITY

As I suggested above, Kalin is broadly correct in his observation that there is more to the Bergman story than a Nietzsche- or Kaila-inspired 'egoism'. Kalin does not slow down to say exactly what he means by this term, but it would seem to be a label for some form of moral nihilism (there are no true moral judgements) coupled with the cynical thesis that the satisfaction of individual desires or needs is the only real (or rational?) motivation of anyone's behaviour (no one is really moved by what they believe to be good or bad, right or wrong). In my view, there is no consistent support for either of these two notions in Bergman's works. In what follows I shall mention only a small part of the evidence that could be brought forth in support of this general interpretation of Bergman.

First of all, it is entirely uncontroversial to observe that Bergman's films are carefully designed to give rise to emotional responses of a particular kind and at particular moments in the viewer's experience of the film. This assumption is supported by Bergman's statement that, when working on a film, the film-maker has to be perfectly clear about what ideas are being expressed and what emotional responses they are meant to 'release'. The next step in this argument is to point out that, amongst the reactions targeted by the film-maker, there are many specifically moral emotions, such as sympathy for a victim, or injustice and outrage over some character's intentionally harmful behaviour.

The act of making a work of fiction and presenting it to a public can be broadly understood as a kind of invitation to engage in a specified sequence of imaginings or make-believe. Yet it is generally not the case that this action is limited to a bare invitation to entertain a series of morally neutral thoughts or propositions. Some of the events that are to be imagined are to be imagined as morally good, others as bad or evil, and the spectator is meant to experience emotions, or at least emotion-like states, that correspond to these morally valenced positions. For example, in Bergman's (1968) *Skammen* (*Shame*), the violinist Jan (portrayed by Max von Sydow) kills a tired and desperate young soldier for his boots, and his wife Eva (Liv Ullmann), who protests, expresses her complete horror and grief (Figure 6.13). The spectator is clearly meant to experience something similar to, or at least in line with, Eva's anguished reaction to this heartless deed. A spectator who thought that Jan was

Figure 6.13. Moral emotion in *Shame*: Liv Ullmann as Eva Rosenberg.

rightfully advancing his own interests and so behaving in a perfectly rational and correct manner would be diverging wildly from the targeted response, as would one who thought that the attitudes of neither Jan nor Eva could be justified because there is no real right or wrong.

Another example is provided by Bergman's manner of portraying the witch burning in *The Seventh Seal*. The entire sequence is clearly designed to inspire the spectator's sympathy for the victim. To evoke Murray Smith's helpful terminology, the rhetorical design of the film 'aligns' the implicit spectator with the squire, Knight, Jof, and Maria, who clearly express disapproval of this cruel action (Figures 6.14–6.16).[8] The squire says that he has considered intervening to try to save the girl from the soldiers, but believes this hopeless because the girl has already

---

[8] Murray Smith, *Engaging Characters: Fiction, Emotion and the Cinema* (Oxford: Clarendon Press, 1995). The notion of the implicit spectator rests upon claims about how the film was successfully designed to elicit a particular type of response. Actual spectators may (and sometimes should!) react in ways that are not invited or called for by the effective design of a work. For example, I doubt that I am alone in being unimpressed by the paintings made by the character played by William Holden in *The World of Suzy Wong* (1960, dir. Richard Quine), but I reckon the viewer was meant to think that these works are artistically admirable.

been mortally wounded. The best he and the Knight can do is to give her something to attenuate the pain. These details support the spectator's alignment with these characters. If we imagine the scene without these factors in place, we can easily imagine spectators having qualms about the Knight's and squire's passive and unquestioning complicity in the murder of an innocent girl. Instead, we are clearly meant to align with the squire when, peering up at her on the ladder on which the witch will be burnt, he says 'we see what she sees'.

It could be responded to these considerations that the fact that Bergman's artistic designs target the activation of morally valenced imaginings in response to *fictions* does not entail any stance with regard to the status of moral knowledge in the actual world; nor does this fact provide any reasons to doubt a nihilistic thesis that nothing is really right or wrong. Bergman could in fact have accepted the thesis that value is just a manifestation of subjectivity while opportunistically manipulating these very manifestations so as to advance his own personal

Figure 6.14. A victim and sympathetic onlookers in *The Seventh Seal*: Maud Hansson as the victim, and Max von Sydow as Antonius Block, Gunnar Björnstrand as his squire Jöns, Nils Poppe as Jof, and Bibi Andersson as Mia.

Figure 6.15.

Figure 6.16.

ambitions. Making fictions in which the implicit authorial persona and target audience are aligned with the victims is just the most effective way to make dramas that function well for certain audiences. Either the film's rhetorical devices function for the audience and the target responses are experienced (and found to be worthwhile or somehow rewarding), or the fictional invitation is 'declined' or fails to take effect. But neither case has any bearing on the actual status of moral knowledge, because this is simply a separate (and notoriously difficult) philosophical question.

In response to these considerations, it is important to note that Bergman's works do not explicitly take a theoretical stance with regard to ongoing debates over theories in normative ethics or second-order debates over the status of values more generally. There is no explicit taking sides, for example, in the dispute between consequentialists, Kantians, and virtue theorists. Bergman's films do not tell us, for example, whether it would be correct to sacrifice one innocent person to save a large number of other innocent persons. I suspect, but cannot prove, that he would be more inclined to espouse an 'anti-sacrificial' principle and take his distance from 'cold-hearted' calculations of the greatest good. One can, however, at least observe with some certainty that in his works there is a systematic and unshakeable condemnation of cruelty and of actions involving a selfish disregard for the suffering of others. With regard to meta-ethics or the question of the truth and justification of moral beliefs, Bergman makes no explicit statements about the ultimate basis or 'grounding' of moral judgements, at least in so far as such a grounding would require making a choice amongst the several competing philosophical views on this topic. I think it is safe to say, however, that his artistic practice is compatible with any meta-ethical position that allows first-order moral claims (such as references to certain actions as being evil) and emotional responses to go through unchallenged and unrevised. It is also safe to say that, in that part of his career that is under discussion here, Bergman has no recourse to any form of religious authority that might be appealed to in defence of moral judgements.

Reference to another, relatively unknown document sheds light on the status of moral judgements in Bergman's work. Around 1975 Bergman wrote a draft that carries the title 'Utkast till TV film om Jesu död och uppståndelse och några mänskor som deltog i dessa händelser' ('Draft of a TV film about the death and resurrection of Jesus and about some people who took part in these events'). The text includes an afterword in which Bergman begins by saying that anyone who approaches this topic as an artist must take a stand and account for his intentions. He sets out to say what he means with his film on Jesus, and writes:

First, and most importantly, I am not a believer. Every form of otherworldly salvation seems blasphemous to me. To put it simply: my life has no meaning. I cherish no hopes, foster no secret longing. If I try to think of my children's and my descendants' future, and that of humankind, I become deeply depressed.

Against all that I set the abundance, cruelty and beauty of life, reality, and existence, as well as man's inconceivable potential for good and evil.

Everything is enacted within and between human beings, nothing above or outside them.

Holiness and its opposite, which I call non-existence or emptiness, are within and between human beings.

For me Jesus Christ is forever the incontestable advocate of life, of everything living, and of spiritual life. He steps forth in a world of law, logicality, emptiness, fear, hate and mortal desperation. A world which from a superficial perspective conquers and kills him and, practically speaking, destroys his message.

But that tremendous concentrate of life cannot be destroyed. Through some excellent, frightened and imperfect people, the knowledge is clarified and carried forward, distorted, exalted, and desecrated, but is nonetheless passed along.

For me the holiness of Jesus is conceivable. I understand it, but perhaps without my reason. It shines in my eyes but does not dazzle and blind me because its luminosity is human. For me Jesus is a human being who speaks to human beings and who lives and dies in a human world.

Only in this way does he come close to me and only in this way can I understand what he says to me.

My film is thus about a human world that is admittedly remote in time but is unchangingly close and the same. In this world Jesus dies and life is violated. But the resurrection's earthly miracle, humanity's holiness, life's indestructibility manifest themselves just as well.

In Bergman's treatment for the film, the story is told by focusing on seven figures: Caiaphas ('high priest of the high priests'), Livia (the wife of Pontius Pilate), James the Lesser (son of Alphaeus), Mary, Rufus (a Roman centurion), Mary Magdalen, and Simon Peter. The characterization of the Roman centurion is perhaps the most important of the seven in this context. This man is ordered by Pontius Pilate to subject Jesus to a 'moderate' torture and humiliation. After this has been done Rufus looks at Jesus and is gripped by an 'inexplicable angst'. Rufus is ordered to supervise the crucifixion. He twice offers Jesus some wine to lessen the pain, but Jesus refuses. When Jesus looks him in the eyes, Rufus cannot bear it. He overhears Jesus say 'Father, forgive them, they know not what they do'. Suddenly the young captain in the Roman colonial army cannot stand it any longer. He says he is ill and hands the command over to a subordinate. Bergman writes:

In a quarry some hundred meters from the scene of the execution (the cross is visible above the edge) he falls on his knees and tries to bury his face in the ground. He cries desperately without tears. Finally in his deep confusion he finds some words to say: Father forgive us, we know not what we do. Forgive us, forgive us.

One might observe that, for such a scenario to be dramatically effective, the spectators must already be inclined to exhibit and agree with the kind of moral sympathy for suffering persons that the Roman officer suddenly begins to experience in response to the humiliation and torture of Jesus. Presumably many such officers never had any such qualms about the countless scenes of crucifixion they observed and in which they took part. Although it could be dramatically quite effective, Bergman's scenario does not even attempt to tell us why Rufus responds, and more crucially, *why he ought to respond*, in the way he does. In short, although the film could have been dramatically quite effective, and it is a pity that Bergman never went on to make the film, there are no implications here for moral knowledge in the real world.

Yet the latter remark overlooks a few points. First of all, Bergman's statements here (and elsewhere) do not just pertain to fiction. Bergman asserts that people have a potential for good and evil. Secondly, at least part of Bergman's basis for his condemnation of cruelty and victimization, both within and without the frame of fiction and make-believe, is cognitive. One way to couch this point would be to say that many (or, far more ambitiously, all) morally incorrect judgements can be disqualified by identifying their basis in some form of epistemic (non-moral) irrationality. The victimizers are irrational; they are driven and deluded by their fear of death, for example, and the multiple diversions and surrogate desires to which this fear gives rise. In the script of *The Seventh Seal*, a monk literally proclaims that the 14-year-old girl accused of witchcraft is 'guilty of the pestilence that touches all of us'—a preposterous attribution of an enormous causal power to a single, defenceless victim. Actions resting on such blatant errors are discredited. In the script about Jesus, the corresponding moment would be Bergman's emphasis on the irrational interests motivating the decision to crucify Jesus. The judgement and actions of the priest Caiaphas, for example, are shown to be vitiated by his desire to maintain absolute power and authority. These desires give rise to unreasonable thoughts and emotions that then motivate horrific and unnecessary aggressivity. Thus this script resembles other scapegoating and persecution dramas in Bergman, such as the sequence from *The Seventh Seal* discussed above, in that the life-destructive evil of persecution is again characterized as resting upon a fundamental cognitive failing, and, more precisely, a lack of self-knowledge.[9] The centurion's 'conversion', then, involves not only the emergence of an 'inexplicable' moral emotion in response to the humanity of the victim, but an acceptance of the truth of that victim's statement that 'they know not what they do'. The centurion becomes aware of his own blind spot, for he does not know what reasons there are for his involvement in the humiliation and killing of another person. (Presumably the premiss here is that various justifications involving duty and the needs of the empire have collapsed in his mind.) This knowledge of ignorance is part of the *knowledge* (vetskapen) that Bergman attributes to Jesus in his reconstruction of a secular, moral revelation.

It is significant that Bergman uses the term *vetskap* in this context, but important as well that he does not even try to spell out its content. What is this knowledge or wisdom that gets carried on in spite of human imperfection and deliberate attempts to destroy it? Bergman does not at this point in his career have explicit recourse to the Pauline, 'God is love' doctrine that he espoused in the late 1950s and early 1960s, but then went on to challenge in various ways (for example, the line is included in the dialogue of a radio play that inspires Elisabet Volger's derisive laughter in the script of *Persona*). Would it be fair to say that he has settled for the idea that there is something 'holy' or unquestionable about the emotions of sensitivity, caring, and sympathy that many people are inclined naturally and spontaneously to feel? Or is the implicit moral doctrine limited to a negation of those emotions and actions that are antithetical to those feelings of caring and love—cruelty, hatred, and insensitivity to suffering, or even its sadistic enjoyment? Are these forms of *evil* disqualified because they are based on some kind of essential error of inauthenticity or irrationality? Although it seems quite reasonable to believe that in many instances this is the case, it would be hard to establish the strong thesis that every act of cruelty involves the kind of motivated irrationality that Kaila describes, for this

---

[9] For a lengthier discussion of the central, anti-scapegoating theme in Bergman's work, see my *Ingmar Bergman and the Rituals of Art* (Ithaca, NY: Cornell University Press, 1982).

would amount to the claim that every desire to inflict suffering is in fact an unrecognized surrogate for either another, surrogate desire, or for some authentic, original desire that did not involve any cruelty. I find no evidence for such a claim in Bergman, and in fact he has on some occasions referred to unmotivated cruelty as an inexplicable form of evil: 'My philosophy (even today) is that there exists an evil that cannot be explained—a virulent, terrifying evil—and humans are the only animals to possess it. An evil that is irrational and not bound by law.'[10] Here it looks as though Bergman has indeed gone beyond Kaila's perspective and rejected what Evald's schoolbook says about there being no right and wrong.

In my next section I consider some of the implications these considerations about irrationality and value have for an understanding of the art of cinema and the artist's goals and values.

BERGMAN AND THE MODERNIST CRITIQUE OF FANTASY

All works of fiction express sequences of imaginings, and fictions are most often made with the primary intention of inviting an audience to engage in a sequence of imaginings guided by the work. Imagining, or make-believe, is understood here as a kind of thinking that is neutral between belief and disbelief. Although all fiction is intended to give rise to imagining in this sense, it may be helpful to distinguish between fictions that are primarily or even exclusively a matter of fantasy, and those that are not.[11]

---

[10] Ingmar Bergman, *Images: My Life in Film*, trans. Marianne Ruuth (London: Faber and Faber, 1995), 306. The context in which the remark appears is Bergman's discussion of *A Passion*, which includes the horrific victimization of the fisherman Erik. See also Bergman's remarks on scapegoating in *Bergman on Bergman: Interviews with Ingmar Bergman* by Stig Björkman, Torsten Manns, and Jonas Sima, trans. Paul Britten Austin (New York: Simon and Schuster, 1973), 40.

[11] As Peter Lewis points out, R. G. Collingwood distinguishes between imagining and make-believe, where the latter is driven by desire and is ruled inimical to 'art proper'. See Peter Lewis, 'Collingwood on Art and Fantasy', *Philosophy*, 64 (1989), 547–56, and R. G. Collingwood, *Principles of Art* (Oxford: Clarendon Press, 1938). My disagreement with this way of setting up the issues emerges below. Basically, I see no need for a honorific idea of 'art proper', nor do I agree with the broad concept of fantasy as make-believe governed by the 'desire that the situation imagined were real' (Collingwood, *Principles of Art*, 137).

By 'fantasy' I do not mean any particular literary, artistic, or cinematic genre. Instead, I have in mind a psychological usage of 'fantasy' that refers to pleasurable imaginings of actions that are, for the fantasizers, 'out of reach' in two possible ways. Some actions are out of reach in the sense that the fantasizer at least temporarily lacks the capacity or opportunity to perform them. For example, many people appear to enjoy watching fiction films in which a protagonist engages in fearless, extraordinarily skilful, and of course victorious combat; most of these spectators are not, I presume, themselves capable of any such actions. Other actions are out of reach in the sense that the fantasizer deems them imprudent or wrong. For example, many successful films prompt us to indulge in fantasies of highly efficient, violent revenge, and it is likely that many of the people who enjoy these films would not approve of anyone's actually performing such vengeful actions. The primary aim of fantasy is the pleasure yielded by imagining actions that are out of reach in at least one of these two senses.

Fantasy as described in the last paragraph *sometimes* has nothing to do with works of art. Yet it should be obvious that some fantasizing is stimulated and guided by works of fiction, some of which are works of art of greater or lesser merit. Amongst the works that stand in opposition to fantasy experience is the category of modernist fictions. As Herbert Read observed, a central goal of modernist art is its 'immense effort to rid the mind of the corruption which, whether it has taken the form of fantasy-building or repression, sentimentality or dogmatism, constitutes a false witness to sensation or experience'.[12] Combatting irrationality, beginning with the perceived irrationality of fantasy, is one of the guiding ambitions of various modernist artists, and many of their distinctive artistic strategies follow from this goal. Instead of offering spectacles of success achieved through highly improbable skill and luck, modernists evoke ineffective action, including prevalent forms of self-defeating behaviour and inner conflict. Such fictions may offer us a kind of enjoyment, but it is not a matter of fantasizing about performing actions that are out of reach for the spectator or reader. Rather, what we enjoy and admire are the modernist's creative and unflinching explorations of aspects of life about which we are curious or concerned.

---

[12] Herbert Read, *A Concise History of Painting* (London: Thames and Hudson, 1968), 290.

Returning now to Ingmar Bergman, it is safe to observe that the modernist orientation just evoked was central to his long career in theatre and cinema. Heavily influenced by the great modern Scandinavian dramatists, Ibsen and Strindberg, the young Bergman struggled to win the autonomy needed to write and direct his own pictures. But what is the basis of the modernist's critique of fantasy? For Bergman, truth and authenticity are intrinsically valuable, even when they are obstacles to pleasure or other practical pay-offs. It is better to face the grim truth, including the fact that we cannot have what we want, than to make the mistake of finding satisfaction through surrogates. Wishful thinking and actions based on it are anathema. Actions directed at some surrogate object are inauthentic because they are based on a mistake in which significantly different objectives are conflated. This mistake may be due to an irrational process of belief formation involving distortion by motivational forces; it may also be the result of a 'cold' cognitive bias alone, such as a tendency to draw inferences on the basis of salient similarities as opposed to more important, but less tangible, differences. The error may also be a matter of an inability to recognize the 'dependency relations' between experience and behaviour. In any case, the implicit perspective is one that rejects epistemic irrationality, or a breakdown in the fixation of belief through good and sufficient reason. At least some of the moral responses that are called for in Bergman's works are based on this perspective.

Yet it is not clear how this motivates the critique of fantasy in film and elsewhere. Fantasy is a kind of thinking that remains neutral between belief and disbelief; so it should not be condemned for committing the fantasizer to false or unwarranted beliefs. Nor does it seem plausible to argue that all fantasies involve some kind of faulty reasoning. Does it follow that Bergman's critique of fantasy must ultimately rest on a moral judgement, and, if so, what would that be?

It may be instructive in this regard to consider Roger Scruton's moral condemnation of fantasy, which I shall contrast to what I take to be a Bergmanian perspective.[13] Scruton understands fantasy as a desire for something that is the subject of a 'personal prohibition'. The fantasizer deems the fantasized actions wrong, but nonetheless enjoys fantasizing about them. Scruton does *not* say fantasizers are people who think

---

[13] Roger Scruton, 'Fantasy, Imagination, and the Screen', in *The Aesthetic Understanding* (London: Methuen, 1983), 149–59; 'Porn and Corn', http://www.artspacegallery. co.uk/OtherWWW/FULLER_BE/articles/Roger%20Scruton_01.htm.

thoughts they deem it immoral to think, and that fantasizers are indeed immoral because they fail to exert direct control over these guilty thoughts. What is wrong with fantasy, Scruton argues, is that, while it may satisfy a desire, it does not satisfy the whole person who has that desire, since the person cannot really identify with the fantasized actions. In many cases, fantasy involves an immoral objectification of the object of desire; as Scruton puts it, fantasies 'obliterate the human person'.

Scruton's definition of fantasy is overly narrow. It rules out fantasizing about actions that one deems perfectly acceptable, but outside one's range. Consider the case of someone who loves music and practises diligently in an effort to improve her performances. She is not immensely talented, and sometimes pauses to enjoy imagining what it would be like to give a perfect performance of an extremely difficult piece. I think this ought to be recognized as a type of fantasy, and it does not strike me as an instance of immorality.

Scruton correctly observes that some fantasies involve thoughts about actions that the fantasizer deems prohibited or immoral. Yet Scruton's Kant-inspired moral critique of this sort of fantasy misses the mark. Pleasurable experience, including pleasurable imaginative experience, figures amongst the intrinsic values that it can be rational to pursue, so it is unclear why any particular episode of fantasy would have to be immoral. No actual person has to be harmed whenever someone has an intrinsically valuable imaginative experience; nor is there necessarily any breakdown of personal identification on the part of the fantasizer. There is an important difference between enjoying thinking about doing something prohibited, and actually performing the prohibited action. Someone can coherently identify with a desire for the make-believe without identifying with the desire actually to perform the prohibited action. If this is correct, no violation of the integrity of a person is inherent in fantasy. There may, of course, be cases where someone objects to having a particular fantasy yet irrationally indulges in it.

If fantasy is not necessarily immoral, at least in Scruton's sense, we may still ask whether it should be criticized along other lines. What motivates or justifies the modernist aversion for fantasy? One answer, which I find consonant with Bergman's work and in keeping with various remarks he has made in interviews and essays, is simply that fantasy's pursuit of pleasure does not contribute to the modernist goal of providing a true and authentic witness to all aspects of human experience, which includes life's dark and unpleasant moments, our uncertainties and our failures. Another answer, which is more directly critical of fantasy, targets its practical incoherence or irrationality—here in the sense of imprudence. Even if particular episodes of fantasy need not involve any contradiction, fantasy can be self-defeating in the long run, at least in so far as fantasizing takes the place of activities oriented towards valuable goals within the agent's reach. People who indulge in a lot of fantasizing may cultivate a bad mental habit of thinking that the truly valuable experiences are the ones that are out of reach; their fascination with the pleasures associated with thoughts about out-of-reach actions can lead them to neglect the value of achievements that they could actually realize. For example, instead of practising diligently and thereby enjoying an improved performance, a mediocre pianist basks in the pleasures of fantasized virtuosity. This behaviour runs contrary to the agent's own long-term goals, and so is irrational; it may also be judged immoral, given some account of duties and virtues. (W. D. Ross, for example, counts self-improvement as one of our *prima facie* duties.[14]) A habit of enjoying vivid imaginings of dubious activities may in turn lead the agent in the direction of surrogate satisfactions and wishful thinking. In this manner, fantasy is contingently linked to the kinds of cognitive errors mentioned earlier. In some cases, fantasy may lead to disastrous attempts to realize the fantasized scenarios in the actual world. For example, the easy formulae that provide answers to all the important questions raised in a fiction are wrongly extended to the intractable issues that emerge in actual life. Some of Bergman's films are about people whose fantasizing leads them to such self-defeating behaviour. Bergman's characterization of the crusading Knight and religious fanatics in *The Seventh Seal* is in large part a criticism of this type of irrationality.

In sum, modernists such as Bergman target the irrationality of an imagination placed in the service of surrogate satisfactions and a flight from the challenges and pleasures of reality. At the same time, Bergman affirms the imagination's positive role in the exploration of the human condition. In spite of its dangers, the imagination may be a reasonable source of both learning and pleasure. Works of fiction cannot give us any empirical confirmation or statistics about the relative frequency of hot and cold irrationality, but they can be used vividly to illustrate, and sometimes even inspire, hypotheses about the springs of human behaviour. And modernists such as Bergman use fiction to challenge us

---

[14] William David Ross, *The Right and the Good* (Oxford: Clarendon Press, 1930).

to improve and apply our conceptual models of both irrationality and rationality.

Consider in this regard some of Bergman's remarks about his own artistic activities. I have in mind, in particular, his 1965 Erasmus Prize reception speech, 'The Snakeskin'. The negative and critical thrust of the essay consists of a sweeping rejection of various traditional justifications for art. And the only positive contention is the purely personal claim that Bergman's own artistic work finds its sole source in an innate curiosity: 'The reason is curiosity. An unbounded, never satisfied, continuously renewed, unbearable curiosity, which drives me forward, never leaves me in peace, and completely replaces my past hunger for fellowship.' And a few lines later, Bergman adds: 'As a basis for artistic activity, during the next few years it is entirely adequate, at least for me.'[15]

Bergman's manner of describing his curiosity squares neatly with Kaila's points by identifying a spontaneous drive or need as the sole basis for complex cognitive and artistic processes; at the same time, the specific nature of this 'drive' holds out some promise, since curiosity is an inclination that can lead one to try to find out how things really are, which could in turn give rise to some insightful or cognitively valuable work. Thus we have a kind of 'escape' clause that allows us to see how a philosophy that stresses the primacy of motivation can avoid being self-defeating. Yes, thinking is always in danger of being wishful thinking, as Kaila proclaims, but not all wishes are the same, and the quality of thoughts can vary with that of the wishes, or, better, needs and desires, that determine them. Someone who is basically driven by curiosity may enjoy a kind of local lucidity that is not shared by someone whose ruling passion is vanity or sensual lust. Curiosity makes you observant, and, coupled with the desire to record or capture what has been observed, leads to art-making impulses.

To return to the connection between cinema and philosophy, if the philosopher's defining virtue is a love of wisdom, a sense of wonder and curiosity, in this respect the philosopher resembles the artist as Bergman describes himself, driven by a curiosity to seek to represent and express at least some fragments of our experience of the world. Bergman often follows Kaila in emphasizing the primacy of

---

[15] Ingmar Bergman, 'The Snakeskin', in *Persona and Shame: The Screenplays of Ingmar Bergman*, trans. Keith Bradfield (New York: Grossman, 1972), 11–15, at 14, 15. Bergman reprinted this material in *Images: My Life in Film* (pp. 46–51) and added that these ruminations were written in 'direct connection with the work on *Persona*' (p. 51).

motivational forces over reason, yet he is also motivated to affirm a basic cognitive value—namely, the idea that it is better to recognize unpleasant facts or 'terrible truths' than to indulge in fantasy and wishful thinking. Bergman carries forward Kaila's affirmation of the epistemic value of fictions, creating works that help us explore the multiple tangles of human thought and passion, the underlying assumption being that this is a good, though often distressing, thing to do. Even the scientific perspective that Kaila wants to promote depends on this evaluative stance, and, in Bergman's case, this first affirmation of the sway of value extends to a moral antipathy for violence and victimization. Bergman certainly does not give us anything resembling a naive return to Enlightenment myths, but nor does he present nihilism as the only alternative. He may or may not have been theoretically persuaded by Kaila's restatement of a positivist anti-realism about values, but it is clear that, in his artistic practice, value and its various qualities are an immanent feature of the value-laden experience which the director prepares for the spectator in the design of a film.

Conclusion

In this conclusion I shall briefly revisit and clarify some of my central claims about cinema's contributions to philosophy. I shall also make some additional remarks about the implications of Ingmar Bergman's works for this general issue.

To begin by recapitulating some of my basic points, films or audio-visual displays do not literally have thoughts or goals and cannot raise questions or attempt to answer them. A film does not have any beliefs, so it cannot hold or promote views about metaphysical topics, such as the nature of space, time, or causation. On the assumption that concepts are thoughts or modes of classification, a film does not have, entertain, or create any concepts. Authors who describe films as independently proposing or somehow incarnating an innovative metaphysics or some other philosophical stance are in fact projecting their own ideas onto the audio-visual display. This fact is not changed by the strategy of explicitly attributing the philosophizing to an imagined, postulated, or 'hypothetical' author, since these are just other labels for the interpreter's projections.

A film can be used by both its maker(s) and audience to serve a wide variety of ends, none of which has to be philosophical. A film-maker's motives and goals can involve such things as the desire for fame and fortune, or various ambitions directly related to artistic, scientific, polemical, or other sorts of success. The author of a film usually acts on expressive or communicative intentions: he or she means to stir the audience in a certain way, and tries to evoke or advocate attitudes or ideas. Spectators may in turn be interested in finding out what the film-makers were trying to get across with a film, but clearly that is not the only goal (or the only good goal) people have in watching movies.

Bergman's long career as a film-maker represents no exception to these truisms. Early in his career, the Swedish author repeatedly stated his desire to use film to communicate with people in an authentic and probing manner about some of life's most fundamental topics, and many spectators have responded to his work along precisely these lines. When the Swedish film studios were closed for a year and he had debts to pay, Bergman adapted to this adverse situation and made clever soap commercials. Later in his career Bergman identified personal curiosity as the motive behind his film-making. Yet he also declared that, with the help of his various collaborators, he designed the scenes in his films with specific responses, both emotional and intellectual, in mind. In the many interviews he gave, Bergman was forthcoming about his intellectual and personal preoccupations as well as his artistic and philosophical sources. The members of Bergman's various audiences have watched his films for an enormous variety of reasons and with any number of different interests. Some of his films, such as *Summer with Monika* and *The Silence*, were box-office successes outside Sweden partly (or perhaps even largely) because of their sexual content. Yet many of Bergman's spectators have taken a keen interest in the ideas expressed in his films, interviews, theatrical works and productions, essays, and autobiographical books.

A variety of goals can also be pursued when people talk and write about films. One goal is to discover and say what the author or authors meant, and to gauge whether the finished audio-visual display is congruent with those intentions. Another goal is to say what some *possible* author could have meant by the film, where the interpretation is understood as an imaginative exercise, as opposed to an enquiry into the actual author's intentions. In what can be called *extrapolative* interpretations, the goal is to bracket what may be known about the author's intentions and to try to use the film as a point of departure for saying something creative and of independent interest. The extrapolative interpreter's conception of what counts as interesting can depend, for example, on the assumptions and preoccupations of contemporary philosophy, such as an interest in the relation between consequentialist moral doctrines and virtue ethics. The extrapolative interpreter looks for elements in the film that resonate with his or her own conception of such a philosophical or theoretical topic. Given a sufficiently elaborate *problématique* in relation to which the cinematic display can be interpreted, a philosophical allegorical reading of elements in the film can be developed.

Other goals pursued by people who discuss films could easily be enumerated. I have not seen any good arguments establishing that any one type of interpretative project should always have priority over all others. It is possible, however, to show how the pursuit of one sort of interpretative goal can be in conflict with the realization of other goals, and it is also possible to say something about the kinds of advantages and disadvantages that are correlated with specific types of interpretative projects, and, in particular, philosophically minded ones.

Although some film-makers are guided by subtle and sophisticated philosophical ideas, many are not. In the latter case, the philosophically minded interpreter faces the following dilemma. Either the commentator faithfully describes the film-maker's philosophizing, but says nothing of any great philosophical import, or the commentator says something of genuine philosophical import, but fails to describe philosophizing actually done by the film-maker. The overarching tendency in the 'film as philosophy' literature has quite understandably been to steer towards the latter of these two options. The philosopher writing about cinema wants to present an argument or line of thought, and recruits some of a film's story elements and dialogue to that end. This is not in itself an error, but we should be clear about the potential benefits and disadvantages of this approach. On the side of benefits, it is exciting to see how philosophically stimulating issues and distinctions can be applied to the story presented by a vivid and engaging audio-visual display. Students who find a philosophical argument abstract and removed from their actual experience are helped to imagine complex situations where the ideas and distinctions are relevant or even decisive. For example, students who have studied various theoretical positions regarding the nature of personal identity find it bracing to try to isolate the implications that these views have for an understanding of particular fictional characterizations. Given the pedagogical value of this source of intellectual excitement and elucidation, why should not philosophers feel free to work with any ideas or issues that appear applicable to the film?

Extrapolative interpretations have their rewards, then, but one sort of benefit that is *not* to be had along these lines is *confirmation* of any general theses (philosophical or other) about the actual world.[1] This point should be obvious, but it is remarkable how often interpretations of fictions are presented as though they could function as demonstrations of what is the case outside the fiction. If one's thesis pertains to non-imaginary states of affairs, a fiction can only provide a strong indication

---

[1] There is an exception to this claim. If the commentator's topic is what it is possible for human beings to imagine, the imagined content of a fiction counts as direct evidence, because it is something that has actually been imagined.

concerning the adequacy of that thesis in so far as something in the fiction is already known to resemble something that is not make-believe or part of a fiction. For example, Bergman's Elisabet Vogler is a fictional character, yet some of the things she does in the story of *Persona*, such as tearing a photograph in half, closely resemble the sorts of things we believe actual people have done. Reasoning about Vogler is a good way to reason about actual people—but only if the beliefs about actual people and about the character's particular resemblance to them are sound. Few of the theory-inspired interpreters of fictions provide any independent grounds in support of those sorts of bridging assumptions, which is unsurprising given that doing so would require extensive and difficult empirical investigations. In the absence of such empirically justified bridging assumptions, fiction-based reasoning should be viewed as a kind of hypothesis formation.

Another trade-off can be mentioned here. To the extent that the interpreter brackets the film-makers' premises and orientation in order to develop a complex philosophical problematic within which elements of the film may be found to resonate, it becomes less appropriate to believe that the contents of the interpretation correspond to the philosophy *of the work*. The interpreter's mobilization of assumptions, distinctions, and arguments that are entirely alien to the film-maker's perspective severely attenuates the extent to which claims about characterizations and story events are those of the work, as opposed, say, to one of any number of possible constructions compatible with selectively culled aspects of the audio-visual display. It is important to remember that *any* film that represents characters and their actions can be given an allegorical reading inspired by any number of rival theoretical frameworks, such as some species of psychoanalysis. As long as the interpreter is selective enough and works creatively with possible associations, a story can always be described as illustrating or 'confirming' tenets of the chosen theory, which is why this kind of interpretative exercise has often been referred to as 'cookie-cutter criticism'.

Another trade-off pertains to an extrapolative commentary's relation to film appreciation. As I pointed out at the outset of this study, quite a number of accomplished philosophers have chosen to write about *The Matrix* and other films in that series, and reading their extrapolative essays is a good way to learn about various forms of scepticism. I do not rank these essays highly as bits of film appreciation, however, nor do I reckon their authors had any such aims. Philosophers refer to aspects of the story and to some statements made by the characters about reality, dreaming, and illusion; little or nothing is said, however, about the film's production design, soundtrack, editing, cinematography, use of special effects, and complex choreography of action sequences. Little is made of the fact that large segments of these films are entirely devoted to dazzling representations of fights, gun battles, and high-speed chases. Some philosophers do ask about the morality of the protagonists' killing the 'agents' who are part of the matrix, but this is not a topic that carries a great deal of rhetorical emphasis in the film, the target spectator of which is obviously meant to enjoy the exciting displays of violence the conflict makes possible.

In sum, piecemeal, extrapolative interpretation does not really count as an adequate basis for film appreciation, at least given the prevalent assumption that one of the primary goals of the appreciation of a work of art is to understand and evaluate its artistry, as well as the prevalent assumption that the understanding and evaluation of a work's artistry depend upon some discernment regarding the organization of the parts within the work.

Intentionalist interpretations, on the other hand, potentially contribute to the appreciation of a work of art by making it possible to discuss relations between the use of artistic media and the content of the work. To understand style, or the manner in which something has been done, we need to recognize *what* was done, and that includes the expression of content, and not just camera set-ups, the choice of lenses, editing patterns, average shot lengths, and so on. Without some sense of the *point* of a scene, the appreciator cannot say whether the devices employed in it were effective. If, however, we recognize what the artist was trying to express, we are in a position to attempt to characterize the work's style and the artistic adequacy of the expressive devices the film-maker has employed. An intentionalist approach must refer to the work's content, but it need not target *philosophical* content. It is obvious that, in many cases, the film-maker or film-makers did not actually think along philosophical lines. Instead, the events and characterizations in the story were meant to be fleshed out uniquely in terms of unreflective everyday categories, habitual explanatory schemes, stereotypes, and cinematic conventions familiar to members of the target audience. For example, when interviewed, the director truthfully disavows having had any particular philosophical sources and concerns, and sincerely reports that he was inspired, not by Heidegger and Nietzsche, but by George Stubbs's romantic pictures and a visit to Hong Kong. In such a case, the construction of a philosophically sophisticated framework within which to interpret aspects of the story amounts to an imposition, or, to revert to Wartenberg's distinction, to an audience-oriented as opposed to a creator-oriented interpretative project.

In some cases, however, intentionalism and an interest in film as philosophy harmonize. These are cases where the film-maker, or team of film-makers, has something genuinely valuable to express about a philosophical topic and has successfully done so with a film. The film-maker provides evidence of his or her philosophical interests and background and offers interpreters a way into this framework. The appreciator of the film in turn manages to elucidate the implications of the audio-visual display in ways that not only contribute to the appreciation of the work, but are worthwhile in the light of contemporary philosophical research, either because reference to the film usefully serves to illustrate the philosophical debate, or because it serves to carry that debate one step further.

Intentionalist approaches must shoulder a heavy evidentiary burden. Careful and imaginative scrutiny of the audio-visual display is not enough, as other kinds of evidence can shed light on the film-maker's thoughts, decisions, and intentions. Such evidence, and the inferences based on it, may turn out to be partial or even misleading, but such is the nature of historical research more generally. In the case of Bergman, the interpreter can draw upon testimonies by collaborators, interviews, diaries, and many statements left behind in unpublished notebooks, shooting scripts, and other documents. There are many other cases where such evidence is not available, and it is sour-grapes reasoning to conclude that such evidence is 'therefore' needless or even undesirable. Philosophers interested in the cinema should not make the mistake of extending the literary New Critical approach to the film medium, assuming, then, that 'the text alone' is a sufficient object of interpretative scrutiny.

As I have argued above in Chapters 5 and 6, Bergman emphatically identified one particular philosophical source as having been 'foundational' for his work—Eino Kaila's 1934 treatise in philosophical psychology. It is possible that this remark was misleading and just another one of Bergman's many (and sometimes incompatible) self-promotional moves. I have argued, on the contrary, that the topics, assumptions, and motifs that Kaila set forth in his treatise are likely to have informed Bergman's thinking about a number of his fictions. Many aspects of the films' characterizations and rhetorical patterns are congruent with the hypothesis that Bergman was thinking in terms of issues and ideas explored in Kaila, such as motivated irrationality and surrogate desire satisfaction. I hope to have convinced the reader that this is a case in which an individual film-maker, who drew upon the artistic contributions of many talented collaborators, was to a very high degree the sole author of a number of outstanding, philosophically informed cinematic fictions. With the help of extremely talented collaborators, Bergman used the cinematic and other media to express philosophical ideas of genuine complexity and significance. This should be acknowledged even if one goes on to discover limitations in Kaila-inspired psychological hypotheses. Bergman's vivid and stirring fictional explorations of general issues pertaining to human motivation, knowledge, and value can stimulate and guide philosophical reflection. To take an interest in the Kaila-inspired topics broached in Bergman's films yields an enhanced appreciation of Bergman's artistry and of the skill with which he and his gifted performers bring these issues to life in the fictions.

In sum, most, if not all, films, including the most inept and reprehensible ones, have some kind of philosophical value in the sense that they could be used to illustrate instances of bad reasoning, social stereotypes, and imprudent behaviour. Some films have a more positive philosophical value, because the film-maker or film-makers present characterizations and events designed to evoke subtle problems and ways of responding to them. And a few film-makers should be credited for making works of fiction that are informed by and express sophisticated philosophical thinking. Those who wish to write and think about film in a philosophical vein can explore these different kinds of cinematic contributions to philosophical insight. Finally, while sweeping pronouncements about the cinema's world-historical philosophical significance attract attention and may generate some excitement about this relatively new field of enquiry, more careful studies of particular cases and topics are more likely to yield reliable and credible results.

Bibliography

Allen, Richard, and Murray Smith, eds. *Film Theory and Philosophy*. Oxford: Clarendon Press, 1997.

Andersson, Harriet. *Samtal med Jan Lumholdt*. Stockholm: Alfabeta Pocket, 2006.

Aristarco, Guido. 'Bergman et Kierkegaard', *Études cinématographiques*, 46–7 (1966), 15–30.

Asher, Nicholas, and Alex Lascarides. *Logics of Conversation*. Cambridge: Cambridge University Press, 2003.

Audi, Robert. 'Doxastic Voluntarism and the Ethics of Belief', in Matthias Steup, ed., *Knowledge, Truth, and Duty: Essays on Epistemic Justification, Responsibility, and Virtue*. Oxford: Oxford University Press, 2001, 93–114.

Bach, Kent, and Robert M. Harnish. *Linguistic Communication and Speech Acts*. Cambridge, MA: MIT Press, 1979.

Benedetti, Carla. *The Empty Cage: Inquiry into the Mysterious Disappearance of the Author*, trans. William J. Hartley. Ithaca, NY: Cornell University Press, 1995.

Bergala, Alain. *Monika de Ingmar Bergman: Du rapport créateur-créature au cinéma*. Crisnée: Éditions Yellow Now, Côté Films, 2005.

Bergman, Ingmar. 'Kinematograf', *Biografbladet*, 29 (1948), 240–1.

—— 'Vi är circus!', *Filmjournalen*, 4 (1953), 7, 31.

—— 'Dett att göra film', *Filmnyheter*, 9/9–20 (1954), 1–9.

—— *Varje film är min sista film*. Stockholm: Svenskfilmindustri, 1959.

—— *Wild Strawberries: A Film by Ingmar Bergman*, trans. Lars Malmström and David Kushner. London: Lorimer, 1960.

—— 'The Snakeskin', *Film Comment*, 6 (1970), 9–21; repr. in Ingmar Bergman, *Persona and Shame: The Screenplays of Ingmar Bergman*, trans. Keith Bradfield. New York: Grossman, 1972, 11–15.

—— *Persona and Shame: The Screenplays of Ingmar Bergman*, trans. Keith Bradfield. New York: Grossman, 1972.

—— *Filmberättelser 2: Persona, Vargtimmen, Skammen, En Passion*. Stockholm: Pan/Norstedts, 1973.

—— *Ur Marionetternas liv*. Stockholm: Norstedt, 1980; trans. Hans-Joachim Maass, *Aus dem Leben der Marionetten*. Hamburg: Hoffmann and Campe, 1980; trans. Alan Blair, *From the Life of the Marionettes*. New York: Pantheon, 1980.

—— *Laterna magica*. Stockholm: Norstedts, 1987.

—— *Femte akten*. Stockholm: Norstedts, 1994.

Bergman, Ingmar. *Bilder*. Stockholm: Norstedts, 1990; trans. Marianne Ruuth, *Images: My Life in Film*. London: Faber and Faber, 1995.

Björkman, Stig, Torsten Manns, and Jonas Sima, eds. *Bergman om Bergman*. Stockholm: Norstedts & Soner, 1970; trans. Paul Britten Austin, *Bergman on Bergman*. New York: Simon & Schuster, 1973.

Blackwell, Marilyn Johns. *Gender and Representation in the Films of Ingmar Bergman*. Columbia, SC: Camden House, 1997.

Blake, Richard Aloysius. *The Lutheran Milieu of the Films of Ingmar Bergman*. New York: Arno Press, 1978.

Blessing, Kimberly Ann, and Paul J. Tudico, eds. *Movies and the Meaning of Life: Philosophers Take on Hollywood*. Chicago: Open Court, 2005.

Boden, Margaret. 'What is Creativity?' in Margaret A. Boden, ed., *Dimensions of Creativity*. Cambridge, MA: MIT Press, 1994, 71–117.

Bogue, Ronald. *Deleuze on Cinema*. New York: Routledge, 2003.

—— 'Gilles Deleuze', in Paisley Livingston and Carl Plantinga, eds., *The Routledge Companion to Philosophy and Film*. London: Routledge, 2009, 368–77.

Borden, Diane M. 'Bergman's Style and the Facial Icon', *Quarterly Review of Film Studies*, 2 (1977), 42–55.

Bordwell, David. *The Films of Carl-Theodor Dreyer*. Berkeley and Los Angeles: University of California Press, 1981.

—— *Making Meaning: Inference and Rhetoric in the Interpretation of Cinema*. Cambridge, MA: Harvard University Press, 1989.

—— *The Cinema of Eisenstein*. London: Routledge, 1993.

—— and Noël Carroll, eds. *Post-Theory: Reconstructing Film Studies*. Madison, WI: University of Wisconsin Press, 1996.

Bratman, Michael E. *Faces of Intention: Selected Essays on Intention and Agency*. Cambridge: Cambridge University Press, 1999.

Buckland, Warren, ed. *The Film Spectator: From Sign to Mind*. Amsterdam: Amsterdam University Press, 1995.

Carlshamre, Staffan, and Anders Pettersson, eds. *Types of Interpretation in the Aesthetic Disciplines*. Montreal: McGill-Queen's Press, 2003.

Carney, Raymond. *Speaking the Language of Desire: The Films of Carl Dreyer*. Cambridge: Cambridge University Press, 1989.

Carroll, Noël. 'The Specificity of Media in the Arts', *Journal of Aesthetic Education*, 14/15 (1984–5), 127–53.

—— 'Towards an Ontology of the Moving Image', in Cynthia A. Freeland and Thomas E. Wartenberg, eds., *Philosophy and Film*. New York: Routledge, 1995, 68–85.

—— *Theorizing the Moving Image*. New York and Cambridge: Cambridge University Press, 1996.

—— *Interpreting the Moving Image*. Cambridge: Cambridge University Press, 1998.

—— 'The Essence of Cinema?', *Philosophical Studies*, 89 (1998), 323–30.

—— 'Interpretation and Intention: The Debate between Hypothetical and Actual Intentionalism', *Metaphilosophy*, 31 (2000), 75–95.

—— 'Andy Kaufman and the Philosophy of Interpretation', in Michael Krausz, ed., *Is There a Single Right Interpretation?* University Park, PA: Pennsylvania State University Press, 2002, 319–44.

—— 'Philosophizing through the Moving Image: The Case of Serene Velocity', in Murray Smith and Thomas E. Wartenberg, eds., *Thinking through Cinema: Films as Philosophy*. Malden, MA: Blackwell, 2006, 173–85.

—— *The Philosophy of Moving Pictures*. Malden, MA: Blackwell, 2008.

—— and Jinhee Choi, eds. *Philosophy of Film and Motion Pictures: An Anthology*. Malden, MA: Blackwell, 2006.

Cavell, Stanley. *The World Viewed: Reflections on the Ontology of Film*, enlarged edn. Cambridge, MA: Harvard University Press, 1979.

—— *Pursuits of Happiness: The Hollywood Comedy of Remarriage*. Cambridge, MA: Harvard University Press, 1981.

—— *Contesting Tears: The Hollywood Melodrama of the Unknown Woman*. Chicago: University of Chicago Press, 1996.

—— *Cities of Words: Pedagogical Letters on a Register of the Moral Life*. Cambridge, MA: Harvard University Press, 2004.

Chatman, Seymour. *Coming to Terms: The Rhetoric of Narrative in Fiction and Film*. Ithaca, NY, and London: Cornell University Press, 1990.

Choi, Jinhee. 'Apperception on Display: Structural Films and Philosophy', in Noël Carroll and Jinhee Choi, eds., *Philosophy of Film and Motion Pictures*. Malden, MA: Blackwell, 2006, 165–72.

Chung, Cindy K., and James W. Pennebaker. 'Assessing Quality of Life through Natural Language Use: Implications of Computerized Text Analysis', in William R. Lenderking and David A. Revicki, eds., *Advancing Health Outcomes Research Methods and Clinical Applications*. McLean, VA: Degnon Associates, 2005, 79–94.

Cohen, Hubert I. *Ingmar Bergman: The Art of Confession*. New York: Twayne, 1993.

Collingwood, R. G. *Principles of Art*. Oxford: Clarendon Press, 1938.

Cook, Nicholas. *Analysing Musical Multimedia*. Oxford: Clarendon Press, 1998.

Currie, Gregory. *The Nature of Fiction*. Cambridge: Cambridge University Press, 1990.

—— 'Work and Text', *Mind*, 100 (1991), 325–40.

—— *Image and Mind: Film, Philosophy and Cognitive Science*. Cambridge: Cambridge University Press, 1995.

—— 'Film, Reality, and Illusion', in David Bordwell and Noël Carroll, eds., *Post-Theory: Reconstructing Film Studies*. Madison, WI: University of Wisconsin Press, 1996, 325–44.

Danto, Arthur. *Philosophizing Art: Selected Essays*. Berkeley and Los Angeles: University of California Press, 1999.

Davies, David. 'Works, Texts, and Contexts: Goodman on the Literary Artwork', *Canadian Journal of Philosophy*, 21 (1991), 331–46.

—— 'Medium in Art', in Jerrold Levinson, ed., *The Oxford Handbook of Aesthetics*. Oxford: Oxford University Press, 2003, 181–91.

—— 'Can Film Be a Philosophical Medium?', *Postgraduate Journal of Aesthetics*, 5/2 (2008), 1–20.

—— ed. *The Thin Red Line*. London: Routledge, 2008.

—— 'Ontology', in Paisley Livingston and Carl Plantinga, eds., *The Routledge Companion to Philosophy and Film*. London: Routledge, 2009, 217–26.

Davies, Stephen, ed. *Art and its Messages: Meaning, Morality, and Society*. University Park, PA: Pennsylvania University State Press, 1997.

Davis, Wayne A. *Implicature: Intention, Convention, and Principle in the Failure of Gricean Theory*. Cambridge: Cambridge University Press, 1998.

—— *Meaning, Expression, and Thought*. Cambridge: Cambridge University Press, 2002.

Deleuze, Gilles. *L'Image-mouvement*. Paris: Minuit, 1983.

—— *L'Image-temps*. Paris: Minuit, 1985.

Drouzy, Maurice. *Carl Th. Dreyer né Nilsson*. Paris: Cerf, 1982.

Drum, Jean, and Dale D. Drum. *My Only Great Passion: The Life and Films of Carl Th. Dreyer*. Lanham, MA: Scarecrow, 2000.

Eisenstein, Sergei. 'Methods of Montage', in Jay Leyda, ed., *Film Form: Essays in Film Theory*. New York: Harcourt, Brace & World, 1949, 72–83.

Ellis, John M. *Theory of Literary Criticism: A Logical Analysis*. Berkeley and Los Angeles: University of California Press, 1974.

Epstein, Jean. *Cinéma, bonjour*. Paris: La Sirène, 1921.

—— *L'Intelligence d'une machine*. Paris: Jacques Melot, 1946.

Falzon, Chris. *Philosophy Goes to the Movies: An Introduction to Philosophy*. 2nd edn. New York: Routledge, 2007.

Flaxman, Gregory, ed. *The Brain is the Screen: Deleuze and the Philosophy of Cinema*. Minneapolis, MN: University of Minnesota Press, 2000.

Foucault, Michel. *L'Archéologie du savoir*. Paris: Gallimard, 1969.

Frampton, Daniel. *Filmosophy*. London: Wallflower, 2006.

Fumerton, Richard. 'Skepticism', in Paisley Livingston and Carl Plantinga, eds., *The Routledge Companion to Philosophy and Film*. London: Routledge, 2009, 601–10.

Furhammar, Leif, and Jannike Åhlund. *En liten bok om Hasse: Hasse Ekman som filmregissör*. Göteborg: Filmkonst/Filmbiblioteket 4, 1993.

Gado, Frank. *The Passion of Ingmar Bergman*. Durham, NC: Duke University Press, 1987.

Gaut, Berys. 'Film Authorship and Collaboration', in Murray Smith and Richard Allen, eds., *Film Theory and Philosophy*. Oxford: Clarendon Press, 1997, 149–72.

—— 'Art and Knowledge', in Jerrold Levinson, ed., *The Oxford Handbook of Aesthetics*. Oxford: Oxford University Press, 2003, 436–50.

—— 'Film', in Jerrold Levinson, ed., *The Oxford Handbook of Aesthetics*. Oxford: Oxford University Press, 2003, 627–46.

—— *A Philosophy of Cinematic Art*. Cambridge: Cambridge University Press, 2010.

—— and Paisley Livingston, eds. *The Creation of Art: New Essays in Philosophical Aesthetics*. New York and Cambridge: Cambridge University Press, 2003.

Gerard, Fabien S., T. Jefferson Kline, and Bruce Sklarew, eds., *Bernardo Bertolucci: Interviews*. Jackson, MS: University Press of Mississippi, 2000.

Gilmore, Richard A. *Doing Philosophy at the Movies*. Albany, NY: State University of New York Press, 2005.

Grant, B. K., ed. *Auteurs and Authorship: A Film Reader*. Oxford: Wiley-Blackwell, 2008.

Grau, Christopher, ed. *Philosophers Explore* The Matrix. Oxford: Oxford University Press, 2004.

Grice, Herbert Paul. *Studies in the Way of Words*. Cambridge, MA: Harvard University Press, 1989.

Grodal, Torben, Bente Larsen, and Iben Thorving Laursen, eds. *Visual Authorship: Creativity and Intentionality in Media. Northern Lights Film and Media Studies Yearbook*. Copenhagen: Museum Tusculanum, 2005.

Hägerström, Axel. *Socialfilosofiska Uppsatser*. Stockholm: Bonniers, 1939.

Hegel, G. W. F. *Vorlesungen über die Ästhetik III*, in *Werke in zwanzig Bänden*, ed. Eva Modenhauer and Karl Markus Michel. Frankfurt am Main: Suhrkamp, 1986, vol. xv; *Aesthetics: Lectures on Fine Art*, trans. T. M. Knox. 2 vols. Oxford: Clarendon Press, 1975.

Heijne, Ingemar von. *Lars Johan Werle*. Stockholm: Atlantis, 2007.

Hembus, Joe. *Ingmar Bergman: Die großen Kinofilme*. Lübeck: Amt für Kultur der Hansestadt Lübeck, 1988.

Hermerén, Göran. *Representation and Meaning in the Visual Arts*. Stockholm: Laromedelsforlagen, 1969.

Hjort, Mette, ed. *Dekalog 1: On* The Five Obstructions. London: Wallflower, 2008.

—— and Sue Laver, eds. *Emotion and the Arts*. New York and Oxford: Oxford University Press, 1997.

—— and Scott MacKenzie, eds. *Purity and Provocation: Dogma 95*. London: BFI, 2003.

Hobbs, Jerry R. *Literature and Cognition*. Stanford, CA: Center for the Study of Language and Information, 1990.

Hopkins, Robert. *Picture, Image and Experience: A Philosophical Inquiry*. Cambridge: Cambridge University Press, 1988.

Houlgate, Stephen. *An Introduction to Hegel: Freedom, Truth and History*. Malden, MA: Blackwell, 2005.

Hume, David. 'Of the Standard of Taste', in Eugene F. Miller, ed., *Essays Moral, Political, and Literary*. Indianapolis: Liberty Fund, 1985, 226–52.

Irwin, William, ed. *The Death and Resurrection of the Author?* Westport, CN: Greenwood, 2002.

—— ed. The Matrix *and Philosophy: Welcome to the Desert of the Real*. Chicago: Open Court, 2002.

—— *More Matrix and Philosophy: Revolutions and Reloaded Decoded*. Chicago: Open Court, 2005.

Iseminger, Gary. 'Aesthetic Appreciation', *Journal of Aesthetics and Art Criticism*, 39 (1981), 389–99.

—— 'Experiential Theories of Aesthetic Value', in Richard Shusterman and Adele Tomlin, eds., *Aesthetic Experience*. London: Routledge, 2008, 45–58.

Jarvie, Ian. *Philosophy of the Film: Epistemology, Ontology, Aesthetics*. London: Routledge & Kegan Paul, 1987.

Kaila, Eino. *Persoonallisuus*. Helsinki: Otava, 1934; trans. Jan Gästrin, Introd. John Landquist, *Personlighetens psykologi*. Stockholm: Natur och Kultur, 1935, 2nd rev. edn., 1939; trans. Sunna and Franz From, *Personlighedens psykologi*. Copenhagen: Villadsen and Christensen, 1946, 2nd edn., 1966.

—— *Tankens Oro: Tre Samtal om De Ytterska Tingen*. Helsingfors: Söderström, 1944.

Kalin, Jesse. *The Films of Ingmar Bergman*. Cambridge: Cambridge University Press, 2003.

Källberg, Arne Ruth Knut-Göran. 'Ingmar Bergman berätter om sin nya TV-film "Ur marionetternas liv"', *Expressen*, 15 Mar. 1989, Kultursidan, pp. 5–7.

Kaminsky, Stuart M. *Ingmar Bergman: Essays in Criticism*. London: Oxford University Press, 1975.

Kasher, Asa. 'Conversational Maxims and Rationality', in Asa Kasher, ed., *Language in Focus: Foundations, Methods, and Systems*. Dordrecht: Reidel, 1976, 197–211.

Kau, Edvin. *Dreyers filmkunst*. Copenhagen: Akademisk, 1989.

Ketcham, C. B. *The Influence of Existentialism on Ingmar Bergman: An Analysis of the Theological Ideas Shaping a Filmmaker's Art*. Lewiston, NY: Edwin Mellen Press, 1986.

Kierkegaard, Søren. *Enten-Eller*. *Søren Kierkegaards Skrifter*, vols. 2–3. Copenhagen: Gads forlag, 1997.

Koskinen, Maaret. 'Närbild och narrativ (dis)kontinuitet: Nedslag i Ingmar Bergmans närbilder', *Aura*, 1 (1995), 58–63.

—— *I begynnelsen var ordet: Ingmar Bergman och hans tidiga författarskap*. Stockholm: Wahlström & Widstrand, 2002.

—— ed. *Ingmar Bergman Revisited: Performance, Cinema and the Arts*. London: Wallflower, 2008.

Kupfer, Joseph. *Visions of Virtue in Popular Film*. Boulder, CO: Westview Press, 1999.

Kyrklund, Willy. *Prosa*. Stockholm: Bonnier, 1995.

Lamarque, Peter V. 'Objects of Interpretation', *Metaphilosophy*, 31 (2000), 96–124.

Lauder, R. E. 'Ingmar Bergman: The Filmmaker as Philosopher', *Philosophy and Theology*, 2 (1987), 44–56.

—— *God, Death, Art, and Love: The Philosophical Vision of Ingmar Bergman*. New York: Paulist Press, 1989.

Lawrence, Matt. *Like a Splinter in your Mind: The Philosophy behind* The Matrix Trilogy. Oxford: Blackwell, 2004.

Lee, Gordon A. 'Perceiving Ingmar Bergman's *The Silence* through the I Ching'. Ph.D. diss., San Jose State, 1995.

Levin, Daniel T., and Daniel J. Simons. 'Perceiving Stability in a Changing World: Combining Shots and Integrating Views in Motion Pictures and the Real World', *Media Psychology*, 2 (2000), 357–80.

Levinson, Jerrold. 'Performative vs. Critical Interpretation in Music', in Michael Krausz, ed., *The Interpretation of Music*. Oxford: Clarendon Press, 1993, 33–60.

—— 'Artful Intentions: Paisley Livingston, *Art and Intention: A Philosophical Study*', *Journal of Aesthetics and Art Criticism*, 65 (2007), 299–305.

Lewis, C. I. *An Analysis of Knowledge and Valuation*. La Salle, IL: Open Court, 1946.

—— *Values and Imperatives: Studies in Ethics*. Stanford, CA: Stanford University Press, 1969.

Lewis, David K. 'Postscripts to "Truth in Fiction"', in *Philosophical Papers*, vol. i. New York: Oxford University Press, 1983, 276–280.

Lewis, Peter. 'Collingwood on Art and Fantasy', *Philosophy*, 64 (1989), 547–56.

Light, Andrew. *Reel Arguments: Film, Philosophy, and Social Criticism*. Boulder, CO: Westview Press, 2003.

Litch, Mary. *Philosophy through Film*. New York: Routledge, 2002.

Livingston, Paisley. *Ingmar Bergman and the Rituals of Art*. Ithaca, NY: Cornell University Press, 1982.

—— 'Disciplining Film: Code and Specificity', *Cinema Canada*, 97 (1983), 47–57.

—— *Literary Knowledge: Humanistic Inquiry and the Philosophy of Science*. Ithaca, NY: Cornell University Press, 1988.

—— 'Film and the New Psychology', *Poetics*, 20 (1991), 1–24.

—— *Literature and Rationality: Ideas of Agency in Theory and Fiction*. Cambridge: Cambridge University Press, 1991.

Livingston, Paisley. 'Literature and Knowledge', in Jonathan Dancy and Ernest Sosa, eds., *A Companion to Epistemology*. Oxford: Blackwell, 1992, 255–8.

——*Models of Desire: René Girard and the Psychology of Mimesis*. Baltimore, MD: Johns Hopkins University Press, 1992.

——'Artistic Self-Reflexivity in Strindberg and Bergman', *TijdSchrift voor Skandinavistiek*, 20 (1999), 35–44.

——'Counting Fragments, and Frenhofer's Paradox', *British Journal of Aesthetics*, 39 (1999), 14–23.

——'Om fiktion og fiktions-sandhed', in Lene Tortzen Bager and Ansa Lønstrup eds., *Kunsten og værket*. Aarhus: Aarhus University Press, 1999, 139–56.

——'Pentimento', in Paisley Livingston and Berys Gaut, eds., *The Creation of Art*. New York: Cambridge University Press, 2003, 89–115.

——*Art and Intention: A Philosophical Study*. Oxford: Clarendon Press, 2005.

——'Skepticism, Realism, Fallibilism: On Lem's Epistemological Themes', in Peter Swirski, ed., *The Art and Science of Stanislaw Lem*. Montreal: McGill-Queen's Press, 2006, 117–29.

——'Artistic Nesting in *The Five Obstructions*', in Mette Hjort, ed., *Dekalog 1: On* The Five Obstructions. London: Wallflower Press, 2008, 57–75.

——'Authorship Redux: On some recent and not-so-recent work in literary theory', *Philosophy and Literature*, 32/1 (2008), 191–7.

——'When a Work is Finished: A Response to Darren Hudson Hick', *Journal of Aesthetics and Art Criticism*, 66 (2008), 393–5.

——'Narrativity and Knowledge', *Journal of Aesthetics and Art Criticism*, 67 (2009), 25–36.

Lundemo, Trond. *Jean Epstein—intelligensen hos en maskin—The Intelligence of a Machine*. Stockholm: Svenska Filminstitutet, 2001.

McGinn, Colin. *The Power of Movies: How Screen and Mind Interact*. New York: Pantheon, 2005.

Marty, Joseph. *Ingmar Bergman: Une poétique du désir*. Paris: Cerf, 1991.

Mele, Alfred R. *Springs of Action*. New York: Oxford University Press, 1992.

——'Motivated Irrationality', in Alfred R. Mele and Piers Rawling, eds., *The Oxford Handbook of Rationality*. Oxford: Oxford University Press, 2004, 240–6.

—— and Paul K. Moser. 'Intentional Action', *Noûs* 28 (1994), 39–68.

Meskin, Aaron. 'Authorship', in Paisley Livingston and Carl Plantinga, eds., *The Routledge Companion to Philosophy and Film*. London: Routledge, 2009, 12–28.

Morin, Edgar. *Le Cinéma ou l'homme imaginaire*. Paris: Minuit, 1956.

Mulhall, Stephen. *On Film*. London: Routledge, 2002.

Nehamas, Alexander. 'What an Author Is', *Journal of Philosophy*, 83 (1986), 685–91.

Nystedt, Hans. *Ingmar Bergman och kristen tro*. Stockholm: Verbum, 1989.

Olsen, Stein Haugom. 'Interpretation and Intention', *British Journal of Aesthetics*, 17 (1977), 210–18.

——'Criticism and Appreciation', in Peter Lamarque, ed., *Philosophy and Fiction*. Aberdeen: Aberdeen University Press, 1983, 38–51.

Ostermann, Bernt. 'De Stora Frågornas sorti och Antonius Block', *Finsk tidskrift*, 3 (1989), 177–86.

Peacocke, Christopher. 'Depiction', *Philosophical Review*, 96 (1987), 383–410.

Perkins, V. F. *Film as Film: Understanding and Judging Movies*. Harmondsworth: Penguin, 1972.

Persson, Per. *Understanding Cinema: A Psychological Theory of Moving Imagery*. Cambridge: Cambridge University Press, 2003.

Phillips, James, ed., *Cinematic Thinking: Philosophical Approaches to the New Cinema*. Stanford, CA: Stanford University Press, 2008.

Plantinga, Carl. *Moving Viewers: American Film and the Spectator's Experience*. Berkeley and Los Angeles: University of California Press, 2009.

Ponech, Trevor. *What is Non-Fiction Cinema? On the Very Idea of Motion Picture Communication*. Boulder, CO: Westview, 1999.

—— 'The Substance of Cinema', *Journal of Aesthetics and Art Criticism*, 64 (2006), 187–98.

—— 'The Definition of "Cinema"', in Paisley Livingston and Carl Plantinga, eds., *The Routledge Companion to Philosophy and Film*. London: Routledge, 2009, 52–63.

Ragland, C. P., and Sarah Heidt, eds. *What is Philosophy?* New Haven and London: Yale University Press, 2001.

Read, Herbert. *A Concise History of Painting*. London: Thames and Hudson, 1968.

Robinson, Jenefer. *Deeper than Reason*. Oxford: Oxford University Press, 2005.

Ross, William David. *The Right and the Good*. Oxford: Clarendon Press, 1930.

Rothman, William, ed. *Cavell on Film*. Albany, NY: SUNY Press, 2005.

—— 'Stanley Cavell', in Paisley Livingston and Carl Plantinga, eds., *The Routledge Companion to Philosophy and Film*. London: Routledge, 2009, 344–55.

Rowland, Mark. *The Philosopher at the End of the Universe: Philosophy Explained through Science Fiction Films*. London: Ebury, 2003.

Russell, Bruce. 'On the Philosophical Limits of Film', in Noël Carroll and Jinhee Choi, eds., *Philosophy of Film and Motion Pictures*. Malden, MA: Blackwell, 2006, 387–90.

Schneider, Hans-Helmuth. *Rollen und Räume: Anfragen an das Christentum in Filmen Ingmar Bergmans*. Frankfurt am Main: Lang, 1993.

Schuth, H. Wayne. *Mike Nichols*. Boston: Twayne, 1978.

Scruton, Roger. *The Aesthetic Understanding*. London: Methuen, 1983.

—— 'Porn and Corn'. http://www.artspacegallery.co.uk/OtherWWW/ FULLER_BE/articles/Roger%20Scruton_01.htm.

Sellors, C. Paul. 'Collective Authorship in Film', *Journal of Aesthetics and Art Criticism*, 65 (2007), 263–71.

Sesardic, Neven. 'Gattaca', in Paisley Livingston and Carl Plantinga, eds., *The Routledge Companion to Philosophy and Film*. London: Routledge, 2009, 641–9.

Simon, John. *Ingmar Bergman Directs*. New York: Harcourt Brace Jovanovich, 1972.

Singer, Irving. *Three Philosophical Filmmakers: Hitchcock, Welles, Renoir*. Cambridge, MA: MIT Press, 2004.

—— *Ingmar Bergman, Cinematic Philosopher: Reflections on his Creativity*. Cambridge, MA: MIT, 2007.

Sjöman, Vilgot. *L 136: diary with Ingmar Bergman*, trans. Alan Blair. Ann Arbor: Karoma, 1978.

Skoble, Aeon J., and Mark T. Conard, eds. *Woody Allen and Philosophy: You Mean my Whole Fallacy is Wrong?* Chicago: Open Court, 2004.

Smith, Murray. *Engaging Characters: Fiction, Emotion and the Cinema*. Oxford: Clarendon Press, 1995.

—— 'Film Art, Argument, and Ambiguity', in Murray Smith and Thomas E. Wartenberg, eds., *Thinking through Cinema: Film as Philosophy*. Malden, MA: Blackwell, 2006, 33–42.

—— and Richard Allen, eds. *Film Theory and Philosophy*. Oxford: Clarendon Press, 1997.

—— and Thomas E. Wartenberg, eds. *Thinking through Cinema: Film as Philosophy*. Malden, MA: Blackwell, 2006. Originally published as a special issue of *Journal of Aesthetics and Art Criticism*, 64:1 (2006).

Smuts, Aaron. 'Film as Philosophy: In Defense of a Bold Thesis', *Journal of Aesthetics and Art Criticism*, 67 (2009), 409–420.

Sonnenschein, Richard. 'The Problem of Evil in Ingmar Bergman's *The Seventh Seal*', *West Virginia Philological Papers*, 27 (1981), 137–43.

Stecker, Robert. *Interpretation and Construction: Art, Speech, and the Law*. Oxford: Blackwell, 2003.

—— *Aesthetics and the Philosophy of Art: An Introduction*. Lanham, MA: Rowman & Littlefield, 2005.

—— 'Moderate Actualist Intentionalism Defended', *Journal of Aesthetics and Art Criticism*, 64 (2006), 429–38.

—— 'Intention and Interpretation', *Journal of Literary Theory*, 2:1 (2008), 1–16.

Steene, Birgitta. *Ingmar Bergman*. New York: St Martin's, 1968.

—— ed. *Focus on* The Seventh Seal. Englewood Cliffs, NJ: Prentice-Hall, 1972.

—— *Ingmar Bergman: A Reference Guide*. Amsterdam: Amsterdam University Press, 2005.

Stoehr, Kevin L., ed. *Film and Knowledge: Essays on the Integration of Images and Ideas*. Jefferson, NC: McFarland, 2002.

Sweeney, Kevin. 'Medium', in Paisley Livingston and Carl Plantinga, eds., *The Routledge Companion to Philosophy and Film*. London: Routledge, 2009, 173–83.

Tatarkiewicz, Władysław. *History of Aesthetics*, ed. D. Petsch. 3 vols. Mouton: The Hague, 1974.

Thomson-Jones, Katherine. *Aesthetics and Film*. London: Continuum, 2008.

Verdone, Mario, ed. *Gli intellettuali et il cinema*. Rome: Bianco e nero, 1952.

Wartenberg, Thomas E. *Unlikely Couples: Movie Romance as Social Criticism*. Boulder, CO: Westview, 1999.

—— *Thinking on Screen: Film as Philosophy*. London: Routledge, 2007.

—— and Angela Curran, eds. *The Philosophy of Film: Introductory Text and Readings*. Malden, MA: Blackwell, 2005.

Wexman, Virginia Wright, ed. *Film and Authorship*. New Brunswick, NJ: Rutgers University Press, 2003.

Whittock, Trevor. *Metaphor and Film*. Cambridge: Cambridge University Press, 1990.

Wiers-Jenssen, Hans. *Anne Pettersdotter*. Oslo: Forening for Norsk Bokkunst, 1962.

Wilson, George M. 'Film, Perception, and Point of View', *MLN*, 91 (1976), 1026–43.

—— *Narration in Light: Studies in Cinematic Point of View*. Baltimore, MD: Johns Hopkins University Press, 1986.

Winberly, Amos D. 'Bergman and the Existentialists: A Study in Subjectivity'. Ph.D. diss., University of Texas at Austin, 1979.

Wright, G. H von. *Explanation and Understanding*. Ithaca, NY: Cornell University Press, 1971.

Yanal, Robert J. *Hitchcock as Philosopher*. Jefferson, NC: McFarland, 2005.

Young, Vernon. *Cinema Borealis: Ingmar Bergman and the Swedish Ethos*. New York: Avon, 1971.

Index

Made in the USA
Columbia, SC
02 March 2019